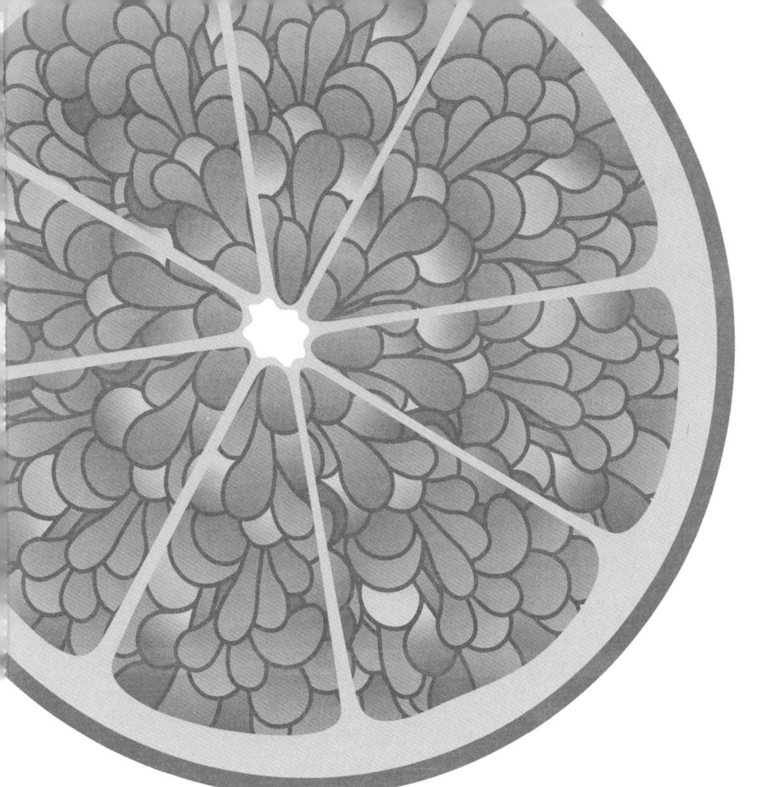

American English File

Student Book 4

Clive Oxenden
Christina Latham-Koenig

OXFORD
UNIVERSITY PRESS

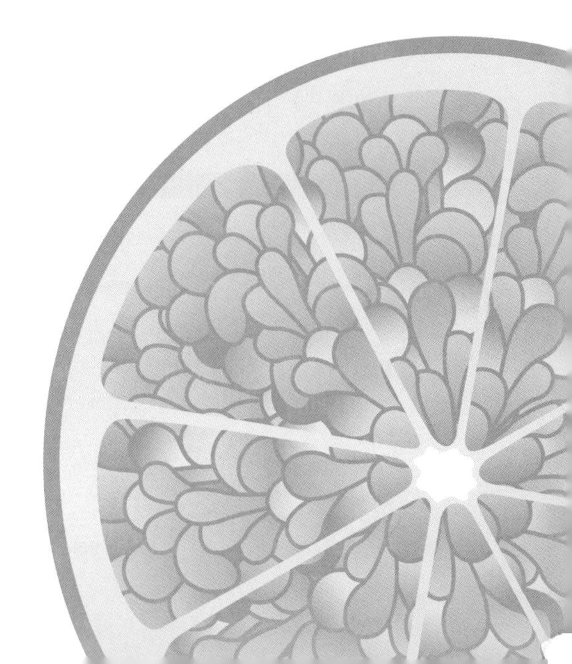

Paul Seligson and Clive Oxenden are the original co-authors of *English File 1* (pub. 1996) and *English File 2* (pub. 1997).

Contents

Look out for Study Link
This shows you where to find extra material for more practice and review.

G review: question formation
V guessing meaning from context
P intonation, stress, and rhythm in questions

Q and A

1 GRAMMAR review: question formation

a Complete the following questions with one or two question words or an auxiliary verb.

1 *How much* do you earn?
2 *Are* you married?
3 How long have you been studying English?
4 Which one do you prefer, small towns or big cities?
5 How often do you go to the theater in a year?
6 How tall are you?
7 What kind of religion are you?
8 Do you want to have children?
9 What kind of music do you listen to?
10 ______ advice do you listen to most?
11 ______ you ever said "I love you" and not meant it?
12 ______ did you vote for in the last election?

b Put an ✘ next to the questions above that you wouldn't ask a person you don't know very well. Are there any questions that you would not even ask a good friend? Which questions would you expect to find in a magazine interview with a famous person?

c Read the two interviews. Which question is ...?

the most personal the most boring the most original

d Read the interviews again and write **N** (Norah) or **L** (Lionel).

Who ...?
1 never has enough time for what he / she wants to do ___
2 has happy childhood memories ___
3 avoids answering one of the questions ___
4 feels guilty about something ___
5 probably doesn't like waking up early ___
6 is very proud of something ___
7 says he / she is an insecure person ___
8 needs help in his / her daily life ___

e In pairs, look at questions 8–12 in the Lionel Richie interview. Find an example of ...

1 a question where an auxiliary verb has been *added* to make the question.
2 a question where there is no auxiliary verb.
3 a question that ends with a preposition.
4 a negative question.
5 a question where the usual subject + auxiliary verb order has been inverted to make the question.

f **p.132 Grammar Bank 1A.** Read the rules and do the exercises.

Young star, old star

Every week the newspaper *The Guardian* chooses people who have been in the news recently and publishes a short interview with them called Q&A. The questionnaire often includes fairly personal questions.

Q&A Norah Jones

Norah Jones was born in New York and is the daughter of the Indian sitar player and composer Ravi Shankar and the concert promoter Sue Jones. Her half-sister is the musician Anoushka Shankar. Norah is a singer-songwriter, and her debut album, *Come Away with Me*, sold more than 20 million copies worldwide and won her five Grammy Awards.

1 **Where would you like to live?**
Barcelona.

2 **What do you most dislike about your appearance?**
I am too short. I am 5 feet, 1 inch (155 centimeters).

3 **Who would play you in the movie of your life?**
Maybe Christina Ricci.

4 **What's your favorite smell?**
Onion, garlic, and butter cooking in a pan.

5 **What's your favorite word?**
"No."

6 **Which living person do you most despise and why?**
No comment!

7 **What single thing would improve the quality of your life?**
Probably a housekeeper.

8 **Who would you invite to your dream dinner party?**
All my friends and Keith Richards – I think he'd be great at a dinner party.

9 **What's the worst job you've ever had?**
A waitressing job where I had the breakfast shift. It wasn't the job that was so bad, just the hours. I had to go in at five in the morning.

10 **If you could go back in time, where would you go?**
Summer camp in Michigan, age 14.

11 **How do you relax?**
A hot bath.

12 **What keeps you awake at night?**
Music. A song will keep going around in my brain and keep me awake.

Q&A Lionel Richie

Lionel Richie was born in Alabama, US. He became famous in the 1970s as lead singer with The Commodores and then in the 1980s as a solo singer. He is best remembered for songs like *Three Times a Lady*, *All Night Long*, and *Say You (Say Me)*, for which he won an Oscar.

1 **What's your idea of perfect happiness?**
Sunday by the pool, no phone calls.

2 **What's your earliest memory?**
My first day at preschool. I was terrified. I'd never seen that many children in my whole life.

3 **What's your most treasured possession?**
My Oscar.

4 **If you could edit your past, what would you change?**
The Commodores never did a farewell tour. We just broke up and disappeared.

5 **What has been your most embarrassing moment?**
Forgetting the lyrics to my new single on a TV show.

6 **What words or phrases do you most overuse?**
"I'll call you back" or "I'll see you soon."

7 **What's the most important lesson life has taught you?**
Don't trust the smile, trust the actions.

8 **What don't you like about your personality?**
I'm an egotistical maniac with an inferiority complex.

9 **What makes you depressed?**
That there are 24 hours in a day and I need 36.

10 **When did you last cry and why?**
At the funeral of Milan Williams of The Commodores.

11 **Who would you most like to say "I'm sorry" to?**
To my kids for not being there more.

12 **What song would you like to be played at your funeral?**
All Night Long and Stevie Wonder's *I Just Called to Say I Love You*.

2 PRONUNCIATION intonation, stress, and rhythm in questions

Using the right **intonation** or tone helps you sound friendly and interested when you speak English. **Stressing** the right words in a sentence helps you speak with a good rhythm. **Intonation** + **stress** = the music and **rhythm** of English.

a 1.1 Listen to questions 1–8. In which one does the speaker sound more friendly and interested? Write a or b.

1 ___ 2 ___ 3 ___ 4 ___ 5 ___ 6 ___ 7 ___ 8 ___

b 1.2 Listen and underline the stressed words in these questions.

1 What's your favorite kind of music?
2 Have you ever been to a health club?
3 How often do you go away on weekends?
4 Do you know what's on TV tonight?
5 How long have you been living here?
6 What are you thinking about?
7 Are you a vegetarian?
8 What do you do to relax?

c Listen again and repeat the questions in **b**. Try to sound as friendly as possible. Then ask each other the questions.

3 SPEAKING

a Look at the answers other celebrities gave to some of the questions in *The Guardian* interview series. In pairs, match the answers below to some of the questions in the questionnaires on pages 4 and 5.

Donna Karan, fashion designer

Harry Connick, Jr., musician and actor

David Schwimmer, actor

Bruce Willis, actor

Pamela Anderson, actress and model

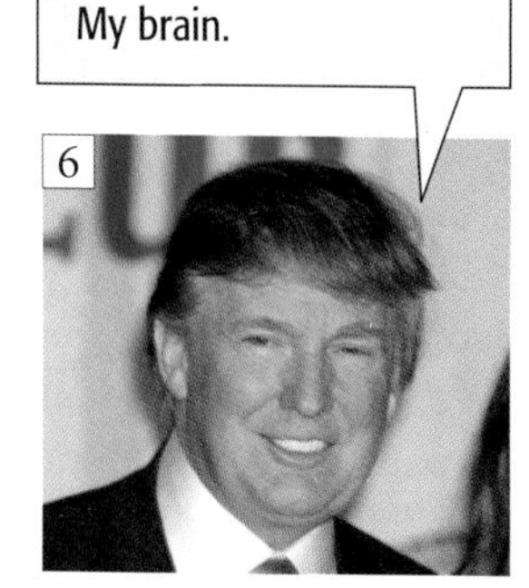

Donald Trump, real estate developer

b Now choose six questions from the interviews to ask a partner. Ask only questions that you would be comfortable answering yourself.

Three minutes to get to know the love of your life

4 READING & VOCABULARY

a Do you know what "speed dating" is? Read the first half of the article to check, or to find out how speed dating works.

> **Guessing meaning from context**
>
> When you are reading and you find a word or phrase you don't know, try to guess the meaning from the context (the other words around it). Think also about what part of speech the unknown word is (e.g., a verb, an adjective, etc.), whether it is similar to another English word you know, or whether it is similar to a word in your language.
>
> If you still can't figure out what the word or phrase means, either ignore it and continue reading or use a good dictionary (or glossary if there is one) to help you.

b Read the first half of the article again carefully. With a partner, say or guess what the highlighted words and phrases mean. Then check with **Glossary 1**.

c Using your own words, answer questions 1–4 with a partner.

1. According to the writer, how did people use to get to know a prospective partner?
2. What kind of people is speed dating designed for?
3. Why does Adele Testani think three minutes is enough?
4. Why do you think the journalist pretended to be a lawyer?

d Now read the second half of the article on page 7 and find out...

1. the advantages of speed dating (according to the participants).
2. if the journalist thinks speed dating is a good idea.

e Read the second half of the article again more carefully. With a partner, say or guess what the highlighted words and phrases mean.

Glossary 1

prospective partner sb who might become your boyfriend / girlfriend or husband / wife in the future

courtship the period of time when two people have a romantic relationship before they get married

Mr. or Ms. Right (informal) the man / woman who would be the perfect partner for sb

quick-fire (a series of things) done very quickly

a scorecard a card or paper where you write the points, e.g., in a game

a "match" when two things or two people fit together

not your type not the kind of person who you would normally like or get along with

In recent years speed dating has become popular all around the world. Journalist *Anushka Asthana* tried it out.

FINDING A PARTNER has always been a complicated process. It is a ritual that has evolved over the centuries, from a man taking food to a prospective partner in the Stone Age to young couples having tea together in Victorian times (under the watchful eye of an unmarried aunt) to dancing in a club with deafening music in the 21st century.

But now busy men and women who don't have the time for a slow, gentle courtship have a quicker way to find a partner: speed dating, where single people have exactly three minutes to decide if the person they are talking to could be Mr. or Ms. Right. The idea involves bringing together people for an evening of frenzied, "quick-fire" dating. This is how it works.

Small tables are placed in a line and the women sit down at the one assigned to them. They stay at their table all evening. The men take turns sitting next to each woman and having a very quick conversation. After three minutes a bell rings and, even if you are in mid-sentence, it is time for the man to move to the next table. If you like the person you have just spoken to, you put a check in the "yes" box on a scorecard. If the other person chooses you too, this is called a "match," and the organizers will send you the other person's e-mail address a couple of days later, and they will be sent yours, too.

"Three minutes is enough time to talk to someone," says Adele Testani, who runs a speed dating company, "because you can get an idea of what a person is like in that time, and you can eliminate them if you see right away that they're not your type."

One of the largest-ever speed dating evenings took place this week at the Hydro Bar, so I decided to go along and see what it was all about. I pretended to be a single 24-year-old lawyer...

WHEN I ARRIVED at the Hydro Bar, the women, who were wearing fashionable dresses and stylish suits, were giggling nervously as they each put on a tag with a number on it. "Maybe my jeans are a bad idea," I thought. I chatted with other people while we waited. People I spoke to said they had doubled the number of dates they had in a year with just one night of speed dating. The men included a chef, a banker, a photographer, an engineer, a management consultant, and a novelist. They were just pleased they could stop having to try to make small talk with strangers in bars. "It's so hard to meet women. With speed dating you meet 20 or 30 single women in one night," said one man. "You can't talk to women in salsa classes," said another. Matt, 28, said, "After doing this once I got several dates. There's a good atmosphere; it's safe and it's really good. It's like being at a party with lots of single women."

Then it started. I made eye contact with the woman next to me so we could compare our opinions of the men; we raised our eyebrows for a possibility, exchanged a smile if the man was good-looking, and made a grimace if he made three minutes feel like three hours.

I thought it was boring just to ask questions like "What do you do?" or "Where are you from?" so I tried to think of more interesting and imaginative questions to ask, like "If you could be an animal, what animal would you be and why?"

In the end I checked six boxes. A couple of days later, I was told that four of the men had checked me, too. Four new dates. Pretty good for 66 minutes.

Adapted from a newspaper

Glossary 2

1 ______________ a small piece of paper, metal, plastic, or cloth with a name or some identification on it
2 ______________ an expression on your face that shows you are in pain
3 ______________ laugh in a silly way because you are amused or nervous
4 ______________ move the line of hair above your eye upwards
5 ______________ polite conversation about unimportant things
6 ______________ talk in a friendly, informal way

f Complete **Glossary 2** with the correct highlighted word or phrase. Use the base form of the verbs.

g Using your own words, answer questions 1–4 with a partner.
1 Why did the journalist feel a little uncomfortable at first?
2 What kind of men went to this speed dating evening?
3 What kind of signs did she make to the woman next to her? What for?
4 What kind of questions did she think worked best?

h Do you think speed dating is a good way of meeting people? If you were looking for a partner, would you try it? What questions would you ask?

5 LISTENING

a 1.3 Listen to a radio program about speed dating. A man and a woman who have both tried it talk about their experiences. How successful was it for them?

b Listen again. Then answer the questions with **E** (Emily), **A** (Alex), or **B** (both).

Who ...?
1 preferred to ask usual questions ☐
2 was asked an unusual question ☐
3 was asked the same question over and over ☐
4 got fewer matches ☐
5 had a disastrous date because he / she wasn't feeling well ☐
6 was invited on a date that never took place ☐
7 had a good date in spite of hearing bad news that day ☐
8 realized on a date that his / her first impression was wrong ☐
9 says he / she isn't planning to go speed dating again ☐

c Does hearing about Emily and Alex's experiences make you feel more or less positive about speed dating?

6 SPEAKING

GET IT RIGHT reacting and asking for more information
When you ask someone a question and they answer, it is usual to show interest by saying expressions like *Really?*, *Is that right?*, *Yes, me too*, *Me neither*, *I know what you mean*, or by asking for more information, either with another question, e.g., *And what happened then?* or simply with a question word, e.g., *Why? When?*, etc.

a You are going to do "speed questioning" with other people in the class. Before you start, think of five questions to ask.

b When your teacher says "Start," you have three minutes to talk to the person next to you. Ask and answer each other's questions and ask for more information. When the teacher says "Change," stop and go and talk to another student.

c Which questions were the best for finding out about other students?

1B Do you believe it?

G auxiliary verbs; *the … the …* + comparatives
V personality
P using a dictionary to check word stress; intonation and sentence rhythm

1 READING & SPEAKING

a Look at the signatures. Can you identify any of the people?

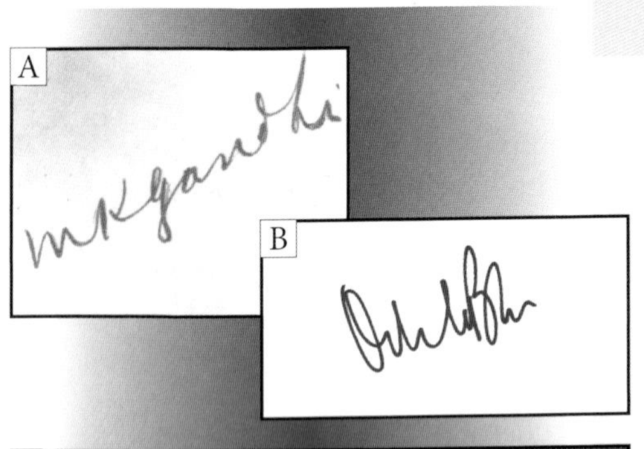

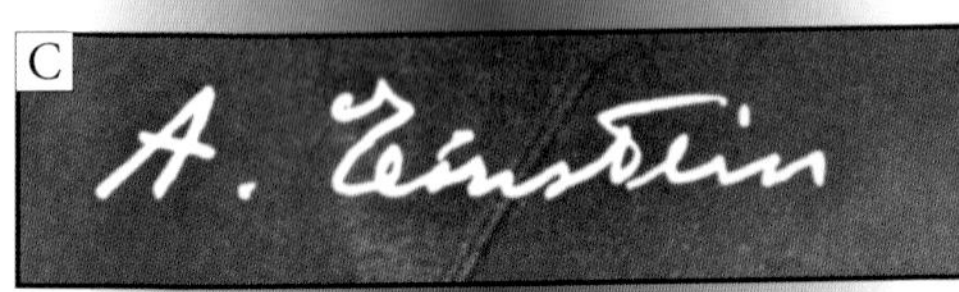

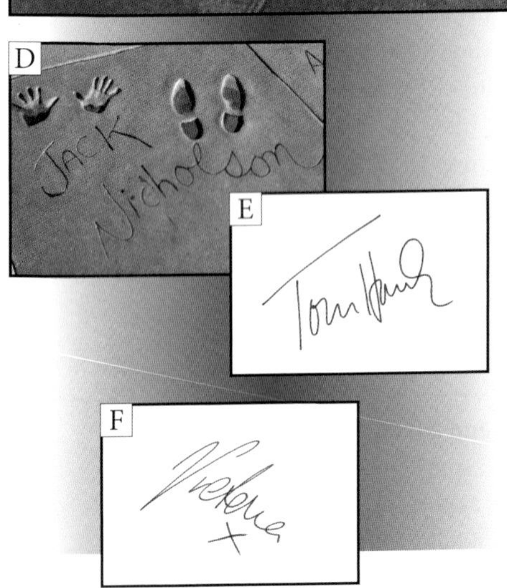

What your *signature* says about you

Your signature is the part of your handwriting that says the most about your personality. It is common for your signature to change during your life, as your signature reflects how you evolve as a person. It is also common to have several signatures, for example, a more formal signature (first and last name) when you sign a credit card or passport and an informal signature (just your first name) when you sign a birthday card.

Your formal signature A signature usually contains either a first name and a last name, or initials and a last name, or, less frequently, a first name and initials. Your first name represents your private or family self, and your last name represents your public self – how you are socially and at work.

If your first name is more prominent in your signature, this implies that you have positive feelings about your childhood and that your "private" self is more important to you than your "public" self.

If your last name is more prominent, this means that your "public" self is more important to you. The more space there is between your first and last name, the more you wish to keep your public and private self separate.

If you use only initials, either for your first or last name in your signature, this means that you are more secretive about this part of your personality (your private or public persona).

Legibility A legible signature, with names that can be clearly read, implies that you are a person with clear ideas and objectives. The more illegible your signature is, the less assertive you are as a person, and the more you tend to avoid conflict.

Angle Most signatures are horizontal, rising, or descending. A rising signature means that you are the kind of person who, when faced with problems, will work to overcome them. Usually optimistic, you are in control and ambitious. A descending signature means that you have a tendency to get depressed and give up when faced with problems and lack self-confidence. Some people's signatures go through a temporary phase when they go down, which shows that they are going through a hard time or an illness. A horizontal signature suggests an emotionally stable person who is well-balanced and generally satisfied with the way their life is going.

Size If the letters in your signature are bigger than the letters in the rest of the text you have written, that means that you are self-confident and have a high opinion of yourself. Some people actually sign in capital letters, which suggests they are arrogant rather than self-confident. People whose signature is smaller than the rest of the text may be insecure and have low self-esteem.

b Read the first paragraph of an extract from a book about graphology. On a piece of paper, write the sentence *I look forward to hearing from you*, and then sign your name under the sentence.

c Now read the rest of the extract and answer the questions. According to the extract, which of the people A–F …?

1. has / had no separation between their public and private self, and is / was not very assertive
2. is / was more identified with their public self, optimistic, and ambitious
3. is / was more identified with their private self, and without much self-confidence
4. is / was probably rather arrogant
5. keeps / kept their public and private life separate, is / was ambitious, and has / had positive feelings about their childhood
6. is / was secretive about their private life, and keeps / kept it very separate from their public life

d Try to guess the meaning of the highlighted words and phrases from the context. Check with your dictionary or the teacher.

e Now look at your partner's piece of paper with his / her signature, and explain what it means.

f Did you agree with your partner's interpretation? Do you think graphology is a serious science? Why (not)?

2 VOCABULARY personality

a Without looking at the text, how many of the ten highlighted adjectives / phrases can you remember?

b **p.146 Vocabulary Bank** *Personality.*

c Add either a suffix (e.g., *-able* or *-ful*) or a prefix (e.g., *un-* or *dis-*) or both to the **bold** words to make an adjective that fits the sentence.

1 You can invite him to the party, but he won't go. He's totally *unsociable*. **social**
2 You'll have a lively evening if Jane comes because she's very ________. **talk**
3 You can't trust John to help. He's completely ________. **rely**
4 You look very ________. Have you had some good news? **cheer**
5 He's kind of ________. He said he liked my sister, but he obviously doesn't. **sincere**
6 She's not very ________. She never has any good ideas. **imagine**
7 People say he's ________. You can't trust him with money. **honest**
8 She's so ________! She never calls when she's going to be late. **consider**

3 PRONUNCIATION using a dictionary to check word stress

In a dictionary, word stress is shown by this mark (') before the stressed syllable, e.g., *begin* /bɪ'gɪn/. Some words, especially compound words, have a primary (or main stress) and a secondary stress, e.g., *good-looking* /ˌgʊd'lʊkɪŋ/. Secondary stress is shown by a low stress mark (ˌ). It is not as strong as primary stress.

a Use the phonetics to underline the *main* stressed syllable.

1 arrogant /'ærəgənt/
2 assertive /ə'sərtɪv/
3 irritable /'ɪrətəbl/
4 creative /kri'eɪtɪv/
5 considerate /kən'sɪdərət/
6 conscientious /ˌkɑnʃɪ'ɛnʃəs/
7 possessive /pə'zɛsɪv/
8 loyal /'lɔɪəl/
9 stubborn /'stʌbərn/
10 impatient /ɪm'peɪʃnt/
11 unsociable /ˌʌn'soʊʃəbl/
12 immature /ˌɪmə'tʃʊr/

b 1.4 Listen and check. Are the negative prefixes stressed? Are the suffixes stressed?

c Practice saying the sentences below.

1 He's terribly irritable – you need to be careful with him.
2 She's so conscientious – she always does her best in everything.
3 He's very easygoing – he never gets stressed.
4 His mother's really possessive – she doesn't want him to get married.
5 She's so immature – she behaves like a child.

4 SPEAKING

GET IT RIGHT paraphrasing
If you don't know the exact adjective you need, use a phrase like *She's the kind of person who…*, *He tends to…*

⚠ Remember the third person *s*.

Talk in small groups. Where you can, give examples of people you know or have known.

What kind of person makes…?
- a bad roommate
- a bad traveling companion
- a bad boss
- a good teacher
- a good friend
- a good politician

MINI GRAMMAR
the… the… + comparatives

The more illegible your signature is, the less assertive you are as a person.
Use *the* + comparative adjective or adverb to show that one thing depends on another, for example:
The sooner you do it, the easier it'll be. = How easy it will be depends on when you do it.
The colder it is, the more clothes you need to wear.

Rewrite the sentences using *the… the…* + a comparative adjective or adverb.

1 If you study more, you learn more.
The ________, the ________.
2 If we leave soon, we'll get there earlier.
The ________, the ________.
3 If you are sociable, you have more friends.
The ________, the ________.
4 If you are happy, you are nicer to other people.
The ________, the ________.

5 1.5 SONG ♫ *You gotta be*

6 LISTENING & READING

a Read the beginning of a magazine article. Do you know what a psychic is? Do you believe psychics have special powers or are you skeptical?

b You're now going to listen to Jane describing her visit to a psychic, Sally. After each part, discuss the questions with a partner.

Part 1 1.6
Answer the questions.
1 What was Jane's first impression of the room and of Sally?
2 What are the first questions Sally asked her?
3 Why is Jane surprised by two things Sally mentions?

Part 2 1.7
True or False?
1 Jane lived in Ireland when she was a child.
2 The psychic says Jane will meet someone new.
3 Jane is above average height.
4 Sally thinks Jane will be attracted to the man by his looks.
5 Jane thinks she knows who the man is.

Part 3 1.8
Choose a, b, or c.
1 Sally says that, in the future, Jane ___.
  a will have the same health problems as her mother
  b will live longer than her mother
  c should have plastic surgery
2 According to Sally, ___ is good at reading and writing.
  a neither Jane's son nor her daughter
  b neither Jane's ex-husband nor her daughter
  c neither Jane's ex-husband nor her son
3 What Sally says about Jane's children makes Jane feel ___.
  a convinced that Sally is a genuine psychic
  b less skeptical about Sally being a psychic
  c sure that Sally is not a genuine psychic

c Read about some typical techniques used by psychics. Match the titles with the paragraphs.

A **Getting information from the client**
B **Using a name**
C **The flattering statement**
D **Identifying common medical problems**

d Listen to Jane talking about her visit again. Which techniques did Sally use?

e 1.9 Now listen to Jane talking a few weeks later. What was her final opinion about Sally's psychic abilities? What has happened since she went to see Sally?

f Do you know anyone who has ever been to a psychic? What happened?

Can psychics really see the future?

Jane Dickson investigates.

I am almost the only person I know who has never been to a psychic. Everyone I asked had a story about how key events in their lives had been predicted in some way. So I was really looking forward to my first visit to a psychic...

Tricks of the trade?

These are some of the techniques used by psychics...

1 ☐ Something psychics always do is say something that's true of almost anyone on the planet, preferably something positive. An all-time favorite is "You're intelligent with a great sense of humor." Who is going to answer, "Well, actually, I'm not. I'm really stupid and have no sense of humor at all"?

2 ☐ Statistics confirm that a headache is the most common female health problem, and almost 50 percent of men have a scar on their leg, so it's not really surprising when a psychic "sees" these problems.

3 ☐ A psychic can deduce a lot from your age and appearance, and most of them actually ask direct questions. It's difficult to avoid answering if you want results because saying nothing is like going to the doctor and refusing to discuss your symptoms.

4 ☐ Coming up with a few names is always impressive. The usual method is to let the client figure out who it might be. "Does the letter *s* mean anything to you?" is a frequent strategy.

7 GRAMMAR auxiliary verbs

a Look at some extracts from the listening. Circle the correct auxiliary verb.

"Australia is very important in your life."
"It [1]*is / isn't / was?* I've never been to Australia."
"Another place that is very important in your life is Ireland."
"Yes, that's true. Ireland [2]*is / does / has* play a big role in my life."
"Let's see… Your mother suffers from headaches, [3]*doesn't / isn't / does* she?"
"Yes, she [4]*is / does / has*, as a matter of fact."
"Well, you'll need to watch out for headaches, and so [5]*is / does / will* your mother."

b 1.10 Listen and check. Underline the auxiliaries that are stressed.

c In pairs, decide which auxiliary is used …

A as a short answer. [*4*]
B to add emphasis. [ ]
C to check information. [ ]
D to show surprise. [ ]
E to avoid repeating a verb or phrase. [ ]

d **p.132 Grammar Bank 1B.** Read the rules and do the exercises.

8 PRONUNCIATION intonation and sentence rhythm

a 1.11 Listen to the conversation and circle the auxiliary verbs that are stressed.

A What's your sister like?
B Well, she's kind of shy and quiet.
A She **is**? So **is** my brother!
B **Isn't** your brother a doctor?
A That's right. And your sister works in a bank, **doesn't** she?
B No, she **doesn't**. She's a journalist.
A Oh, that's right, you **did** tell me, but I forgot. I think they'd probably get along well.
B You **do**? But if my sister **doesn't** talk much and neither **does** your brother…
A Yeah, I see what you mean. We probably **shouldn't** introduce them.

b Listen and repeat the conversation, copying the intonation and rhythm. Then practice it in pairs.

c 1.12 Listen and respond to the sentences you hear with an echo question, for example, *You are? You didn't?*, etc. Use a rising intonation.

d Complete the sentences on the left so that they are true for you. Then read them to your partner, who will respond with an echo question and then say whether he / she is the same as you or different.

I'm not very good at ______. (activity)	You aren't?	Neither am I. / I am.
I'm very ______. (adjective)	You are?	So am I. / I'm not.
I hate ______. (a food)	You do?	So do I. / I don't. I like it.
I don't ______ very often. (verb)	Don't you?	______.
I've been to ______. (town / country)	______?	______.
My favorite season is ______.	______?	______.

e **Communication** *You're psychic, aren't you? A p.116 B p.119.* Make guesses about your partner and then check if they are true.

G present perfect (simple and continuous)
V illness and treatment
P consonant and vowel sounds

1C You're the doctor!

1 SPEAKING & VOCABULARY illness and treatment

a Read about the two situations and try to figure out the meaning of the highlighted words. Then decide which you think is the correct answer for each situation.

You're the doc!

1 You're at home with some friends watching a game on TV. In the excitement, one of your friends suddenly starts having a nosebleed.

DO YOU ...?

a get some ice from the freezer and put it on his nose
b get some toilet paper, tell him to put it in his nose, and suggest that he go to the doctor to check his blood pressure
c tell him to pinch the soft part of his nose for five minutes

2 You're having a barbecue with some friends on the beach. One of your friends accidentally picks up a very hot piece of wood and burns her hand. It hurts a lot, and she has blisters on her skin.

DO YOU ...?

a pour cold water on the hand and then cover it with a plastic bag
b cover the burn with sunscreen
c break the blisters and put on antiseptic cream

b **Communication** *You're the doc! p.116.* Check your answers.

c **p.147 Vocabulary Bank** *Illness and treatment.*

2 PRONUNCIATION consonant and vowel sounds

The phonetic symbols in a dictionary help you check the pronunciation of words that have an irregular sound-spelling relationship.

a 1.13 Use the phonetic symbols to help you pronounce these words. Then listen and check.

1 cough /kɔf/
2 heart /hɑrt/
3 asthma /ˈæzmə/
4 bruise /bruz/
5 blood /blʌd/
6 diarrhea /ˌdaɪəˈriə/

b How do you pronounce the sounds below? Write the words from the list in the correct column.

ache allergy ankle bandage checkup choking GP infection injection pressure rash specialist stomach temperature unconscious

c 1.14 Listen and check. Practice saying the words.

d **p.160 Sound Bank.** Look at the typical spellings for these sounds.

e Ask and answer the questions below with a partner.

1 What are the main symptoms of ...?
   a a cold
   b the flu
   c a twisted ankle
   d a heart attack
   e an allergic reaction
   f food poisoning
2 What should you do if you have the illnesses or injuries above?

3 READING & LISTENING

a You are going to read an article about two people who found themselves involved in life or death situations. Work in pairs. **A** read the first article and **B** read the second.

Help! My friend is choking!

Mrs. Johnson, a library assistant, was having dinner with friends in a restaurant. They were all having steak, and Mrs. Johnson had just swallowed a piece of meat when she suddenly found that she couldn't breathe. Her friends hit her hard on the back, but the piece of steak remained stuck in her throat. She was starting to panic. One of her friends shouted out desperately, "Excuse me, can anyone help my friend? She's choking." At another table in the restaurant, a famous TV talk show presenter saw what was happening and rushed over to try to help. She stood behind Mrs. Johnson and put her arms around her waist, and then pulled hard inward and upward three times...

The day my little boy swallowed a tomato

"Look at me, Mom," giggled my three-year-old son. I could hardly understand him because his mouth was full of cherry tomatoes. He had taken them out of the refrigerator while I was making lunch. "Oh, Peter, don't be silly," I laughed. That was a big mistake. Peter tried to laugh too, and as he did, one of the tomatoes got stuck in his throat. He tried to cough, but nothing happened. He was choking. I hit Peter on the back, but the tomato didn't move. Peter began to turn blue. I ran outside, screaming for help, but the street was completely deserted. I was desperate. I put my whole hand in his mouth and pushed my fingers as far as I could down his throat...

Adapted from a newspaper

b Take turns telling each other your story. Explain ...

1 what the situation was.
2 what the person who was giving first aid did.

c Discuss whether you think they did the right thing or not.

d 1.15 1.16 Now listen to what happened next and answer the questions.

1 What happened to Mrs. Johnson in the end? Did the presenter do the right thing?
2 What happened to Peter in the end? Did his mother do the right thing?

4 SPEAKING

GET IT RIGHT keep going!

Even when you know a lot of vocabulary connected with a topic, you may find that you don't know the exact word or phrase for what you want to say. If this happens, don't freeze! Paraphrase (use other words to say what you mean) and keep going!

Useful language

What I mean is...
I can't remember / I don't know the word, but it's...
She had a sort of / kind of...

Talk to a partner.

Have you ever had to give first aid?

YES — **To who? Why? What happened?**

NO

Has anyone ever had to give *you* first aid?

YES — **What happened?**

NO

First Aid

How much do you know about first aid?
Where did you learn it?

What do you think you should do if...?

a someone is stung by a bee
b someone loses consciousness
c someone accidentally takes too many painkillers

5 GRAMMAR present perfect (simple and continuous)

a **Check what you know:** present perfect / simple past. Right (✔) or wrong (✘)? Correct the wrong highlighted phrases.

1 **A** Have you ever had an operation?
  B Yes, I've broken my leg two years ago.
2 **A** How long was your uncle in the hospital?
  B Since last Tuesday. He's coming home tomorrow.
3 You haven't taken your medicine yet.
4 **A** Why did you get up so early this morning?
  B Because I have gone to bed early last night.
5 They were married for 50 years! Today is their anniversary.
6 I know my doctor for ten years. She's very good.

Any problems? ➲ **Workbook p.11**

b 1.17 **New grammar.** Read the jokes and use your instinct to cross out the wrong form (present perfect simple or continuous). Listen and check.

Patient Doctor, my son *has swallowed / has been swallowing* my pen. What should I do?
Doctor Use a pencil until I get there.

Doctor You look exhausted!
Patient Yes. *I've run / I've been running* after a cat.
Doctor After a cat?
Patient Yes, doctor. I think I'm a dog.
Doctor I see. How long *has this gone on / has this been going on*?
Patient Since I was a little puppy.
Doctor OK. Just lie down here on the couch, and we'll talk about it.
Patient I can't!
Doctor Why not?
Patient I'm not allowed on the furniture.

Patient *Have they sent / Have they been sending* you the results of my tests yet?
Doctor Yes. The news isn't good, I'm afraid.
Patient How long do I have to live, doctor?
Doctor Ten…
Patient Ten WHAT? Months? Weeks?
Doctor Nine, eight, seven, six…

c ➲ **p.132 Grammar Bank 1C.** Read the rules and do the exercises.

d In pairs, use the prompts to ask and answer the questions. Is there anything you could do to improve your health?

1 / drink enough water? How many glasses / drink today?
2 / get any physical exercise? What kind? How long / do it?
3 / eat a lot of fruits and vegetables? How many servings / have today?
4 / walk to school/work? How far / walk today?
5 / smoke? How long / smoke? How many cigarettes / have today?
6 / take any vitamins right now? How long / take them?
7 How many hours / sleep a night? / sleep well recently?
8 / allergic anything? / ever have a serious allergic reaction?

6 READING

a What symptoms do people have when they feel stressed?

b Which *three* of these things do you think are the most stressful? Number them 1–3 (1 = the most stressful) and compare with a partner.

- ☐ Packing for a trip at the last minute.
- ☐ Being stuck in a traffic jam when you have an appointment.
- ☐ Writing a report for your boss when you don't have much time to finish it.
- ☐ Running for a bus or train.
- ☐ Taking care of a family member who has a chronic illness.
- ☐ Shopping on your lunch break.
- ☐ Programing a DVD player using the instruction manual.

c Read the article once quickly. Then put a check (✔) next to the activities above that are bad for your health. What does the article say about the others?

d Read the article again more slowly. Circle the correct *main idea* for each paragraph.

1 a Being in traffic jams is bad for our health.
b Some people think that not all kinds of stress are bad for us.
c Doctors don't agree on how we can reduce our levels of stress.

2 a Young people suffer more from stress than older people.
b Alzheimer's is one of the illnesses many old people suffer from.
c Good stress can stop us from getting sick.

3 a Situations that produce good stress are always short-term.
b Some stress can make our cells stronger.
c Too much protein can make us sick.

4 a We need some stress to exercise our cells' self-repair mechanism.
b Getting physical exercise makes us feel less stressed.
c Packing your suitcase in a hurry is an example of good stress.

e Complete the sentences using words from the article.

1 When we try to do less of something, we try to **c**________ **d**________. (paragraph 1)
2 An illness that you have for a very long time is called a **c**________ illness. (1)
3 Something that is good for us is **b**________. (2)
4 The verb to make something stronger is **s**________. (2)
5 Our bodies are made up of millions of **c**________. (2)
6 When we treat our bodies badly, we **d**________ them. (3)
7 Another word for illness is **d**________. (3)
8 Something that is bad for us is **h**________. (3)
9 Exercising helps make our **m**________ bigger and stronger. (4)

f Use your dictionary to check the pronunciation of the words in **e**.

g Discuss these questions with a partner.

1 Do you agree with what you have read in this article? Why (not)?
2 What kinds of "good stress" do you have in your life?
3 What other health stories have you heard about recently? Do you pay much attention to them? Do you believe them?

➲ **p.157 Phrasal verbs in context** *File 1.*

Get stressed, stay young

1 For decades doctors have warned us about the dangers of stress and have given us advice about how to cut down our stress levels. Everyone agrees that long-term stress, such as having to take care of someone with a chronic illness, or stressful situations where there is nothing we can do, such as being stuck in a traffic jam, is bad for our health and should be avoided whenever possible. However, some medical experts now believe that certain kinds of stress may actually be good for us.

2 Dr. Marios Kyriazis, an anti-aging expert, claims that what he calls "good stress" is beneficial to our health and may, in fact, help us stay young and attractive and even live longer. Dr. Kyriazis says that "good stress" can strengthen our natural defenses, which protect us from illnesses common among older people, such as Alzheimer's, arthritis, and heart problems. He believes that "good stress" can increase the production of the proteins that help repair the body's cells, including brain cells.

3 According to Dr. Kyriazis, running for a bus or having to work to a deadline are examples of "good stress," that is, situations with short-term, low, or moderate stress. The stress usually makes us react quickly and efficiently, and gives us a sense of achievement – we did it! However, in both these situations, the stress damages the cells in our body or brain, and they start to break down. But then the cells' own repair mechanism "switches on" and produces proteins that repair the damaged cells and remove harmful chemicals that can gradually cause disease. In fact, the body's response is greater than needed to repair the damage, so it actually makes the cells stronger than they were before.

4 "As the body gets older, this self-repair mechanism of the cells starts to slow down," says Dr. Kyriazis. "The best way to keep the process working efficiently is to 'exercise' it, in the same way you would exercise your muscles to keep them strong. This means having a certain amount of stress in our lives." Other stressful activities that Kyriazis recommends as good stress include redecorating a room in your house over a weekend, packing your suitcase in a hurry to reach the airport on time, shopping for a dinner party during your lunch break, or programing your DVD player by following the instruction manual.

So next time your boss tells you that she wants to see that report finished and on her desk in 45 minutes, don't panic; just think of it as "good stress," which will have benefits for your long-term health!

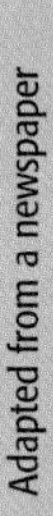

THE INTERVIEW

a You are going to listen to an interview with Joyce Levine, an astrologer. Before you listen, read the glossary and look at how the words are pronounced to help you understand what she says.

Glossary
body of knowledge /'badi əv 'nalɪdʒ/ a large collection of information
rapport /rə'pɔr/ a friendly relationship between people
counseling /'kaʊnsəlɪŋ/ professional advice given to people with problems
birth chart /bərθ tʃɑrt/ a diagram that shows the position of the planets when a person was born
temperament /'tɛmprəmənt/ the emotional side of a person's character
range /'reɪndʒ/ the limits within which things can vary
fate /feɪt/ the power that is believed to control everything that happens
free will /fri wɪl/ the power to make your own choices

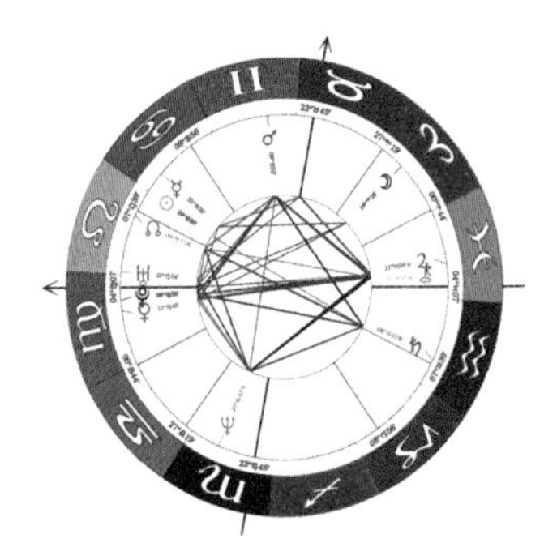

b 1.18 Listen to part 1. Answer the questions with a partner.
1 What does an astrologer need to know about the planets?
2 What are some of the skills an astrologer should have?
3 What does Joyce do when someone comes to see her?
4 What kinds of things does an astrologer learn about people from their birth charts?
5 How much can a person's birth chart tell about their future?

c 1.19 Listen to part 2. Answer the questions with a partner.
What does she say about ...?
1 why people come to see her
2 the kinds of people who go to see her
3 the questions businesses want answered
4 how she warns people about bad news
5 predicting her own future

d 1.20 Listen and complete the phrases. What do you think they mean?

COMMON PHRASES
1 ... you have to know the meanings of the planets _____ _____ of how they affect human nature.
2 ... what we do is _____ go over what that means.
3 The clients I have really are a _____ _____ of people ...
4 "You might want to spend more time with your mother," or _____ _____ that.
5 Ideally, I wouldn't scare them, but they'd get _____ _____.
6 Of course, you _____ _____ it!

e Listen to the interview again with the audioscript on page 121. Would you like Joyce Levine to do your birth chart? Why (not)?

ON THE STREET

a 1.21 Listen to five people talking about horoscopes. Write the number of the speakers next to their star sign. Who believes that star signs can definitely influence someone's personality?

1 Duey

2 Dennis

3 Fern

4 Curt

5 Tiffany

Aries /'ɛriz/	Leo /'lioʊ/	Sagittarius /sædʒə'tɛriəs/
Taurus /'tɔrəs/	Virgo /'vərgoʊ/	Capricorn /'kæprɪkɔrn/
Gemini /'dʒɛmənaɪ/	Libra /'librə/	Aquarius /ə'kwɛriəs/
Cancer /'kænsər/	Scorpio /'skɔrpioʊ/	Pisces /'paɪsiz/

b Listen again and write the name of the person. Who ...?
1 doesn't like to admit they really believe in astrology
2 learned something about astrology while studying another subject
3 reads their own horoscope almost every day
4 thinks star signs influence people only when they read about them too often
5 thinks that people and places have more influence than star signs

c 1.22 Listen and complete the phrases with one word. What do you think they mean?

COMMON PHRASES
1 I think it's what you _____ into it. pv
2 I do every once in a _____ ...
3 ... probably where you grow up and the people you talk to have a bigger influence on how you _____ out. pv
4 ... I don't go out of my _____ every day to find my horoscope and read it ...
5 However, they might apply to several other people as _____.

d Listen to the interviews again with the audioscript on page 122. Then answer the same questions with a partner.

Study Link MultiROM

An informal e-mail / letter

If you are writing an informal e-mail, it is usual to start with *Hi*. If you are writing an informal letter, you should start with *Dear*.

a Read the e-mail from Chris. It has 12 mistakes: four grammar, four punctuation, and four spelling mistakes. With a partner, correct the mistakes.

b Read Chris's e-mail again and find phrases that mean…

I haven't written or called.
I've been reading and replying to my e-mails.
Say hello to your family from me.

New Message

Send Chat Attach Address Fonts Colors Save As Draft

From: Chris
To: Eva
Subject: News

Hi Eva,

Sorry that I havent been in touch for a while but I've been sick. I got the flu last week and I had a temprature of 102°F, so I've been in bed since four days. I'm feeling a little better today, so I've been catching up on my e-mails. Luckly my classes at the university don't start until next week.

How are you? What have you been doing? Anything exciting. Here everyone are fine – except for me and my flu! My brother Ian just started his new job with a music-company – I think I told you about it when I last wrote – anyway, he's really enjoying it. How is your family? I hope they're well.

I have a good news – I'm going to a conference in your town in may, from the 16th to the 20th. Could you recomend a hotel where I could stay downtown? It needs to be somewhere not too expensive because the university is paying. I'll have a half day free for siteseeing. Do you think you'll can show me around? That would be great.

Well, that's all for now. Please give my regards to your family.

I hope to hear from you soon.

Take care,

Chris

c You're going to answer Chris's e-mail. Look at the **Useful language** expressions and try to complete them.

Useful language

Opening expressions

Thanks [1]______ your e-mail / letter.
It was great [2]______ hear from you.
Sorry for [3]______ writing earlier / that I haven't been in touch for a while.
I [4]______ you and your family are well.

Responding to news

Sorry [5]______ hear about your exam results.
Glad [6]______ hear that you're all well.
Good luck [7]______ the new job.
Hope you [8]______ better soon.

Closing expressions

Anyway, / Well, that's all [9]______ now.
Hope to hear from you soon. / Looking [10]______ to hearing from you soon.
[11]______ my regards (love) to…
Take [12]______ / [13]______ wishes / Regards / (Lots of) love from…
[14]______ (= something you forgot and want to add after your signature) Please send me the photos you promised.

PLAN the content.

1 Underline the questions in the e-mail that Chris wants you to answer.
2 Underline other parts of the e-mail that you think you need to respond to, e.g., *I've been sick*.
3 Think about how to respond to each of the things you underlined.

WRITE 120–180 words, in two or three paragraphs. Use informal language (contractions, conversational expressions, etc.), and expressions from **Useful language**.

CHECK your e-mail for mistakes (grammar, punctuation, and spelling).

1 What do you remember?

GRAMMAR

a Complete the sentences with one word.

1 What were you and Sarah talking ______?

2 You didn't like the movie, ______ you?

3 My father loves opera, and so ______ my mother.

4 **A** I've been to Peru twice.
B You ______? I'd love to go.

5 What have you ______ doing since I last saw you?

b Circle the right answer, a, b, or c.

1 Could you tell me what time ______?
a the bus leaves
b leaves the bus
c does the bus leave

2 How many people usually ______ to this class?
a do come
b come
c did come

3 ______ at least three books so far this month.
a I've been reading
b I'm reading
c I've read

4 That was the best movie ______!
a I've ever seen
b I've never seen
c I've ever been seeing

5 The sooner you start, ______ you'll finish.
a sooner
b the sooner
c the sooner than

VOCABULARY

a Word groups. Underline the word that is different. Say why.

1 vain	stubborn	possessive	wise
2 cheerful	loyal	insincere	conscientious
3 flu	blister	cold	asthma
4 GP	ER	specialist	doctor

b Complete the sentences with a preposition.

1 Who were you talking ___ on the phone?

2 She's very good ___ listening to people.

3 Sam is a real pain ___ the neck.

4 She's allergic ___ milk.

5 What are you waiting ___?

c Complete the sentences with an adjective made from the word in **bold**.

1 Daniel is very ______. He never remembers our anniversary. **forget**

2 I'm ______ – I want to go far in my profession. **ambition**

3 My sister is very ______. I can always depend on her for anything. **rely**

4 Luke is very ______ – happy one moment and sad the next. **mood**

5 Michi is very ______. It's very easy to hurt her feelings. **sense**

d Write words for the definitions.

1 **b**______	(verb)	when blood comes out of, for example, your finger
2 **s**______	(adj)	bigger than normal, especially because of an injury or infection
3 **b**______	(noun)	a piece of cloth used to tie around a part of the body that has been hurt
4 **i**______	(adj)	(a person who) gets angry easily
5 **b**______	(adj)	(a person who is) always telling other people what to do
6 **a**______	(adj)	(a person who) thinks he / she is superior to other people

PRONUNCIATION

a Underline the word with a different sound.

1	cheerful	headache	choking	stitches
2	sociable	unconscious	pressure	bossy
3	funny	impulsive	blood	flu
4	cough	open	swollen	throat
5	heart	scorecard	earache	arm

b Underline the stressed syllable.

arrogant immature injection allergic specialist

What can you do?

CAN YOU UNDERSTAND THIS TEXT?

a Read the article and choose a, b, or c.

1 The survey was paid for by ___.
 a Dr. Petrie b City University c CentralNic
2 If your password is "family oriented," you ___.
 a probably have a large family
 b probably don't use a computer very often
 c are likely to be an animal lover
3 If your password is "Brad Pitt," you probably ___.
 a want to identify yourself with a famous person
 b watch a lot of TV
 c go to the movies very often
4 People who belong to the "cryptic" group probably ___.
 a worry about other people reading their e-mails
 b don't spend much time trying to invent a password
 c can't think of an interesting password
5 Passwords say something about our personalities because ___.
 a we think for a long time before choosing one
 b we choose words that we will remember easily
 c we choose something without thinking about it consciously

b Look at the highlighted words and phrases. Can you guess what they mean?

Passwords reveal your personality

THE WORD OR PHRASE that you use to open your e-mail account may provide a key to your personality as well as your correspondence, according to a psychologist. Helen Petrie, professor of human / computer interaction at City University in London, analyzed the responses of 1,200 people who participated in a survey funded by CentralNic, an Internet domain-name company.

Petrie identifies three main password "genres." "Family-oriented" respondents numbered nearly half of those surveyed. These people use their own name or nickname, the name of a child, spouse, or pet, or a birth date as their password. They tend to be occasional computer users and have strong family ties. "They choose passwords that symbolize people or events with emotional value," says Petrie. One third of respondents were "fans," using the names of athletes, singers, movie stars, fictional characters, or sports teams. Petrie says fans are young and want to associate themselves with the lifestyle represented by a celebrity. Two of the most popular names were Madonna and Homer Simpson. The third main group of participants are "cryptics" because they pick unintelligible passwords or a random string of letters, numerals, and symbols such as "Jxa+157." Petrie says cryptics are the most security-conscious group. They tend to make the safest, but least interesting, choices.

Passwords are revealing for two reasons. First, because they are invented on the spot. "Since you are focused on getting into a system, for example, your e-mail account, you're likely to write down something that comes to mind quickly," says Petrie. "In this sense passwords tap into things that are just below the surface of consciousness. Also, to remember your password, you pick something that will stick in your mind. You may unconsciously choose something of particular emotional significance."

CAN YOU UNDERSTAND THESE PEOPLE?

a 1.23 Listen and circle the correct answer, a, b, or c.

1 How did the woman meet her current partner?
 a By speed dating.
 b Through a friend.
 c On an Internet dating site.
2 How does the man describe the woman he met?
 a shy
 b outgoing
 c hardworking
3 How will the man be traveling?
 a By train and taxi.
 b By bus and taxi.
 c By train and bus.
4 What does the doctor tell Mr. Strong to do?
 a Take antibiotics.
 b Drink a lot.
 c Stay in bed.
5 What do the two sports commentators agree about?
 a That the player won't be playing in the game next Sunday.
 b That the player twisted his ankle.
 c That the player won't be able to play again for two months.

b 1.24 You will hear two women who visited psychics talking to a man from the Psychic Association about their experiences. Answer the questions.

1 Why did Mara go to a psychic?
2 What did the psychic tell her?
3 Was it good advice?
4 What is the man's opinion of the psychic Mara saw?
5 Why doesn't Alice agree with Mara?
6 What did the psychic tell Alice?
7 How did the psychic's advice help Alice?
8 What advice does the man give Alice?

CAN YOU SAY THIS IN ENGLISH?

Can you ...?

- ☐ ask questions with or without auxiliaries and with prepositions
- ☐ describe your personality and your friends' / family's personalities
- ☐ talk about health problems and describe symptoms to a doctor

G adjectives as nouns, adjective order
V clothes and fashion
P vowel sounds

National stereotypes: truth or myth?

1 LISTENING & SPEAKING

a You're going to listen to four people talking about the typical characteristics of people from their country (Canada, Australia, England, and the US). Before you listen, work with a partner and try to predict what positive and negative characteristics the speakers might mention.

b 2.1 Listen and try to match the speakers 1–4 with their nationality. Use their accent and what they say about people from their country to help you.

Canadian ☐ English ☐
Australian ☐ American ☐

c Listen again. Write down at least one negative and two positive characteristics about each nationality. Does each person think he / she is typical or not? Why (not)?

d 2.2 Now listen to two extracts from each speaker. Try to write in the missing words. What do you think they mean?

1 a I'd say we're a down-to-earth people, friendly and ______.
  b We believe in working hard, but we really enjoy our ______ time.

2 a We think that if we work hard, we can ______ anything.
  b I think I've ______ the typical optimism and drive.

3 a It's difficult to generalize about us as a people, especially as our big cities now have such a ______ population.
  b Just think of our inability, or our ______, to learn foreign languages!

4 a We try to accept everyone's culture and welcome their ______, their food, their traditions.
  b We're physically reserved, compared to other cultures that might have more touching or ______ or kissing.

e In pairs or small groups, discuss the questions.

1 What do you think are the strengths of your nationality?
2 What are the weaknesses?
3 In what way would you say *you* are typical?

2 GRAMMAR adjectives as nouns

a In many parts of the world there is a joke based on national stereotypes. With a partner, complete *The best place in the world* with five different nationalities. Then do the same for *The worst place in the world*. Compare your version of the joke with another pair.

The best place in the world is where …
the police are ______,
the cooks are ______,
the mechanics are ______,
and everything is organized by the ______.

The worst place in the world is where …
the police are ______,
the cooks are ______,
the mechanics are ______,
and everything is organized by the ______.

b Read the article *Do we see ourselves as we really are?* and answer the questions.

1 How was the research done?
2 What does it tell us about national stereotypes?

c Read the article again. Which nationality / nationalities …?

1 were friendlier than they thought
2 were less outgoing than they thought
3 were more hardworking than they thought
4 knew themselves the best
5 knew themselves the least
6 thought they were calm and reasonable, but they weren't

d After reading the article, do you think any of the strengths and weaknesses of your nationality you mentioned before (in **1e**) may not be completely true?

Do we see ourselves as we really are?

A worldwide survey casts doubt on national stereotypes

The English are cold and reserved, Brazilians are lively and fun-loving, and the Japanese are shy and hardworking – these are examples of national stereotypes that are widely believed, not only by *other* nationalities but also by many people among the nationality themselves. But how much truth is there in such stereotypes? Two psychologists, Robert McCrae and Antonio Terracciano, have investigated the subject, and the results of their research are surprising. They found that people from a particular country do share some general characteristics, but that these characteristics are often very different from the stereotype.

In the largest survey of its kind, a team of psychologists used personality tests to establish shared characteristics among 49 different nationalities around the world. They then interviewed thousands of people from these same groups and asked them to describe typical members of their own nationality. In most cases the stereotype (how nationalities saw themselves) was very different from the results of the personality tests (the reality).

For example, Italians and Russians thought of themselves as outgoing and sociable, but the personality tests showed them to be much more shy than they imagined. The Spanish saw themselves as very outgoing, but also as rather lazy. In fact, the research showed them to be only moderately outgoing and much more conscientious than they thought. Brazilians were rather anxious – the opposite of their own view of themselves. The Czechs and the Argentinians thought of themselves as irritable and unfriendly, but they turned out to be among the friendliest of all nationalities. The English were the nationality whose own stereotype was the furthest from reality. While they saw themselves as reserved and closed, Dr. McCrae's research showed them to be among the most outgoing and open-minded of the groups studied.

The only nationality group in the whole study where people saw themselves as they really are was the Poles – not especially outgoing, and slightly anxious.

Dr. McCrae and Dr. Terracciano hope that their research will show that national stereotypes are inaccurate and unproductive and that this might improve international understanding – we're all much more alike than we think we are!

e Right (✔) or wrong (✘)? Correct the sentences that are *grammatically* wrong.

1 English talk about the weather a lot. ✘ *The English*
2 English people often travel abroad.
3 The Spanishs enjoy eating out.
4 Chinese and Japanese have different cuisines.
5 I know an Italian who doesn't like spaghetti.
6 My sister married a Polish.

f **p.134 Grammar Bank 2A.** Read the rules for adjectives as nouns, and do exercise **a**.

g In pairs, say if you agree or disagree with the sentences below.

The British are usually less friendly than the Americans.
The Italians dress better than any other nationality.
The rich are always stingier than the poor.
The elderly are best taken care of in nursing homes.
The unemployed should not receive government benefits.
Small towns are better places to live than big ones.
It's better to buy expensive clothes if you can afford to because they last longer than cheap ones.

3 READING

a Look at the photos on page 23. Do you think the people are typically English in the way they dress? Who do you think is dressed in the most eccentric way?

b You are going to read an article about how the English dress. Before you read the first part, discuss with a partner whether you think the following statements are true or false. Write T or F in the box.

1 The English dress badly. ☐
2 The English wear very good suits. ☐
3 English people need rules to dress well. ☐
4 Punks and Goths wear a kind of uniform. ☐
5 The English person with the best fashion sense is the queen. ☐
6 Young people around the world copy "street fashion" invented by the English. ☐
7 The English don't like people who dress "differently." ☐

c Now read the first part of the text and find out if the writer agrees with your answers.

d Look at the photo below. What "tribe" of young people does he belong to? Read the second part of the text and find out why the anthropologist spoke to this person and what she discovered.

e Look at the highlighted adjectives and try to figure out the meaning from the context. Check with your dictionary or the teacher.

f Choose the best summary of the article. From what you know about English people, do you think it is true?

A The English often dress badly because they are insecure about what to wear. However, they often have a sense of humor about it.

B The English are a nation of individuals, who each dress in a rather eccentric way. The queen and the Goths are good examples of this.

C The English love wearing uniforms, and the more outrageous they are, the better.

4 VOCABULARY clothes and fashion

a Look at the photos on page 23 again. What are the people wearing?

b ➲ **p.148 Vocabulary Bank** *Clothes and fashion.*

c ➲ **Communication** *Clothes quiz A p.116 B p.119.*

Watching the English: how the English dress

Kate Fox, an English anthropologist, spent 12 years researching various aspects of English culture in order to try to discover the "defining characteristics of Englishness." The following is an extract from her book *Watching the English*.

THE ENGLISH have a difficult and, generally speaking, dysfunctional relationship with clothes. Their main problem is that they have a desperate need for rules and are unable to cope without them. This helps to explain why they have an international reputation for dressing in general very badly, but with specific areas of excellence, such as high-class men's suits, ceremonial costume, and innovative street fashion. In other words, we English dress best when we are "in uniform."

You may be surprised that I am including "innovative street fashion" in the category of uniform. Surely the parrot-haired punks or the Victorian vampire Goths are being original, not following rules? It's true that they all look different and eccentric, but in fact they all look eccentric in exactly the same way. They are wearing a uniform. The only truly eccentric dresser in this country is the queen, who pays no attention to fashion and continues to wear what she likes, a kind of 1950s fashion, with no regard for anyone else's opinion. However, it is true that the styles invented by young English people are much more outrageous than any other nation's street fashion and are often imitated by young people all over the world. We may not be individually eccentric, apart from the queen, but we have a sort of collective eccentricity, and we appreciate originality in dress even if we do not individually have it.

IN OTHER AREAS OF RESEARCH another "rule" of behavior I had discovered was that it is very important for the English not to take themselves *too* seriously, to be able to laugh at themselves. However, it is well known that most teenagers tend to take themselves a bit too seriously. Would a "tribe" of young people be able to laugh at the way they dress? I decided to find out and went straight to a group whose identity is very closely linked to the way they dress, the Goths.

The Goths, in their macabre black costumes, certainly look as if they are taking themselves seriously. But when I got into conversation with them, I discovered to my surprise that they too had a sense of humor. I was chatting at a bus stop with a Goth who was in the full vampire costume – with a white face, deep purple lipstick, and spiky black hair. I saw that he was also wearing a T-shirt with "Goth" printed on it in large letters. "Why are you wearing that?" I asked. "It's in case you don't realize that I'm a Goth," he answered, pretending to be serious. We both looked at his highly conspicuous clothes and burst out laughing.

Adapted from *Watching the English* by Kate Fox

5 PRONUNCIATION vowel sounds

Some English vowel sounds are fairly similar and might be confusing. Practice distinguishing them.

a 2.3 Look at the pairs of sound pictures below. Put two words from the list in each column. Listen and check.

awful checked cotton high-heeled hooded leather linen long
loose patterned sandals sleeveless slippers polka-dot suit wool

b Practice saying the phrases.

a loose wool suit
pink silk slippers
red leather sandals
green high-heeled shoes
a polka-dot cotton top
a long hooded sweater

c p.159 Sound Bank. Look at the typical spellings for these sounds.

6 SPEAKING

GET IT RIGHT *wear* and *dress*

Circle the right word.

1 The English don't *wear* / *dress* very stylishly.
2 The Goths *wear* / *dress* a lot of black clothes.

Talk in small groups.

How your nationality dresses

Do people in your country have a reputation for dressing well or badly?
Do you think women pay more attention to their appearance than men, or vice versa?
Are people generally very fashion conscious?
What is in fashion right now for men and women?
What are the current "tribes" of young people? What do they wear? Do you like the way they dress?
Are there any celebrities in your country who dress in a very eccentric way? What do you think of them?
Do people tend to judge others by the way they dress?
Do *you* think you dress like a typical person from your country? Why (not)?

7 GRAMMAR adjective order

a Use your instinct. Complete each sentence with the **bold** words in the right order.

1 The Goth in the photo has ______________. **hair black spiky**
2 For the wedding I'm wearing a ______________. **suit linen beige**
3 I want to buy a ______________. **bag black big leather**
4 I'm looking for some ______________. **shorts running nylon white**

b p.134 Grammar Bank 2A. Read the rules for adjective order and do exercise **b**.

c Imagine you were given two items of clothing for your birthday that you don't like. You have decided to sell them on eBay™, the auction website. Write a detailed description, making them sound as attractive as possible.

d Now tell other students about your two items. Try to find someone who wants to buy them and agree on a price.

8 2.4 SONG ♫ *Englishman in New York*

G narrative tenses, past perfect continuous; *so / such … that*
V air travel
P irregular past forms

2 B Air travel: the inside story

1 READING

a Read the back cover of a book about air travel. Can you guess the answers to any of the questions?

Air Babylon **is a best-selling book, cowritten by Imogen Edwards-Jones and anonymous airline employees whose identities must remain secret. It tells the "inside story" about flying and answers all these questions and many more…**

What are the check-in agents really doing when they type at their computers?

Why is the heat often suddenly turned up halfway through a flight?

Out of 1,000 passengers, how many will probably lose their luggage?

Why do airport employees sometimes have a problem with wheelchairs?

Why can you sometimes smell roast chicken in a plane when they are serving you fish?

b Now quickly read the extract from *Air Babylon*. Did you guess correctly?

c Now read the extract again. Complete each paragraph with one of the sentences below. Be careful: there is one sentence you do not need to use.

A Wheelchairs are a big problem for us.
B It flies into the engine, totally destroying itself and the machinery.
C I'll never forget the last time it happened to me.
D So you can see, it really does pay to be nice to the person at the counter.
E This is mainly because the transport times between the terminals are so tight.
F And, as every flight attendant knows, a snoring plane is a happy plane.

d Do you believe everything you read in the extract?

Air BABYLON

Depending on what computer system the airline uses, check-in agents can talk to each other via simultaneous e-mail. So when they seem to be taking a very long time to type your rather short name into the computer, they are probably sending one of their coworkers a message – usually about you or about someone in the line behind you. These messages range from "Have you seen this incredibly good-looking woman / man?" to "I've got a really difficult passenger here – does anyone have a seat next to a screaming child?" 1 ☐

There is a sensible drinking policy on all airlines, which means that we are not supposed to serve passengers if they start getting noisy, but some cabin crew members think that if you give them enough to eat and drink, they will eventually fall asleep and give you no trouble at all. 2 ☐ That's the reason, of course, why we like to turn the heat up halfway through a flight…

Some airports are notorious for losing passengers' luggage. Heathrow Airport has a poor reputation – most airports lose about two in every thousand bags, but Heathrow loses 80 per thousand, which means for every 500 people who check in, 40 won't get their bags or suitcases at the other end! 3 ☐ When the airport is busy, which it always is, there is so much baggage being transported between the terminals and so little time to do it that a lot of the transferred luggage gets left behind.

4 ☐ Not only is there always a shortage of them for the people who really need them, but worse still, some of the people who request them often don't need them at all. I've lost count of the number of times I've pushed someone through the airport, taken them through customs and passport control, and gotten a porter to pick up their luggage, and then seen the person jump up in Arrivals and sprint toward their waiting relatives. One flight attendant I know gets so annoyed when this happens that as soon as the passenger gets out of the chair, she shouts, "Ladies and gentlemen! I give you another miracle, courtesy of the airline industry! After decades in a chair, he walks again!" The passenger is usually so embarrassed that he (and it's usually a *he*) disappears as quickly as he can.

Birds are one of the major problems for any airport when planes are taking off and landing. A swan or any large bird can easily cause an accident. 5 ☐ Smaller birds are less of a problem. In some cases they can do some damage, but more often than not they are just roasted. When this happens, there is often such a strong smell of roast bird that passengers on the plane think that chicken is being cooked, and they're often surprised when they are given a choice of fish or beef for dinner!

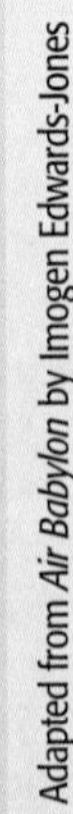

2 VOCABULARY air travel

a Complete the column on the right with a word or phrase. (All the words come from the *Air Babylon* extract).

At the airport

1 Most big airports have several different buildings called ____. *terminals*
2 Passengers leave from Departures and arrive at ____. ________
3 Two general words for bags and suitcases are ____ and ____. ________ / ________
4 When you arrive at the airport, you go to ____ to get your boarding pass. ________
5 Before you take an international flight, you have to show identification at ____ ____ and go through security. ________
6 After you arrive, you go to baggage claim to ____ your luggage. ________
7 When you go through ____, you may be asked, "Do you have anything to declare?" ________
8 A person whose job is to carry your bags for you is called a ____. ________
9 JetBlue and easyJet are two discount ____. ________

On the plane

10 The people who work on the plane are the (cabin) ____. ________
11 The people who pay to travel on a plane are ____. ________
12 The person who serves you during a flight is the ____. ________
13 You can usually ask for a window or aisle ____. ________
14 The noun from the verb *fly* is ____. ________
15 When a plane is going up into the sky, it is ____. ________
16 When a plane is coming down from the air, it is ____. ________

b Which of the words in **a** can also be used if you are traveling by bus or train?

c Cover the words on the right and read the definitions again.
Can you remember all the words and pronounce them correctly?

MINI GRAMMAR *so / such ... that*

The passenger is usually so embarrassed that he disappears as quickly as possible.
When this happens, there is often such a strong smell of roast bird that passengers on the plane think that chicken is being cooked.
We often use *so / such ... (that)* to express a consequence.

Use *so* + adjective / adverb	*The movie was so good (that) we went to see it again.* *He drives so dangerously (that) nobody wants to go with him.*
Use *so much / so many* + noun	*There was so much traffic (that) we nearly missed our flight.*
Use *such a / an* + adjective + single countable noun	*It was such a good movie (that) we went to see it again.*
Use *such* + adjective + uncountable or plural noun	*They played such awful music (that) nobody wanted to dance.* *They were such beautiful shoes (that) I bought them.*

Complete the sentences with *so*, *such*, or *such a*.

1 The flight was ______ long that I got really bored.
2 I had ______ noisy child sitting beside me that I couldn't sleep at all.
3 There was ______ long delay because of fog that we had to sleep at the airport.
4 My suitcase was ______ heavy that I had to pay for excess baggage.
5 I slept ______ badly on the plane that it took me two days to recover.
6 We were served ______ terrible food that I couldn't eat a thing.
7 There were ______ many people at check-in that we had to stand in line for an hour.
8 We had ______ heavy suitcases that we had to ask for a porter.

3 GRAMMAR narrative tenses, past perfect continuous

a Read a newspaper story about an incident during a recent flight. What happened?
Do you think the flight attendant should lose her job?

We're going to crash!

Hysterical flight attendant causes panic on transatlantic flight

Everything was going smoothly on Virgin Atlantic flight VS043 from London Gatwick to Las Vegas. The 451 passengers were relaxing after lunch when the plane hit some turbulence over Greenland. There was no advance warning, so a number of passengers were out of their seats or were not wearing seat belts when the plane started dropping violently.

Suddenly, one of the flight attendants screamed , "We're going to crash!" Panic immediately broke out. In the 30 minutes of chaos, passengers desperately clung to their seats as drinks and magazines flew around the cabin. Amid the terror, the flight attendant screamed every time the plane dropped.

Businesswoman Angela Marshall was traveling with her boyfriend. "Until then the flight had been fine," she said afterward. "I'd been reading my book and my boyfriend had been taking a nap. But when the flight attendant started screaming, I was totally convinced that we were about to die."

Another passenger said, "It was unreal, like something from a movie. People started crying and throwing up. That woman shouldn't be a flight attendant. After we landed, she was joking and laughing as if nothing had happened, but we all staggered off the plane in a state of shock."

Adapted from a newspaper

Glossary

turbulence sudden and violent changes in wind direction
break (broke, broken) out pv start suddenly
cling (clung, clung) hold on tightly to sb / sth
nap a short sleep, especially during the day
be about to be going to do sth very soon
stagger walk as if you are about to fall

b Copy the highlighted verbs into the chart.

simple past: regular __________
simple past: irregular __________
past continuous __________
past perfect __________
past perfect continuous __________

c In pairs, look at the sentences and circle the more logical verb form. Be ready to say why.

When the plane hit turbulence ...
1 the passengers *screamed / were screaming*.
2 the passengers *relaxed / were relaxing*.
3 they *finished / had finished* lunch.
4 they *had flown / had been flying* for two hours.

d **p.134 Grammar Bank 2B.** Read the rules and do the exercises.

e In pairs or groups, try to complete each of the two sentences in four different ways using the four narrative tenses.

1 The police stopped the driver because he ...
2 I couldn't sleep last night because ...

4 PRONUNCIATION irregular past forms

a Match the sentences 1–8 with the correct sounds A–H according to the pronunciation of the vowel sound.

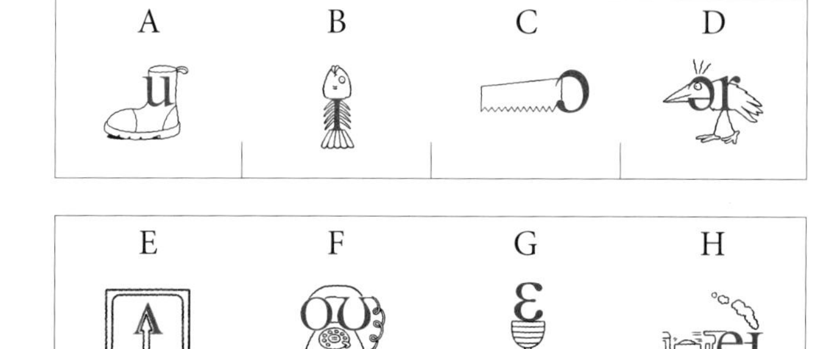

1 ☐ I thought he'd caught that flight. I saw him checking in.
2 ☐ The hotel was built in 1950. The date was written above the door.
3 ☐ The company has become successful since it won the prize for Best Airline.
4 ☐ I flew to Mexico City. I knew the city very well.
5 ☐ She read for a while before she fell asleep in her bed.
6 ☐ We chose a bad day to travel. We hadn't known about the bad weather.
7 ☐ I heard that they'd been hurt in the accident, but they weren't.
8 ☐ She said she'd paid for the tickets with money she'd taken from my wallet.

b 2.5 Listen and check. Then practice saying the sentences.

5 LISTENING

a You are going to listen to an interview with two pilots. Before you listen, discuss questions 1–6 with a partner and guess how the pilots will answer them.

1 What weather conditions are the most dangerous when flying a plane?
2 Which is more dangerous, taking off or landing?
3 Is it really worthwhile for passengers to wear seat belts?
4 Is it worth listening to the safety instructions?
5 Are some airports more dangerous than others?
6 How important is it for pilots to speak English well?

b 2.6 Listen to the first part of the interview. How many of the questions did you answer correctly?

c Listen again for more detail. Then, with a partner, try to remember as much as possible about the pilots' answers.

d 2.7 Now listen to the second part. What three questions do they answer?

e Listen again and try to remember the anecdotes.

f Do you think you would like to work as a pilot? What are the main advantages and disadvantages?

6 SPEAKING

GET IT RIGHT **active listening**

When someone tells us a story or anecdote, we normally interact with the person who is telling the story.

Useful language

ASKING FOR MORE INFORMATION	SHOWING SURPRISE	SHOWING APPROVAL	SHOWING SYMPATHY
What happened next?	*Really?*	*Wow!*	*Oh no!*
Then what happened?	*You're joking!*	*That's great / fantastic!*	*That's awful!*
How did you feel?	*No! I don't believe it.*		*What a shame!*
What was it like?			*That's too bad.*

a **Communication** *Flight stories A p.116 B p.119.* Read a newspaper story to retell to your partner.

b You are going to tell an anecdote. **The story can either be true or invented.** If it is invented, try to tell it in such a convincing way that your partner thinks it's true.

Choose one of the topics below and plan what you are going to say. Look at the **Story plan** below, and ask your teacher for any words you need.

Talk about a time when you (or someone you know) ...

- had a frightening / funny / unusual experience when traveling by plane / bus / train.
- got sick or had an accident while traveling.
- missed a bus / train / flight, which caused serious complications.
- arrived home from a trip and had a surprise.

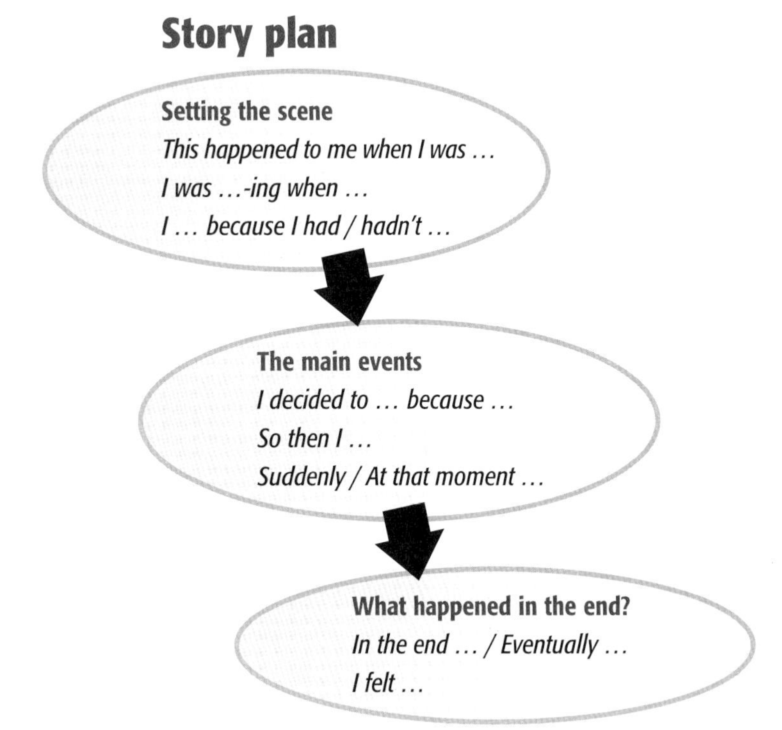

c In pairs, A tell B your story. B ask A for more details and decide whether the story is true or not. Then change roles.

G adverbs and adverbial phrases
V confusing adverbs and adverbial phrases
P word and sentence stress

2C Incredibly short stories

Mini sagas

A mini saga is a story that is told in exactly 50 words. The original idea came from science fiction writer Brian Aldiss.

A ______

She recognized the writing on the envelope immediately. The Gypsy had warned her that she had no future with this man, yet here he was – five lonely years after their last meeting, begging her to join him in New York.
She felt unbelievably happy as she stepped on board the *Titanic*.

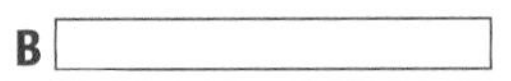

B ______

He was worried. Unfortunately, since his wife's death, his teenage daughter had become increasingly difficult.
They had agreed 2:00 a.m. as the latest return time from nightclubs. It was now 3:30.
He prepared himself for confrontation as the door opened.
"Dad!" she shouted angrily. "I've been frantic. You're late again."

C ______

"He always has dinner at six," she told the maid. "No beef. He has dessert in the garden. Fill the bath at eight – he goes to bed early."
"When will I meet the master?" the maid asked, as she tripped over a sleeping poodle.
"You already have," laughed the housekeeper.

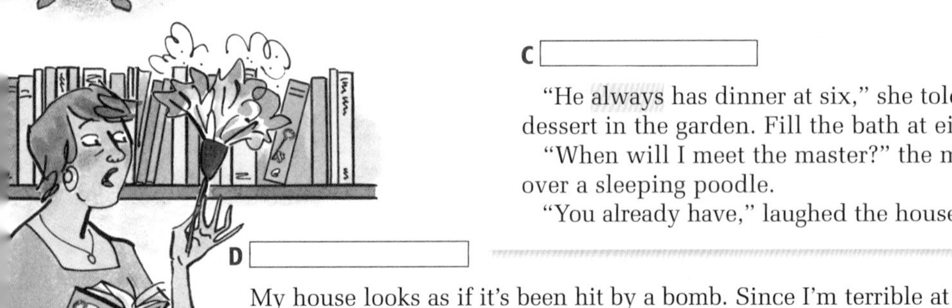

D ______

My house looks as if it's been hit by a bomb. Since I'm terrible at organizing, I bought a new book, *Key to Organizing Your Life*. I felt so proud.
I started cleaning the bookcase. Five minutes later I couldn't believe my eyes.
I'd bought the same book last year.

From *Mini Sagas*

Glossary

beg ask sb very strongly or anxiously for sth
confrontation a situation where there is angry disagreement
frantic very worried
maid female servant
master man who has people working in his house as servants
poodle a small dog with very curly hair
housekeeper woman employee in charge of a house and its servants

1 GRAMMAR adverbs and adverbial phrases

a Read the four mini sagas and match them with the titles below. You don't need to use one of the titles.

Generation gap **The last laugh** **Good intentions** **In the cards** **Meeting the boss**

b Read the mini sagas again. Some of them are fairly cryptic, and the story is not immediately obvious. In pairs, explain each story in your own words. Which story do you like most / least?

c Look at the highlighted adverbs or adverbial phrases in the stories. Think about what they mean and notice their position in the sentence. Write them in the correct place in the chart.

Types of adverbs

Time (when things happen, e.g., *now*) *immediately* ______ ______ ______
Manner (how you do something, e.g., *slowly*) ______
Frequency (how often sth happens, e.g., *sometimes*) ______
Degree (describing / modifying an adjective, e.g., *very*) ______ ______ ______
Comment (giving an opinion about a phrase, e.g., *luckily*) ______

d Use your instinct. Where should the adverb go in these sentences?

1 He speaks three languages. **fluently**
2 I have breakfast during the week. **hardly ever**
3 My brother was in a car crash, but he wasn't hurt. **fortunately**
4 It's often hot in New York in July and August. **extremely**
5 When I know the date, I'll call you. **right away**

e **p.134 Grammar Bank 2C.** Read the rules and do the exercises.

f 2.8 Listen to some sound effects or short dialogues. Then use the adverb in **bold** to complete the sentence.

1 When he got to the bus stop, *the bus had just left.* **just**
2 They were having a party when … **suddenly**
3 He thought he had lost his boarding pass, but … **luckily**
4 The woman thought Andrea and Tom were friends, but, in fact, … **hardly**
5 The driver couldn't see where he was going because … **hard**
6 The Chinese man couldn't understand the other man because … **incredibly**

2 VOCABULARY confusing adverbs and adverbial phrases

a Match each pair of adverbs with a pair of sentences.

right now / actually	5	in the end / at the end	☐
especially / specially	☐	late / lately	☐
ever / even	☐	near / nearly	☐
hard / hardly	☐	still / yet	☐

	Adverb
1 a Her Spanish isn't very good. She can ______ say anything.	______
b He works very ______ – at least ten hours a day.	______
2 a My boss always arrives ______ for meetings.	______
b We haven't seen Mary ______. She's been very busy.	______
3 a ______ of the concert, everybody applauded.	______
b I didn't want to go, but ______ they persuaded me.	______
4 a I love all sports, but ______ basketball.	______
b All her clothes are ______ made for her in Paris.	______
5 a She looks younger than me, but ______ she's two years older.	______
b He's unemployed ______, but he's looking for a job.	______
6 a It's ______ stopped raining. We'll be able to leave soon.	______
b Does your boyfriend live ______ here?	______
7 a Have you found an apartment ______?	______
b No, we're ______ looking.	______
8 a Have you ______ been to Texas?	______
b I've been all over the US – I've ______ been to Alaska!	______

b Now decide which adverb goes where and write it in the adverb column. Compare with a partner, and say what you think the difference is between the two adverbs.

c Cover the adverb column and look only at sentences 1–8. Try to remember the adverbs.

3 PRONUNCIATION
word and sentence stress

a Underline the main stressed syllable in these adverbs.

absolutely actually almost apparently definitely especially even extremely fortunately ideally incredibly luckily unfortunately

b 2.9 Listen and check.

> Remember: adverbs, like other "information" words, are usually stressed in a sentence.

c 2.10 Now underline the stressed words in each sentence. Listen and check. Practice saying the sentences.

1 There was a lot of traffic, and unfortunately we arrived extremely late.
2 We definitely want to go abroad this summer, ideally somewhere hot.
3 It's incredibly easy – even a child could do it!
4 I thought he was Portuguese, but actually he's Brazilian.
5 You said they'd already gone, but apparently they're still here.
6 I absolutely love Italian food, especially pizza.

4 WRITING

a You are going to write a mini saga.

Your story must be exactly 50 words (not including the title) and you must include at least two adverbs. Contracted forms (e.g., *I'd*) count as one word. First, choose one of the titles below.

A summer romance **Revenge is sweet**
The lie **Never again**

b Think of a plot. Then write a first draft without worrying about the number of words.

c Now count the words and then try to cut or add words until the story is the right length. Write your final version.

d Read two other students' stories. Which do you like best?

5 SPEAKING

Communication *Reading habits p.117.*

6 READING & LISTENING

Reading for pleasure

When you read a longer text, e.g., a short story, you usually don't read once quickly for gist and then read it again. You read, perhaps at a slightly slower speed, and keep going, focusing on following the story. It is also especially important to try to guess words from context. Look up a word while you are reading only if it's holding you up or you really want to know what it means. Looking up words frequently may get in the way of your enjoyment. However, it can help to pause from time to time and look back, just to check you are clear about what is happening.

a Read and listen to a short story. Answer the questions 1–13 in pairs.

Little Brother™

by Bruce Holland Rogers

Peter had wanted a Little Brother™ for three Christmases in a row. His favorite TV commercials were the ones that showed just how much fun he would have teaching Little Brother™ to do all the things that he could already do himself. But every year, Mommy had said that Peter wasn't ready for a Little Brother™. Until this year.

This year when Peter ran into the living room, there sat Little Brother™ among all the wrapped presents, babbling baby talk, smiling his happy smile, and patting one of the packages with his fat little hand. Peter was so excited that he ran up and gave Little Brother™ a big hug around the neck. That was how he found out about the button. Peter's hand pushed against something cold on Little Brother™'s neck, and suddenly Little Brother™ wasn't babbling anymore, or even sitting up. Suddenly, Little Brother™ was limp on the floor, as lifeless as any ordinary doll.

2.11

1 What kind of toy is Little Brother™? What does the ™ mean?
2 What do you think "babbling" means?
3 What happened when Peter hugged Little Brother™?

"Peter!" Mommy said.

"I didn't mean to!"

Mommy picked up Little Brother™, sat him in her lap, and pressed the black button at the back of his neck. Little Brother™'s face came alive, and it wrinkled up as if he were about to cry, but Mommy bounced him on her knee and told him what a good boy he was. He didn't cry after all.

"Little Brother™ isn't like your other toys, Peter," Mommy said. "You have to be extra careful with him, as if he were a real baby."

She put Little Brother™ down on the floor, and he took tottering baby steps toward Peter. "Why don't you let him help open your other presents?"

So that's what Peter did. He showed Little Brother™ how to tear the paper and open the boxes. The other toys were a fire engine, some talking books, a wagon, and lots and lots of wooden blocks. The fire engine was the second-best present. It had lights, a siren, and hoses just like the real thing. There weren't as many presents as last year, Mommy explained, because Little Brother™ was expensive. That was okay. Little Brother™ was the best present ever! Well, that's what Peter thought at first.

2.12

4 How did Peter's mother stop Little Brother™ from crying?
5 What do you think "wrinkled up" means?
6 What does the last line make you think?

Glossary

in a row /roʊ/ one after the other
wrapped (up) covered with paper
pat hit lightly with your hand
limp not firm or strong
lap the top part of your legs that forms a flat surface when you are sitting down
bounce move (sb or sth) up and down, e.g., a ball
tottering walking like a baby, nearly falling over
tear /tɛr/ **(tore, torn)** to damage sth by pulling it apart, e.g., paper, cloth
keep up pv to move at the same speed as sb or sth
stacked up placed one on top of another
swat /swɑt/ hit, (esp. an insect) using your hand
howl /haʊl/ make a long loud cry, like a dog or wolf
calm down pv become quiet and calm
wad into balls /wɑd/ make (e.g., paper) into tight balls
let drop allow sth to fall

At first, everything that Little Brother™ did was funny and wonderful. Peter put all the torn wrapping paper in the wagon, and Little Brother™ took it out again and threw it on the floor. Peter started to read a talking book, and Little Brother™ came and turned the pages too fast for the book to keep up.

But then, while Mommy went to the kitchen to cook breakfast, Peter tried to show Little Brother™ how to build a very tall tower out of blocks. Little Brother™ wasn't interested in seeing a really tall tower. Every time Peter had a few blocks stacked up, Little Brother™ swatted the tower with his hand and laughed. Peter laughed, too, for the first time, and the second. But then he said, "Now watch this time. I'm going to make it really big."

But Little Brother™ didn't watch. The tower was only a few blocks tall when he knocked it down.

"No!" Peter said. He grabbed hold of Little Brother™'s arm. "Don't!"

Little Brother™'s face wrinkled. He was getting ready to cry.

Peter looked toward the kitchen and let go. "Don't cry," he said. "Look, I'm building another one! Watch me build it!"

Little Brother™ watched. Then he knocked the tower down.

Peter had an idea.

2.13

7 What funny things did Little Brother™ do at first?
8 What do you think "grabbed hold of" means?
9 What do you think Peter's idea was?

When Mommy came into the living room again, Peter had built a tower that was taller than he was, the best tower he had ever made. "Look!" he said.

But Mommy didn't even look at the tower. "Peter!" She picked up Little Brother™, put him on her lap, and pressed the button to turn him back on. As soon as he was on, Little Brother™ started to scream. His face turned red.

"I didn't mean to!"

"Peter, I told you! He's not like your other toys. When you turn him off, he can't move, but he can still see and hear. He can still feel. And it scares him."

"He was knocking down my blocks."

"Babies do things like that," Mommy said. "That's what it's like to have a baby brother."

Little Brother™ howled.

"He's mine," Peter said too quietly for Mommy to hear. But when Little Brother™ had calmed down, Mommy put him back on the floor, and Peter let him toddle over and knock down the tower.

Mommy told Peter to clean up the wrapping paper, and she went back into the kitchen. Peter had already picked up the wrapping paper once, and she hadn't said thank you. She hadn't even noticed.

Peter wadded the paper into angry balls and threw them one at a time into the wagon until it was almost full. That's when Little Brother™ broke the fire engine. Peter turned just in time to see him lift the engine up over his head and let it drop.

2.14

10 Why didn't Peter's mother even look at the tower?
11 What makes Little Brother™ a different kind of toy?
12 Why did Peter feel annoyed with his mother?
13 What do you think is going to happen next?

b **2.15** Listen to the end of the story. In pairs, discuss what you think happened.

1 What did Peter do to Little Brother™ after he broke the fire engine?
2 How did his mother react?
3 What did Peter threaten to do?
4 How did Peter's mother punish him for his behavior?

c Listen again with the audioscript on page 123. Were you right?

d Do you think Little Brother™ or Little Sister™ may exist in the future? Why do you think people might want to have them?

p.157 Phrasal verbs in context *File 2.*

THE INTERVIEW

a You are going to listen to an interview with Heidi Evans, a flight attendant with JetBlue Airways. Before you listen, read the glossary and look at how the words are pronounced to help you understand what she says.

Glossary
safety drill /ˈseɪfti drɪl/ practice for an emergency
CPR /ˌsi pi ˈɑr/ cardiopulmonary resuscitation, a procedure used to rescue an unconscious person by breathing air into the mouth and pressing on the chest
defibrillator /difɪbrəˈleɪtər/ a device that gives electric shocks to someone's heart to make it beat again after a heart attack
cranky /ˈkræŋki/ bad-tempered
go the extra mile to make a special effort to achieve sth after you have already made a great effort
take a toll to have a very bad effect
red-eye flight /ˈrɛdaɪ flaɪt/ late night or overnight flight
sleep in /slip ɪn/ to sleep late in the morning
clenching their fists squeezing their closed hands tightly

b 2.16 Listen to part 1. Answer the questions with a partner.
1 Why did Heidi apply for a job as a flight attendant?
2 What are some of the things she learned during training?
3 What kind of person makes a good flight attendant?
4 What are the good sides of being a flight attendant?
5 What are the bad sides?

c 2.17 Listen to part 2. Answer the questions with a partner.
What does she say about ...?
1 what to do *before* you go on a long flight
2 what to do *during* a long flight
3 how she deals with passengers who are afraid of flying
4 how to identify passengers who are scared
5 a time when she smelled smoke in the cabin

d 2.18 Listen and complete the phrases. What do you think they mean?

COMMON PHRASES
1 We learn how to ______ with many different situations ...
2 ... someone who is ______ to work with other people.
3 You ______ ______ travel for free ...
4 It takes a toll on your body, so you ______ ______ sleep the rest of the day when you get home.
5 And at ______ ______ he got on the phone with the ground people to make an emergency landing.
6 Everyone worked together, nobody got hurt, thankfully, and that ______ ______.

e Listen to the interview again with the audioscript on page 123. Does Heidi make her job sound attractive to you? Why?

ON THE STREET

a 2.19 Listen to four people talking about air travel. Match the speakers to what they most <u>dislike</u> about air travel. Which speakers are afraid of flying?

1 Shelly

2 Sophie

3 Tiffany

4 Juan

landing ☐
turbulence ☐
waiting in long lines ☐
feeling bored ☐

b Listen again. Who ...?
1 sometimes feels sick on a plane
2 was once terrified during a flight
3 thinks it's exciting to fly
4 experienced an overnight delay

c 2.20 Listen and complete the phrases. What do you think they mean?

COMMON PHRASES
1 Taking off and landing is sometimes a little nerve-wracking, but ______, fine.
2 ... off the top of my ______ that's pretty hard. I don't know.
3 I can't think of anything ______ ...
4 And here I am, the big guy, the oldest in the family, crying my ______ out.

d Listen to the interviews again with the audioscript on page 123. Then answer the same questions with a partner.

It was only a small mistake, but it changed my life.

I had been working at JB Simpson's for ten years. It was a small [1]_______ company that exported garden furniture. I was [2]_______ happy with my job – I got along [3]_______ with the owner, Arthur Simpson, but not with his wife, Linda. She was a loud, [4]_______ woman, who [5]_______ used to turn up at the office and start criticizing us for no reason. Everyone disliked her.

One afternoon Mrs. Simpson came in while I was finishing writing a report. She looked at me and said, "If I were you, I wouldn't wear that color. It doesn't look good on you at all." I was wearing a [6]_______ pink shirt that I was [7]_______ fond of, and her comment really annoyed me. I typed a [8]_______ e-mail to Alan Simmonds in Sales. "Watch out! The old witch is on the warpath!" and pressed "send." A couple of minutes later I was surprised to receive an e-mail from Mr. Simpson asking me to come to his office [9]_______. When I opened the door, I saw his wife glaring at the computer screen, and I realized, to my horror, what I had done. I had clicked on Simpson instead of Simmonds. [10]_______ I was packing my things. I had been fired!

a Read the story. What was the "small mistake"? What happened?

b Using adverbs and adjectives helps make a story come alive and makes it more enjoyable to read. Complete the story with an adjective or adverb from the list below.

aggressive an hour later extremely family-run frequently immediately new fairly quick well

c You may want to write some dialogue as part of your story. Rewrite the following with the correct punctuation. Use the dialogue in the story to help you.

sit down mr. simpson said coldly i want to talk to you about an e-mail you sent

"Sit ______________________________

____

____

d You are going to write a story beginning with the sentence *It was three o'clock in the morning when the phone rang.* Look at the underlined time expressions in **Useful language** and correct one word in each.

Useful language

Time expressions

[1] In that moment, the door opened.
[2] As soon than I saw him, I knew something was wrong.
[3] Ten minutes after, I went back to sleep.
[4] A morning in September, I got to work early.
We got to the station [5] just on time to catch the train.

PLAN the content.

1 Invent a plot and write what happened simply, in about 50 words.
2 Then think about how you could improve your story by adding more details, e.g., with adjectives and adverbs.
3 Think about what tenses you need for each part of the story, e.g., how to set the scene, what significant events happened before the story starts.

WRITE 120–180 words, organized in two or three paragraphs. Use a variety of narrative tenses and adverbs and adjectives to make your story more vivid.

CHECK your short story for mistakes (grammar, punctuation, and spelling).

2 What do you remember?

GRAMMAR

Circle the right answer, a, b, or c.

1 Some people think that ______ don't pay enough in taxes.
 a the rich
 b the rich people
 c rich

2 **A** Which shoes do you like best?
 B I like ______.
 a the reds
 b the red
 c the red ones

3 I got a ______ bag for my birthday.
 a beautiful leather Italian
 b Italian leather beautiful
 c beautiful Italian leather

4 We ______ for about five hours when we decided to stop and rest.
 a were driving
 b had been driving
 c have driven

5 When we got to Terminal 2, the flight from Santiago ______.
 a had already landed
 b had already been landing
 c has already landed

6 As soon as we arrived at the airport, we ______.
 a had checked in
 b were checking in
 c checked in

7 Her father ______.
 a speaks very fluently English
 b speaks English very fluently
 c speaks English very fluent

8 I just need another five minutes. ______.
 a I'm nearly finished
 b Nearly I'm finished
 c I'm finished nearly

9 The driver ______ in the accident.
 a seriously was injured
 b was injured seriously
 c was seriously injured

10 It was ______ boring movie that we left in the middle.
 a a so
 b such a
 c a such

VOCABULARY

a Word groups. Underline the word that is different. Say why.

1 striped	checked	hooded	patterned
2 silk	cotton	fur	stylish
3 station	flight	terminal	pilot
4 backpack	scarf	undershirt	cardigan
5 get dressed	match	get undressed	change clothes
6 lately	slowly	nearly	friendly

b Complete the sentences with one word.

1 The plane took ___ at 7:15.
2 I just found ___ that my boss is going to work for another company.
3 You'd better walk a little faster if you don't want to get left ___.
4 People here get dressed ___ a lot for weddings – long dresses and suits.
5 We checked ___ as soon as we got to the airport.
6 My new jeans fit ___ a glove – they're so comfortable.
7 I live near here, ___ the end of this street.

c Circle the right word.

1 We haven't seen each other much *late* / *lately*.
2 The skirt doesn't *fit* / *match* me. It's a little too big.
3 The car is small. There isn't *even* / *ever* a back seat!
4 I've been working so *hard* / *hardly* that I think I need a vacation.
5 How much *suitcases* / *luggage* do you have?
6 I love all pasta, *especially* / *specially* lasagna.
7 Can I go in jeans? I don't feel like *getting dressed* / *changing clothes*.

PRONUNCIATION

a Underline the word with a different sound.

1	aɪ	aisle	flight	linen	striped
2	ər	nearly	early	heard	fur
3	ɛr	wear	airline	carefully	weren't
4	u	crew	loose	suit	took
5	t	crashed	missed	changed	dressed

b Underline the stressed syllable.

stylish   undressed   arrivals   passenger   actually

What can you do?

CAN YOU UNDERSTAND THIS TEXT?

a Read the article and fill in the blanks with a sentence A–E.

A "You see how safe it is," he smiled.
B Apparently, they thought that was what would work best for me.
C It was an experience I would rather not go through again.
D Like many fearful fliers, I often experienced a heightened sense of hearing, noticing small changes in noises and amplifying them dramatically in my mind.
E Which is unfortunate because as a foreign journalist, I can't exactly stay at home.

b Look at the highlighted words and phrases. Can you guess what they mean?

CAN YOU UNDERSTAND THESE PEOPLE?

a 2.21 Listen and circle the correct answer, a, b, or c.

1 What did the woman buy at the sale?
  a A black sweater.
  b A blue jacket.
  c A black jacket.
2 How did the man feel?
  a angry
  b offended
  c confused
3 What is the man's criticism of the book?
  a It's too long.
  b It's boring.
  c It's complicated.
4 The flight to Taipei will leave from ____.
  a Gate B 50
  b Gate P 50
  c Gate B 15
5 The man is stressed because ____.
  a his friends have a problem with their luggage
  b his friends may think he isn't there
  c his friends' flight was late

b 2.22 Listen to a Swede talking about people from his country. Answer the questions.

1 What does he think is the stereotype of the Swedes?
2 How much of the stereotype does he think is true?
3 Why does he mention the Swedish army?
4 What three other aspects of the Swedes does he mention?
5 What does he say about Swedish men?

CAN YOU SAY THIS IN ENGLISH?

Can you …?

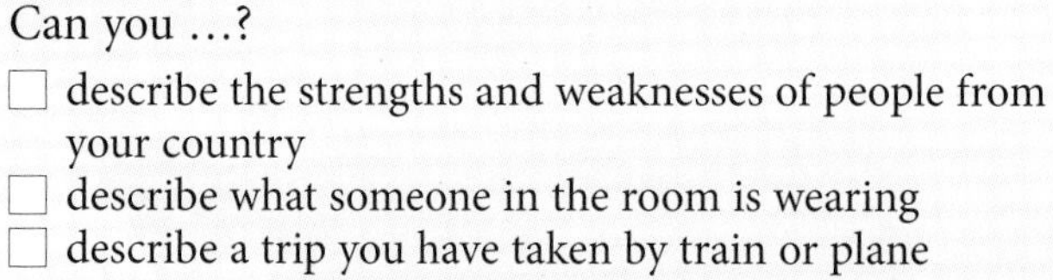

☐ describe the strengths and weaknesses of people from your country
☐ describe what someone in the room is wearing
☐ describe a trip you have taken by train or plane

How I conquered my fear of flying

Journalist and documentary maker Sean Langan talks about his irrational phobia of flying.

My fear of flying is not just a mild case, but a real, oh-no-I'm-going-to-die-any-second kind of fear. 1☐ My job has taken me to dangerous places such as Afghanistan and Iraq, but I'm far more worried about flying planes than flying bullets. After an awful flight earlier this year on a small plane, I decided I would either have to stop flying altogether or I could try to overcome my fears. Which is why, a few weeks later, I agreed to take the flight to end all fears.

The plane was going almost vertically upward before moving sharply to the left. To make matters worse, my seat was shaking violently because of severe turbulence. My stomach was turning. The captain, sensing my fear, took his hands off the controls and turned to face me. 2☐ In fact, Captain Keith Godfrey had designed the flight, or rather the terrifyingly realistic flight simulator, to my needs.

In the two years Virtual Aviation has been offering the course at the airport, they had never put the plane through such extreme flying before. 3☐ And they were right. By showing me just how far you can push a plane and still keep it safely within its limits, they allayed my fears. I had to experience things for myself before I was able to convince myself of the truth. That planes, generally speaking, do not fall out of the sky like rotten apples.

In their careful preflight questioning with a therapist named Susie, they focused on what lay beneath my fear. 4☐ Something moving in an overhead compartment could sound to me like an engine about to fall off. But Susie focused on my heightened sense of movement as my main problem, which is why during the flight the captain flipped the plane over like a pancake.

5☐ But by facing my worst fear, I'd overcome it. And fellow sufferers will be glad to know that I got through my next real flight safe and sound.

Adapted from a newspaper

G passive (all forms), *it is said that …*, *he is thought to …*, etc.
V crime and punishment
P the letter *u*

The one place a burglar won't look

1 SPEAKING & LISTENING

GET IT RIGHT **agreeing and disagreeing**
Use a variety of expressions for agreeing and disagreeing:

I think it must be …	*That's what I was thinking.*
Do you agree with that?	*Exactly!*
Don't you think …?	*I don't think that's true.*

a Take the quiz in pairs. Give reasons for your answers.

BEAT THE BURGLARS!

1 How long do you think a burglar usually takes to search someone's house?
a 10 minutes
b 20 minutes
c 30 minutes

2 Which of these are the most common things burglars steal?
a TVs, digital cameras, etc.
b paintings and antiques
c money and jewelry

3 Which of these is more likely to stop a burglar from coming into your house?
a a dog
b a burglar alarm

4 Which three of these would most influence a burglar to choose a particular house or apartment?
a It looks expensive.
b There is no one at home.
c There aren't many other neighbors nearby.
d There are good places to hide around the house.
e They have burglarized the home before.

5 How are burglars more likely to get into a house?
a through an open door or window
b by breaking a door or window

6 What is the best place to hide your valuables? Number these rooms in the order that burglars usually search them.
☐ the living room
☐ the kitchen
☐ the dining room
☐ the main bedroom
☐ a child's bedroom
☐ the office

Adapted from a newspaper

b **Communication** *There's only one place burglars won't look… p.117.* Read the answers to the quiz – provided by ex-burglars themselves!

c Look at the photos. Have you seen the movie *Oliver Twist* or read the book by Charles Dickens? What do you think the old man is teaching the boys to do?

d 3.1 Listen to a radio interview with an ex-magician who worked as the "pickpocket consultant" for an *Oliver Twist* movie. Answer the questions.

1 What is the main trick pickpockets use when they steal from someone?
2 Why are tourists particularly at risk from pickpockets?

e Listen again for more detail. Then answer with a partner.

What does he say about ...?

1 training boys
2 Prague
3 the director's watch
4 Fagin
5 "misdirection"
6 some keys
7 the journalist's wallet and pen
8 a map
9 subway stations and tall buildings
10 "Watch out for pickpockets!" posters

f What have you learned to do or *not* to do ...?

a to protect your home
b if you are on vacation in a big city

2 VOCABULARY crime and punishment

a Match the words for people who steal with the definitions in the list.

pickpocket mugger burglar robber shoplifter thief

1 A __________ is someone who breaks in and steals from a private home.
2 A __________ is someone who breaks in and steals from, e.g., a bank or business.
3 A __________ is someone who steals something when he / she is in a store.
4 A __________ is someone who steals from you on the street, often without you noticing.
5 A __________ is someone who uses violence to steal from you on the street.
6 A __________ is the general word for someone who steals.

b 3.2 Listen and check. Underline the stressed syllable.

c p.149 **Vocabulary Bank** *Crime and punishment.*

3 PRONUNCIATION the letter *u*

a Look at the words in the list, which all have the letter *u* in them. Put them in the correct column below according to how the vowel sound is pronounced.

accuse burglar caught community drugs fraud guilty
judge jury manslaughter mugger murderer punishment smuggling

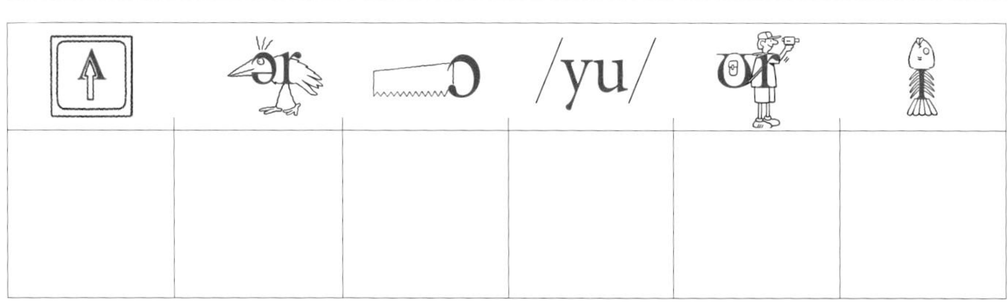

b 3.3 Listen and check. What happens to the pronunciation of ***u*** in *guilty*?

c Practice saying the sentences.

1 He was accused of smuggling drugs.
2 "Murderers must be punished," said the judge.
3 The burglar is doing community service.
4 It wasn't murder; it was manslaughter.
5 The jury said he was guilty of fraud.
6 The mugger was caught by the police.

d Talk to a partner. Find out as much information as possible.

What are the most common crimes in your town or city?
What crimes have been in the news recently?
Do you have trial by jury in your country? Do you think it's a good system?
Do you know anyone ...?

- whose home has been burglarized
- who has been mugged
- whose car has been stolen
- who has been unfairly accused of shoplifting
- who has been stopped by the police while driving
- who has been robbed while on vacation
- who has been offered a bribe
- who has been kidnapped

4 GRAMMAR passive (all forms), *it is said that ..., he is thought to ...*, etc.

a **Check what you know.** You are going to read two true crime stories. In *World Cup thief's own goal,* complete the article with the verb in parentheses in the simple past, active or passive. Then in *Parrot held in prison*, circle the correct form.

Any problems? **Workbook p.25**

World Cup thief's own goal

A thief who [1]______ (steal) a World Cup ticket from a woman's handbag [2]______ (catch) after he sat down to watch the game next to the victim's husband.

Eva Standmann, 42, [3]______ (mug) as she was going to the Munich stadium for the game between Brazil and Australia. The thief, a 34-year-old man, [4]______ (discover) the ticket in her bag and decided to use it.

But when he [5]______ (take) the woman's seat in the stadium, he [6]______ (meet) by her husband, Berndt, 43, who immediately called the police on his cell phone.

A Munich police spokesperson said, "The thief [7]______ (find) the ticket in the bag and decided to watch the game. When he sat down next to his victim's husband, officers on duty at the stadium [8]______ (inform) of the situation and the thief [9] ______ (arrest)."

Parrot held in prison

A parrot has spent five days [1]*interrogating / being interrogated* by the police in a prison in Argentina.

A judge [2]*ordered / was ordered* the parrot, which [3]*calls / is called* Pepo, [4]*to hold / to be held* in custody until he told the police who his real owner was. Two neighbors, Jorge Machado and Rafael Vega, were disputing who the bird [5]*belonged / was belonged* to.

Judge Osvaldo Carlos decided the parrot should [6]*send / be sent* to prison until he said the name of his owner. After five days, Pepo said Jorge's name and also sang the anthem of his favorite soccer team, San Lorenzo. Mr. Machado said, "I knew he wasn't going to let me down. He is a real friend, and we [7]*support / are supported* the same soccer team."

b **New grammar.** Read another true story. How does the hypnotist rob banks?

Hypnotic bank robber

Bank clerks in Moldova have been told by the police not to make eye contact with customers after a series of robberies. The robber is believed to be a trained hypnotist from Russia.

He is said to put cashiers into a trance before making them hand over tens of thousands of dollars' worth of bills.

It is thought that the criminal begins talking to bank tellers and gradually hypnotizes them. After getting them to give him money, he then brings them back out of the trance and leaves them with no memory of handing over the cash. It is believed that the man has robbed at least three banks in the last month.

c Look at the highlighted phrases in **b**. Do people *know* this information for sure about the robber or do they only *suspect it*? How is the structure different after *he* and after *it*?

d **p.136 Grammar Bank 3A.** Read the rules and do the exercises.

e Complete the newspaper crime story using the words in parentheses.

The world's most polite armed robber

Police are looking for a man who [1]____________ (believe / be) the world's most polite armed robber.
The robber, who always says "please" and "thank you" when he orders store employees to give him the money in the cash register, [2]____________ (say / be) a tall man in his early forties.
He wears a mask and rubber gloves during robberies. It [3]____________ (think / he / rob) at least four stores in recent weeks.
A police officer said, "He [4]____________ (report / be) polite to his victims, but there is nothing polite about armed robbery. Last week this man used a knife to threaten employees in a store. They were terrified. Saying 'please' and 'thank you' cannot change that."

5 READING

a What do you think would be an appropriate punishment for…?
  1 a woman who abandoned some kittens in a forest
  2 people caught speeding in a residential area
  3 a man who was caught carrying a loaded gun illegally
  4 some teenagers who vandalized a school bus
  5 noisy neighbors who play rock music very loudly at all hours

b Read the first four paragraphs of the article. What sentences did Judge Cicconetti give these people? Why? Do you think his sentences would be more effective than yours?

> Sometimes when you read a newspaper article for detail, the information is not given in chronological order. You may need to re-read the article to clarify in your mind information about people and events.

c Read through the questions below. Then read the whole article to find the information.

  1 **The judge**
  What was his early life like? How successful has he been professionally?
  2 **The punishments**
  Which three creative punishments get the offenders to learn from a personal experience?
  Which two punishments get them to do something for other people?
  3 **The reasons behind his system**
  What inspired the judge's system of creative punishments?
  Why does he think they are better than conventional punishments?
  What evidence does he have that the punishments are successful?

d What do you think of his system? Would you like to have a judge like Cicconetti in your town?

6 SPEAKING

> **GET IT RIGHT giving your opinion**
> When we are giving our opinion about the best way to punish someone, we often use *should* + passive infinitive:
> *I think they should be made to …*
> *I don't think they should be allowed to …*

a In groups, decide on creative punishments for these crimes or offenses.

- An arsonist who sets fire to a local scenic area, for example, a forest.
- A 15-year-old who is caught drinking and smoking.
- Someone who parks illegally, causing major traffic delays.
- A group of teenagers who paint graffiti all over walls in a small town.
- A couple whose dogs bark incessantly and bother the neighbors.
- A young person who creates a computer virus that infects thousands of computers.

b Compare with other groups and decide which you think are the best solutions.

Making the punishment fit the crime

– Mike Cicconetti, a judge with a difference

Judge Cicconetti

1 When Michelle Murray was arrested for abandoning 35 kittens in a forest, she expected to get a fine or a short prison sentence. Instead, she was sentenced to spend the night in the same cold, dark forest. In the end, it was so cold that she only had to spend three hours in the woods, but Judge Mike Cicconetti had made his point. He wanted the 26-year-old Ohio housewife to feel the same pain and suffering as the animals she had abandoned, many of which later died.

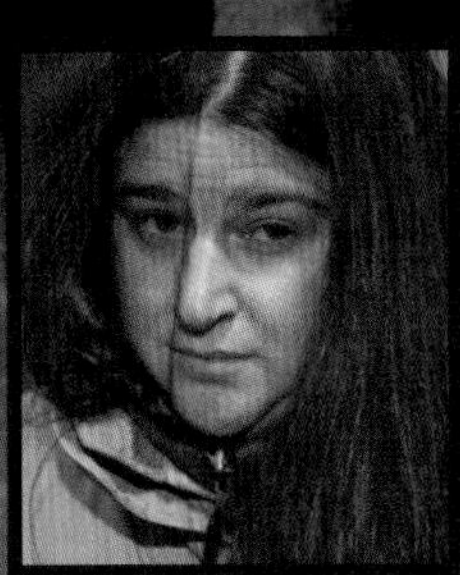
Michelle Murray

2 Judge Cicconetti's unusual ruling was just the latest example of his unique brand of "creative justice," which has won him national acclaim. He was elected unopposed to serve another six years in Lake County, Ohio, last month, and this year he won the presidency of the American Judges Association.

3 Cicconetti allows offenders to choose between jail and an alternative, "creative" sentence. For example, people accused of speeding are offered a choice between having their license suspended for 90 days or having it suspended for a shorter period and spending one day working as a school crossing guard. The judge says that offenders who spend a day helping school children cross the street never appear in his courtroom for speeding again.

4 The judge also sent a man who was caught with a loaded gun to the morgue to view dead bodies and ordered teenagers who let the air out of tires on school buses to organize a picnic for elementary school children. He has ordered noisy neighbors to spend a day of silence in the woods or to listen to classical music instead of rock.

5 Cicconetti attributes his unusual approach to his tough family background. He was the oldest of nine children and had to work part-time collecting garbage to pay his way through college. He studied law at night school. "I didn't go to a prestigious law firm," he says, "I had to get to where I am the hard way. It makes you understand what the working man has to go through and why some of them commit crimes. I want to give people a positive lesson, not a negative one."

6 A drawer in his cramped office in the Painesville Municipal Courthouse is full of thank-you letters from both victims and criminals. "Some people will say that my punishments are cruel or unusual," the judge said. "OK, it's a little bit of embarrassment and humiliation. But when you have people fulfilling these sentences, you are doing it for them and the victims and the community. And above all, I can remember only two people who have been sentenced to alternative punishments and who have reoffended."

3 B

G future perfect and future continuous
V weather
P vowel sounds

Stormy weather

1 READING

a Look at the three photos and read extracts from three blogs. In pairs, guess which country / city the people are writing from.

b Read the blogs again and check (✔) the correct box(es). In which blog(s) does someone ...?

	1	2	3
1 go out in spite of a severe weather warning	☐	☐	☐
2 seem to be a foreigner living abroad	☐	☐	☐
3 have fun in spite of the weather	☐	☐	☐
4 complain about how the weather makes him / her feel	☐	☐	☐
5 talk about problems with transportation	☐	☐	☐
6 describe how surprised people are by the weather	☐	☐	☐
7 criticize some people for doing something	☐	☐	☐
8 talk about the damage caused by the weather	☐	☐	☐
9 complain that people are not well prepared to cope with the weather	☐	☐	☐

c Look at the highlighted words in the blogs and discuss what they mean with a partner.

d Would any of these three types of weather be surprising where you live? Have you had any surprising weather where you live recently?

1

Posted: Tuesday September 4th

Yesterday was unbelievable. Though we were warned there was going to be a terrible storm, no one really expected or could possibly have visualized hurricane-force winds destroying bus stops and ripping trees out of the wet soil. They told us not to cycle anywhere and to stay indoors, but I had a job interview downtown, so I had to go out.

Thank goodness I did manage to get there, but I had to grab hold of traffic lights so I wouldn't be blown into the street. I saw some crazy people on

bikes – some of them got blown over, and one even seemed to be going backward. The canals were full of trash cans that had gotten blown in, and there were piles of bikes in the streets and broken umbrellas everywhere, which people had obviously thought they would be able to use and then couldn't. What a mess!

Comments 8

2

Posted: Sunday July 22nd

Yet another scorching, sunny day...

I never knew this kind of heat was possible here. Last Wednesday was the hottest day ever in this country. The roads were melting in some areas, and the underground was a total nightmare – it was like being slowly cooked in an oven.

The main problem is that people here don't seem to understand the need for air-conditioning during the summer. There is no escaping the heat, and if you actually want to go anywhere, you have to be willing to sweat and learn to enjoy your task sweating. Please tell me, how do you shop? Try on clothes? No, thank you. Even going for an ice-cold drink can be uncomfortable if the pub isn't at least equipped with a large fan.

So I sit here sweating in my living room. The French windows are open, but the coolest room in the apartment is the bathroom, and sadly, there is no Internet connection, so I can't work there!

Comments 22

3

Posted: Thursday November 8th

I got woken up today by my daughter screaming, "Dad... it's snowing... it's snowing!" She just couldn't believe it – not surprising as they said on the news that it hasn't snowed here for nearly 50 years! We decided not to send her to school, and we had a great time – we even made a snowman in the backyard. We used dried cranberries for the eyes and a baby carrot for the nose because it was a baby snowman. People are so amazed by the "totally awesome" weather that I've seen some people just standing there staring as if they were in a trance. You kind of feel it's the work of a skillful set decorator for a high-budget movie.

It was chaos, though, for people going to work – Interstate 5 was closed in some parts, and a whole load of trucks were stuck in the snow. And it's been very bad news for the citrus trees – they're all frozen. Even if it thaws tomorrow, the damage is already done. So I'm afraid we won't be eating any local oranges this year!

Comments 104

2 VOCABULARY weather

a p.150 Vocabulary Bank *Weather*.

b Talk to a partner.

1 What kind of weather do you think is good or bad for ...?
- a camping
- b going for a walk in the mountains
- c running a marathon
- d sailing
- e sightseeing

2 What cities or countries do you associate with ...?
- a typhoons
- b smog
- c heavy snow
- d floods
- e hurricanes

3 PRONUNCIATION vowel sounds

Most vowels, or combinations of vowels, can be pronounced in more than one way. If you are unsure what the vowel sound is in a new word, check with your dictionary.

a Look at the groups of words below. Circle the word with a different sound.

1 blow	snow	showers	below
2 weather	sweat	heavy	heat
3 drizzle	blizzard	chilly	mild
4 hard	warm	yard	farm
5 flood	cool	monsoon	loose
6 fought	ought	drought	brought
7 thunder	sunny	uncomfortable	humid
8 scorching	force	world	storm

b 3.4 Listen and check.

c 3.5 **Dictation.** Listen and write down five sentences. Then practice saying them.

4 LISTENING

a 3.6 You're going to listen to Martin Cinert from Prague talking about the night the River Vltava flooded. Mark the sentences T (true) or F (false).

1. He wasn't at risk at his office, but he was at risk at his apartment.
2. He took his wife and child to his parents' house.
3. He went back to the apartment because he was excited by the situation.
4. Martin went to a place near his apartment to watch the water level rising.
5. He looked out the window and saw that his parking lot was starting to flood.
6. He was the last person to leave his apartment building.
7. All of the roads he tried were flooded now.
8. He decided to follow another car through the water.
9. Martin's car broke down as he drove through the water.
10. All the apartments in his building were seriously damaged.

b Listen again. Then in pairs, correct the false sentences.

c What do you think you would have done in Martin's situation?

5 SPEAKING & WRITING

GET IT RIGHT modifiers

Cross out the wrong form. Put a check (✔) next to the sentences if both are correct.

1. It's very cold! / It's very freezing!
2. It's really windy! / It's incredibly windy!
3. It's really boiling today! / It's incredibly boiling today!
4. I was absolutely frightened! / I was absolutely terrified!

a In small groups, talk about a time when you were somewhere and ...

- there was a flood.
- it was very foggy or there was a lot of smog.
- it was unbearably cold.
- it was pouring rain for days on end.
- there was a gale or hurricane.
- there was a terrible heat wave.
- you were caught outside in a thunderstorm.

What were you doing at the time?
What did you do to protect yourself from the weather?
Did you ever feel scared or in danger?

b Write a short blog (like the ones in **1** on page 40) describing what the weather has been like recently. Write about how it has made you feel and how it has affected what you have been doing.

6 3.7 SONG ♫ *It's raining men*

7 GRAMMAR future perfect and future continuous

a **Check what you know.** Put the verb in parentheses in the correct future form (*will* + base form, *going to,* or present continuous). Sometimes more than one form is possible.

Future forms

1 **A** It's freezing in here!
 B OK, OK. I __________ the window. (**close**)
2 The sky is really clear! I'm sure it __________ a beautiful day tomorrow. (**be**)
3 **A** Do you think __________ while we're in Seoul? (**rain**)
 B I don't know, but I __________ my umbrella just in case. I've already put it in my suitcase. (**take**)
4 **A** Let's have lunch on the patio.
 B __________ it __________ warm enough? (**be**)
 A I think it __________ fine. I __________ the table outside. (**be, set**)
5 **A** What time __________ you __________? (**leave**)
 B Soon, in about ten minutes. It's very foggy, but don't worry. I __________ really slowly, I promise. And I'm sure there __________ too much traffic. (**drive, not be**)

Any problems? ➲ **Workbook p.28**

b **New grammar.** Read some of the predictions scientists are making about climate change and complete them with a word from the list below.

become closed down doubled having (x2) melted risen (x3) suffering

c Read the predictions again. Which ones worry you most? Have you noticed the effects of climate change in your country?

Storm clouds on the horizon

Climate change is now something that we cannot close our eyes to, and governments all over the world have finally realized that they have to sit up and take notice. These are some of the things that many scientists predict will happen if we keep on polluting the atmosphere with CO_2 emissions.

Short term: by the year 2050

- More than a third of the world's plant and animal species will have [1]______ extinct.
- The ice in the Arctic Sea will melt every summer, causing the extinction of polar bears. Many glaciers, for example, on Mount Kilimanjaro, will have [2]______ completely.
- Fifty percent of the world's ski resorts will have [3]______ due to lack of snow.

Mid term: by the year 2100

- Sea levels will have [4]______ by 6–27 inches (16–69 centimeters). This means that low-lying islands like the Maldives will no longer be habitable.
- The number of serious coastal storms and tsunamis will have [5]______.
- Northern European cities, e.g., Paris and London, will be [6]______ 50 days a year of heat waves when temperatures are over 86°F (30°C) (there are currently 6–9 days).

Long term: by the year 3000

- Temperatures will have [7]______ by about 59°F (15°C).
- Sea levels will have [8]______ by more than 36 feet (11 meters), flooding large areas of Bangladesh, and many low-lying cities, such as New York. Hundreds of millions of people will be displaced.
- One third of the world will be [9]______ from extreme droughts, and half the world will be [10]______ moderate droughts. Tens of millions of Africans will have to emigrate.

d Match the sentences A–C with pictures 1–3.

A At this time tomorrow it will be snowing.
B By tomorrow evening it will have snowed.
C It will snow tomorrow.

e **p.136 Grammar Bank 3B.** Read the rules and do the exercises.

f What do you think? Explain why (not). What are the alternatives? Talk to a partner.

In 20 years ...
we'll all be using solar power to heat our homes.
discount airlines will have disappeared, and tickets will be extremely expensive.
private swimming pools and golf courses will have been banned.
everyone will be using public transportation to get to work.
we'll have stopped using gas, and we will be using electric cars.
people won't be going on skiing vacations anymore.

I think it will have become so warm that we won't need any heat.

I disagree. I think we'll be using nuclear power.

8 LISTENING & SPEAKING

a 3.8 Listen to the first part of a news story about a woman named Barbara Haddrill. What did she do? Why?

b Listen to the first part again and answer the questions.

1 What was Barbara's dilemma? Why?
2 What changes has she made to her lifestyle over the last six years? Why?
3 How did Barbara travel? Through which countries?
4 How was she able to take such a long vacation?

Barbara Haddrill

c 3.9 Listen to the second part and complete the information in the chart.

UK TO AUSTRALIA ONE-WAY

	Cost	Distance	Time	CO_2 emissions
Barbara	$______	______ miles	______ days	______ metric tons
plane	$______	______ miles	______ hours	______ metric tons

d What do you think of Barbara's trip?

e Read *What can you do to help?* about what *you* can do to help prevent climate change. Talk to a partner or in small groups.
Which of the tips below ...? a do you already do b are you willing to try to do c are you not willing to try

What can YOU do to help? The top tips

1 Fly less. Use buses or trains instead where possible. If you have to fly, give money to an organization like Carbon Footprints to compensate for the CO_2 emissions of your flight.

2 Drive as little as possible. Use bikes or public transportation. And if you need to drive, buy a hybrid, a car with an extra electric motor that charges up when you stop. You could also carpool with a friend.

3 Use only energy-saving lightbulbs.

4 Plant trees. Two or three dozen trees can absorb a whole household's emissions of CO_2.

5 Unplug electrical appliances when they're not in use; they use electricity even in "standby" mode.

6 Use the cold water wash on your washing machine, and use a short-wash cycle on your dishwasher, which uses less energy and water than handwashing dishes.

7 If possible, try to buy organic food that has been grown locally. Take your own bags when you go to supermarkets.

8 Turn your heat down and wear a sweater if you're cold. If you use air-conditioning, don't set it lower than 78°F (26°C).

9 Take showers, not baths.

10 Support an environmental organization, for example, Friends of the Earth or Greenpeace.

11 Regularly recycle paper, glass, plastic, and household waste.

12 Call or write to government officials to let them know your opinion on combatting climate change.

Taking a risk

1 READING

a Which of these things scares you more?

- being shot or drowning?
- mad cow disease or bacteria in the kitchen?
- flying or driving?
- terrorist attacks or heart disease?

b Read the article once fairly quickly and find out which of the things in **a** is riskier.

c Read the article again and answer the questions.

1 Molly's parents ...
  a worry too much about their daughter.
  b are scared of the wrong thing.
  c don't take danger seriously.

2 Having bacteria in our kitchen doesn't worry us because ...
  a it isn't really dangerous.
  b we can keep our kitchen clean.
  c we are too worried about mad cow disease.

3 People are more afraid of flying than driving because ...
  a on a plane, they are in a situation where they can't do anything.
  b more people die in plane crashes than car crashes.
  c flying is more dangerous.

4 People ...
  a believe that terrorism is more of a threat than heart disease.
  b shouldn't worry so much about heart disease.
  c are less worried about dangers in the near future.

5 People tend ...
  a to worry too much about danger.
  b to confuse terror with danger.
  c not to do enough to stop accidents.

The risk factor

Our daily lives are full of dangers, from driving our cars to eating cholesterol in our food. But how good are we really at assessing these risks?

Not very good at all, according to Steven Levitt and Stephen Dubner in their best-selling book *Freakonomics*. Parents, they say, take danger very seriously, but they often worry about completely the wrong things. The authors give as an example the fictitious case of a little girl they call "Molly." Her parents know that the parents of one of her friends keep a gun in their house, so Molly's parents decide that she is not allowed to play there. Instead, they feel that Molly would be much safer spending time at another friend's house, where there are no guns, but there is a swimming pool. You may think this is the right choice, but according to the statistics, you would be wrong. Every year, one child per 11,000 private swimming pools is drowned in the United States. However, only one child is killed by a gun for every million guns. This means that a child is 100 times more likely to die in a swimming accident than because of playing with a gun.

Molly's parents are not unique. Generally, people are just not very good at assessing risk. Peter Sandman, a risk consultant in Princeton, New Jersey, says, "The risks that scare people and the risks that kill people are very different things." He compares the dangerous bacteria in our kitchen and diseases such as mad cow disease: the first is very common, but for some reason not very frightening; the second is extremely rare, but it terrifies us. "Risks that you can control are much less worrisome than risks you can't control," says Sandman. "We can't tell if our meat is infected, whereas we can control how clean our kitchen is."

This "control factor" probably explains why flying tends to scare people more than driving. Levitt argues, "Their thinking goes like this: 'since I control the car, I am the one keeping myself safe; since I have no control of the airplane, I am at the mercy of external factors.'" Actually, the question of which is more dangerous is not as simple as many people think. Statistics for the United States show that although many more people die each year in car accidents than in plane crashes, driving isn't necessarily more dangerous. This is because, generally, people spend far less time flying than driving. In fact, statistically, the number of deaths for each hour of driving compared with each hour of flying is about the same. So flying and driving carry a very similar risk. It is just our lack of control when we are flying that makes it seem more scary.

Levitt also says that people tend to be much more scared of short-term dangers than long-term ones. The probability of someone being killed in a terrorist attack is infinitely smaller than the probability that this same person will eat too much fatty food and die of heart disease. "But a terrorist attack happens now," says Levitt. "Death from heart disease is a distant, quiet catastrophe. Terrorist acts lie beyond our control – French fries do not."

Finally, there is what Peter Sandman calls "the dread factor," that is, how horrific we consider something to be. We are horrified by the thought of being killed in a terrorist attack, but for some reason we are not horrified by the thought of death from heart disease. Sandman uses the following equation: for most people risk = hazard (or danger) + outrage (or horror). "When the hazard is high but the terror is low, people underreact. When the hazard is low and the outrage is high, people overreact." Which is why so many parents will do more to protect their children from a gun accident than from a swimming pool accident. A gun horrifies us, but a swimming pool does not.

d Look at the highlighted words and phrases in the article and use them to complete these sentences.

1 Motorcycles are much cheaper than cars. ______, they are more dangerous.
2 ______ doctors it isn't a good idea to go swimming right after lunch.
3 The open-air concert was a success, ______ it rained a little bit.
4 People worry about terrorists, but, ______, the risk of an attack is rather small.
5 John loves meat, ______ his wife is a strict vegetarian.
6 ______ the weather forecast is awful, I think we should cancel the trip.
7 There was nothing good playing at the movies, so we went out for a meal ______.

e Is there anything *you* are scared of? Do you think this is a real risk to you?

2 LISTENING

a You are going to listen to a risk expert talking about the risks of driving in the US. Before you listen, in pairs, predict which option you think is correct.

1 The most dangerous thing to be on the road is ______.
   a a pedestrian
   b a driver
   c a motorcyclist
2 Most accidents happen because drivers ______.
   a fall asleep at the wheel
   b are drunk
   c drive too fast
3 Driving at night is ______ as dangerous as driving during the day.
   a three times
   b four times
   c ten times
4 You're most likely to have a nonfatal accident on a ______.
   a Tuesday morning
   b Friday afternoon
   c Saturday night
5 Most fatal accidents happen on ______.
   a highways
   b freeways
   c country roads
6 Mile for mile, women have more ______ than men.
   a minor accidents
   b serious accidents
   c fatal accidents
7 The age at which a driver is most at risk is ______.
   a over 65
   b between 25 and 34
   c under 25

b 3.10 Listen once and check your answers.

c Listen again for more information.

d Talk to a partner.

1 Would these statistics probably be similar in your country?
2 Do you often travel at dangerous times and on dangerous roads?
3 Do you think punishments for dangerous driving should be more severe?

3 VOCABULARY expressions with *take*

a Complete the questionnaire with the words in the list.

advantage after care credit easy notice
part place seriously risks time up

The *take* questionnaire

1 Are you a cautious person or do you enjoy **taking** ______?
2 Do you **take** ______ for your accomplishments, or are you overly modest and shy?
3 Do you **take** climate change ______? What are you doing about it?
4 Are you like your father or your mother? Who do you **take** ______?
5 When you're on vacation, do you relax and **take** it ______?
6 Do you always **take** ______ of rules and regulations, or do you sometimes ignore them?
7 Do you worry about your health? Do you **take** ______ of yourself?
8 Do you get up very quickly in the morning or do you **take** your ______?
9 Have you ever not **taken** ______ of a good opportunity (and regretted it)?
10 Have you ever **taken** ______ in a demonstration?
11 Have you **taken** ______ a new sport or hobby recently?
12 Has any big sporting event ever **taken** ______ in your city?

b In pairs, take turns asking and answering the questions. Ask for more information.

MINI GRAMMAR *likely* and *probably*

A child is 100 times more likely to die in a swimming accident than because of playing with a gun.

This "control factor" probably explains why flying tends to scare people more than driving.

Likely and *probably* are very similar in meaning, but *likely* is more frequently used as an adjective whereas *probably* is always an adverb.

Use *be* + *likely* + infinitive, e.g., *She's likely to be off work for a long time.*

Use *probably* before the main verb in an [+] sentence, e.g., *She'll probably be off work for a long time*, but before the auxiliary verb in a [−] sentence, e.g., *He probably won't come.*

Complete the sentences with *likely* or *probably*.

1 I don't think the boss is very ______ to agree.
2 They ______ won't be here before 6:00.
3 That isn't ______ to happen in the near future.
4 I'll ______ be home late tonight.

4 GRAMMAR conditionals and future time clauses

a Check what you know. Circle the correct verb form.

1 If *I like / I'll like* the car when I see it, I'll buy it.
2 I *don't go / won't go* to work tomorrow unless I feel better.
3 We'll keep on playing until it *gets / will get* dark.
4 If it rains tonight, we *won't have to / don't have to* water the lawn tomorrow.
5 I won't make a decision until *I have / I'll have* all the information.
6 I'll tell you when *I hear / I'll hear* from him.

Any problems? Workbook p.31

b New grammar. Match the sentence halves.

	Main clause			Other clause
1	Don't throw your notes away	☐	A	in case it's raining when you finish work.
2	You are more likely to have an accident	☐	B	if you don't hurry up.
3	They'll call us	☐	C	if you're having dinner now.
4	You're going to be late	☐	D	if you're finished cooking.
5	I'll probably be driving	☐	E	if you arrive at two.
6	I'll call back later	☐	F	in case you need them later.
7	Take your umbrella	☐	G	when you call me, so leave a message.
8	Please put everything away	☐	H	until everybody puts their seat belt on.
9	I'll have already had lunch	☐	I	as soon as they've landed.
10	I'm not starting the car	☐	J	if you drive too fast.

c Answer the questions with a partner.

1 Which sentence is a zero conditional and refers to something that always happens, not a future possibility?
2 In the other sentences, what tenses can be used in the main clause? What tenses can be used in the other clause after *if*, *in case*, *when*, etc.?
3 What does *in case* mean in sentences 1 and 7?

d **p.136 Grammar Bank 3C.** Read the rules and do the exercises.

e In pairs, complete each sentence to make some useful safety tips.

1 Don't let children play near a swimming pool unless …
2 Never leave a dog locked up in a car if …
3 Keep a first aid kit in your house in case …
4 You shouldn't leave children alone in the house until …
5 Always unplug electrical appliances (e.g., a hairdryer) as soon as …
6 Always keep medicine in a safe place in case …
7 Don't allow strangers into your house unless …
8 If you are frying something and the oil catches fire, …

5 PRONUNCIATION sentence stress and rhythm

a 3.11 **Dictation.** Listen and write six future sentences to complete the dialogues.

1 **A** If we rent a summer house in June, will you come and stay?
B *I'll tell you* ____________________
2 **A** Do you think you'll be able to repair them soon?
B ____________________
3 **A** How will I know where to find you?
B ____________________
4 **A** What time did Mandy say she was coming?
B At 8:00. But ____________________
5 **A** What do you have in that bag?
B ____________________
6 **A** Will it be a problem if they stay for lunch?
B ____________________

b Listen again and underline the stressed words.

c In pairs, practice the dialogues. Try to say the sentences as fast as possible with the correct rhythm.

6 LISTENING

a Look at the photo and read an extract from an article about a children's playground in Japan. What are the main safety measures? What do you think of them?

Japan's children play safe

When Ryosuke and Taemi Suzuki take their 18-month-old daughter to Fantasy Kids Resort in Japan, they are guaranteed total peace of mind. Fantasy Kids Resort is one of several similar playgrounds in Japan that provide for the growing number of parents who constantly worry about possible dangers threatening their children, such as disease and accidents.

First-time visitors to the playground must provide proof of identification before they enter, and shoes must be removed at the door because they carry germs. Even the wheels of baby carriages are sprayed with an antibacterial solution.

Inside, children are watched over by about 20 staff members, dressed in bright yellow uniforms, and more than a dozen security cameras are mounted on the ceiling. Pets are banned from the playground, its large sandpit contains sterilized sand that is cleaned daily to remove any potentially harmful objects. Most of the bigger toys are inflatable to reduce the risk of injury. This is to protect the resort as much as the children because parents of a child injured while at the playground might easily sue the resort.

"We've been here before and we'll definitely come again," says Mr. Suzuki. "This place has everything under one roof, but most importantly, it puts absolute priority on safety."

Mr. and Mrs. Suzuki are not alone in wanting to remove just about every element of risk from their children's lives. According to a recent government survey …

Adapted from a newspaper

b 3.12 Now listen to an interview with Sue Palmer, director of a preschool in England. How is her attitude different from that of Mr. and Mrs. Suzuki?

Risk-taking preschool is a breath of fresh air

c Listen again and complete the information about the school with a word or phrase.

1 The preschool is in a ____________ in southern England.
2 Children spend most of their time ____________, even in the ____________.
3 They learn about the world by ____________.
4 Sue thinks children today don't have enough ____________.
5 They need to be allowed to ____________ when they play.
6 She thinks that schools are obsessed with eliminating risk because if children ____________, their parents will sue the school.
7 Parents at her school are ____________ about what the school is doing.

d Do you agree with Sue Palmer's philosophy about young children and risk?

7 SPEAKING

Talk in small groups.

GET IT RIGHT comparing past and present

Cross out the wrong form. Check (✔) the sentences if both are correct.

1 I *must / had to* walk to school by myself when I was little.
2 I *was allowed to / could* play in the street.
3 I *used to / use to* go to the park alone when I was *a child / young*.
4 *Nowadays / Today* parents think this is too risky.
5 They don't let children *go / to go* on the bus by themselves.

Did you use to do the following things when you were younger?

- play in the street
- walk to school
- go to a nearby park or playground alone or with friends
- use public transportation by yourself or with friends
- stay at home alone
- go swimming without an adult supervising
- use the Internet
- choose whatever TV programs you wanted to watch
- travel in a car without a seat belt

Do you think it was safe?

Do you think it is safe for children to do them today?

Are there any other things you used to do as a child that you think would be risky today?

➲ **p.157 Phrasal verbs in context** *File 3.*

THE INTERVIEW

a You are going to listen to an interview with EZ, a "free runner" who started the organization Urban Freeflow. Free runners use obstacles in a town or city to create movement by running, jumping, and climbing. Before you listen, read the glossary and look at how the words are pronounced to help you understand what he says.

Glossary

the South Bank /saʊθ bæŋk/ the area of London on the south side of the River Thames
lamppost /ˈlæmpˌpoʊst/ a tall post with a lamp on top used to illuminate the street
scheme /skim/ (British English) a program or plan for organizing sth
PE physical education, especially as a school subject
skateboard /ˈskeɪtbɔrd/ a short narrow board with small wheels at each end, which you stand on and ride as a sport
BMX a kind of mountain bike
calluses /ˈkæləsɪz/ areas of thick hard skin on a hand or foot
straight away /streɪt əˈweɪ/ (British English) immediately, right away

b 3.13 Listen to part 1. Answer the questions with a partner.
1 Can you do free running anywhere?
2 Does EZ usually do it alone or with other people?
3 What sports did he practice before free running?
4 Why did he take up free running?
5 How many athletes are there on the Urban Freeflow team? What kind of work do they do?
6 How is free running helping youth offenders and schoolchildren? Why do they like it?

c 3.14 Listen to part 2. Answer the questions with a partner.
What does he say about ...?
1 being safety conscious
2 the sense of freedom
3 blisters and sprained ankles
4 a tree
5 gymnastics

d 3.15 Listen and complete the phrases. What do you think they mean?

COMMON PHRASES
1 If you wanted to, you could _____ _____ do it anywhere.
2 ... someone leading _____ _____ and the rest following.
3 I had to just change my life around and become sensible all of _____ _____.
4 To _____ _____, the risk element played a part.
5 ... does a bit of running and _____ _____ up straight away. pv
6 As _____ _____ you start out very small scale ...

e Listen to the interview again with the audioscript on page 125. Do you think free running is a good thing for young people to do? Why (not)?

ON THE STREET

a Look at this list of high-risk sports. Do you know what they all are?

bungee jumping	☐☐	rock climbing	☐☐
jet skiing	☐☐	scuba diving	☐☐
parachuting	☐☐	skydiving	☐☐
race car driving	☐☐	white-water rafting	☐☐

b 3.16 Listen to four people talking about high-risk sports. Write the number of each speaker next to the sport(s) they have tried. Which sports haven't any of the speakers tried yet?

1 Tim

2 Duey

3 Josh

4 Christina

c Listen again. Who ...?
1 wants to try out a sport with a family member
2 had a sports injury
3 says they're too nervous to try skydiving
4 learned a high-risk sport as a child

d 3.17 Listen and complete the phrases. What do you think they mean?

COMMON PHRASES
1 ... and I never _____ up on it with them. pv
2 I cannot _____ myself doing any high-risk sports.
3 ... and jumping out of a plane _____ for me.
4 ... so I would definitely love to _____ into white-water rafting.

e Listen to the interviews again with the audioscript on page 125. Then answer the same questions with a partner.

Study Link MultiROM

a Read the title of the composition. Do you agree or disagree? Then quickly read the composition and see if the writer's opinion is the same as yours.

b Complete the composition with a word or phrase from the list below. Use capital letters where necessary.

finally   first   in addition   in conclusion
in most cases   ~~nowadays~~   second   so   whereas

c You're going to write a composition titled *There is nothing that we as individuals can do to prevent climate change.* Look at the **Useful language** expressions and make sure you know how to use them.

Useful language

Ways of giving your opinion

(Personally) I think / I believe ...
In my opinion ...

Ways of giving examples

There are several things we can do, for example / for instance / such as ...
Another thing we can do is ...
We can also ...

PLAN the content.

1 Think about the introduction. This should state what the current situation is and why it is important. Decide what the effects of climate change are now in the world and in your country.
2 Decide whether you agree or disagree with the title. Try to think of at least two or three good reasons to support your opinion, including examples of why you think the alternative point of view is wrong.
3 Think of how to express your conclusion (a summary of your opinion). This should follow logically from the examples you have given.

WRITE 120–180 words, organized in four or five paragraphs (introduction, reasons, and conclusion). Use a formal style (avoid contractions or informal expressions). Use the phrases in **b** and in **Useful Language**.

CHECK your composition for mistakes (grammar, punctuation, and spelling).

Community service is the best punishment for young people who commit a minor offense.

[1] *Nowadays*, when a young person commits a minor offense, he or she is usually sentenced to prison, a fine, or community service. [2] ______ I believe that community service is the best option.

[3] ______, community service often persuades a young person not to reoffend. Working with sick children or old people makes young offenders realize that there are people who have more difficult lives than they do. So community service can be an educational experience, [4] ______ going to prison or paying a fine is not.

[5] ______, spending time in prison results in young people meeting other criminals and learning more about the criminal world, which may tempt them to commit more crimes. [6] ______, in prisons many of the inmates take drugs, and this is a terrible example for young offenders.

[7] ______, I do not think that a fine is an appropriate punishment for young people. They do not usually have much money themselves, [8] ______ it is often their parents who pay the fine for them.

[9] ______, I believe that community service has important advantages both for minor offenders and for the community.

3 What do you remember?

GRAMMAR

a Complete the second sentence so that it means the same as the first.

1 The accident happened when they were repairing the road.
The accident happened when the road ________________ repaired.

2 They'll probably never find the murderer.
The murderer will ________________ found.

3 People think the burglar is a teenager.
The burglar is thought ________________ teenager.

4 They say that crime doesn't pay.
It is ________________ crime doesn't pay.

5 He isn't likely to come.
He probably ________________.

b Complete the sentence with the correct form of the verb in **bold**.

1 Imagine! At this time tomorrow we ________ on the beach. **lie**

2 The game starts at 7:00. By the time I get home, it ________ already ________. **start**

3 You can't use your cell phone until the plane ________. **land**

4 Many people have problems sleeping if they ________ coffee in the afternoon. **drink**

5 I want to spend a year traveling when I ________ college. **finish**

VOCABULARY

a Word groups. Underline the word that is different. Say why.

1 robber	burglar	pickpocket	kidnapper
2 fraud	smuggler	theft	terrorism
3 evidence	judge	jury	witness
4 chilly	cool	scorching	freezing
5 hurricane	mist	blizzard	flood

b Complete the sentences with a verb in the simple past.

1 They **c**______ a terrible crime.
2 The police **c**______ the burglar at the scene of the crime.
3 The judge **s**______ her to five years in jail.
4 They **k**______ the politician's son and asked for a million dollars ransom.
5 Jack the Ripper **m**______ seven women in London in the 19th century.
6 The wind **b**______ so hard that two trees fell down.
7 I **sw**______ so much at the gym that my T-shirt was soaking wet.
8 It **p**______ rain last night and we got soaked coming home.
9 We had nearly three inches of snow when I woke up, but it **m**______ during the morning.
10 We **t**______ advantage of the good weather and spent the day at the beach.

c Complete the sentences with one word.

1 The woman was charged ___ drug dealing.
2 Are you planning to take ___ a new sport when you go to college?
3 Who do you take ___ most, your mother or your father?
4 Watch ___! You nearly hit that cyclist.
5 It's very hot here. Let's move and sit ___ the shade.

PRONUNCIATION

a Underline the word with a different sound.

	Sound				
1	θ	thaw	weather	theft	thunder
2	ər	burned	jury	murder	burglar
3	dʒ	jail	charge	guilty	changeable
4	aɪ	mild	slip	icy	hijack
5	i	steal	dealer	sweat	heat

b Underline the stressed syllable.

accuse   blackmail   community   typhoon   seriously

CAN YOU UNDERSTAND THIS TEXT?

Read the article and choose a, b, or c.

1 Mr. Green did not fight the burglar because ______.
   a he was wearing his best clothes
   b he knew he would lose
   c the burglar was too quick

2 "Flat" (line 6) means ______.
   a broken
   b not round
   c without air

3 Mr. Green used to be ______.
   a an artist
   b a soccer player
   c a journalist

4 "Cruised" (line 15) means ______.
   a drove around slowly
   b looked everywhere
   c went at top speed

5 According to the police, ______.
   a crime victims should take photos
   b a drawing can be better than a photo
   c cell phone photos cannot be used in court

6 "Assault" (line 23) means ______.
   a attacking someone
   b stealing property
   c breaking into someone's house

Burglar caught by clever cartoonist

WILLIAM ELLIS GREEN, 82, was making his breakfast when he heard somebody in his garden. "I went out the back door, and suddenly I saw this guy running toward me. He pushed me out of the way and took my bicycle from the garden shed." Mr. Green did not resist, as he knew he would end up second-best in a fight with the intruder. The burglar tried to cycle away, but the tires on the bike were flat, making it difficult to ride. "He kept falling off the bicycle," said Mr. Green, "at least three or four times." After the man fled, Mr. Green called the local police.

When they arrived, officers asked him to describe the man, but instead he offered to draw them a picture. "When Mr. Green started drawing," said one of the police officers, "I knew right away who the burglar was." In fact, Mr. Green had worked for more than 20 years in daily newspapers doing caricatures of Australian soccer players. "I had no difficulty in remembering the man's face because he was so close to me," he said.

Police cruised the neighborhood in a patrol car with the sketch in search of the alleged burglar and found him within half an hour. "The cartoon was a perfect likeness of the burglar," said another police officer.

The police believe that this is the first time they have ever caught a suspect by using a cartoon sketch. Phil Rushford, a senior police officer, said that in the past some victims had used their cell phones to take photographs at crime scenes, but they had not been as effective.

A 34-year-old man is expected to be charged with theft, burglary, and assault. The missing bike was later found on a nearby street.

Adapted from a newspaper

CAN YOU UNDERSTAND THESE PEOPLE?

a 3.18 You will hear five people talking about teenage crime. Match each speaker with the people A–F. There is one person you don't need.

A a journalist	☐	D a police officer	☐
B a lawyer	☐	E a teacher	☐
C a parent	☐	F a victim of teenage crime	☐

b 3.19 You will hear part of an interview with two mountain climbers. Write **D** next to what Dan says, **M** next to what Marion says, and **N** next to what neither of them says.

1 Climbing is safer than driving.
2 I try to control the element of risk when I climb.
3 Avalanches are a climber's worst enemy.
4 Climbing helps me do my job better.
5 My job is pretty boring.
6 My spouse is not happy that I go climbing.
7 People with young children shouldn't go climbing.
8 Accidents are usually a climber's own fault.

CAN YOU SAY THIS IN ENGLISH?

Can you ...?

☐ talk about appropriate punishments for different crimes
☐ describe things we can do to reduce the effects of climate change
☐ talk about whether life is riskier today than it was in the past

G unreal conditionals
V feelings
P sentence rhythm

Would *you* get out alive?

1 SPEAKING & READING

a Answer the questions with a partner.

1 How do you think *most* people react in a life-or-death disaster situation?
- **a** Most people panic and become hysterical.
- **b** Most people act coolly and calmly.
- **c** Most people "freeze" and can't do anything.

2 What do you do when you are on a plane and the flight attendant starts to explain the safety procedures?
- **a** I don't listen. I've heard it so many times!
- **b** I listen, but I don't take it very seriously.
- **c** I pay attention and also read the safety information in the seat pocket.

3 What would you do if you were in a hotel on the fifth floor and the fire alarm went off in the middle of the night?
- **a** I would pick up essential things like my wallet and phone and find the quickest way down to the lobby.
- **b** I would follow the emergency instructions on the back of the door, which I had read when I arrived.
- **c** I wouldn't pay any attention. I would think it was probably a fire drill.

b Read *How humans behave when the worst thing happens* and check your answer to question 1 above. Then answer the questions below with a partner.

1 What two reasons are given to explain why a lot of people freeze in a crisis?
2 Is it possible to predict how people will react in a crisis?
3 What do you think *you* would do?

c Work in pairs. **A** read about a survivor of the World Trade Center, and **B** read about a survivor from the Tenerife air crash. Then use the questions below to tell each other about what you read.

A
1 Where was Elia on September 11, 2001?
2 How did she react when the plane hit the World Trade Center?
3 What saved her life?
4 How quickly did she leave?
5 According to experts, how could more lives have been saved?

B
1 Where was Paul Heck on March 27, 1977?
2 How did the accident happen?
3 According to experts, how could more passengers have survived?
4 Why did Paul Heck survive?
5 What previous experience influenced Paul?

d Read the whole article and, in pairs, mark the sentences T (true) or F (false).

1 Elia Zedeño's first instinct was to run.
2 If her coworker hadn't shouted, she might not have reacted as she did.
3 She took her time leaving because she didn't know where the exit was.
4 Experts say that some people who died in the World Trade Center could have survived.
5 The 1977 Tenerife air crash happened in bad weather conditions.
6 The Pan Am passengers had plenty of time to escape.
7 Heck had always worried about how he would be able to escape from places.
8 People don't read safety information because they aren't worried about crashing.

e Look at the highlighted words related to disasters. In pairs, try to figure out the meaning of the ones you didn't know from the context.

f What survival tips have you learned from this article? Which were the best options in questions 2 and 3 in exercise **a** above?

How humans behave when the worst thing happens…

WE ALWAYS THINK "It will never happen to me," but disasters can strike, at any time, anywhere – from hotel fires to train crashes to terrorist attacks. How would you cope if the unthinkable happened?

According to experts, people caught up in disasters tend to fall into three categories. About 10% to 15% remain calm and act quickly and efficiently. Another 15% completely panic, crying and screaming and obstructing the evacuation. But the vast majority (70%) of people do very little. They are "stunned and confused," says psychologist John Leach.

Why is this? Research suggests that under great stress, our minds take much longer to process information. So, in a crisis, many people "freeze" just at the moment when they need to act quickly. It also seems that personality is not a good guide to how people might react – a normally decisive person may not act quickly enough in a crisis and vice versa. "Most people go their entire lives without a disaster," says Michael Lindell, a professor at Texas A&M University. "So when something bad happens, they are so shocked they just think, 'This can't possibly be happening to me,' instead of taking action."

Office workers flee the collapsing towers on September 11, 2001.

A

WHEN THE PLANE hit the World Trade Center on September 11, 2001, Elia Zedeño was working on the 73rd floor. She heard an explosion and felt the building actually move, as if it might fall down. Zedeño first shouted out, "What's happening?" You might expect that her next instinct was to run. But she had the opposite reaction. "What I really wanted was for someone to scream back, 'Everything is OK! Don't worry.'"

Luckily, at least one of Zedeño's coworkers responded differently. He screamed, "Get out of the building!" she remembers now. Years later, she still thinks about that command. "My question is what would I have done if that person had said nothing?"

Even then Zedeño still did not immediately run. First, she reached for her bag, and then she started walking in circles. "I was looking for something to take with me. I remember I took my book. Then I kept looking around for other stuff to take. I felt as if I were in a trance." When she finally left, she went slowly. "It's strange because the sound of the explosion and the way the building shook should have made me go faster." But Zedeño made it to safety. Experts have estimated that at least another 130 people would have gotten out of the World Trade Center alive if they had tried to leave the building sooner.

B

ON MARCH 27, 1977 a Pan Am 747, which was waiting to take off from Tenerife airport, collided with a Dutch KLM 747 that was taking off in the fog. It was the worst air crash in history. Everyone on the KLM plane was killed, but 62 passengers on the Pan Am plane survived. Experts say that many more would have survived if they had gotten off the plane immediately.

One of the survivors was 65-year-old Paul Heck. He led his wife Floy toward the exit, and they got out just before the plane caught fire, just 60 seconds after the collision. Why Paul Heck and not others? In the hours just before the crash, Paul did something highly unusual. While he was waiting for the plane to take off, he studied the 747's safety diagram. He looked for the nearest exit and pointed it out to his wife. He had been in a theater fire as a boy, and ever since then, he always checked for the exits when he was in an unfamiliar environment. When the planes collided, Heck's brain had the data it needed. He could work "on automatic pilot," whereas other passengers froze, their minds paralyzed by a storm of new information. Why don't more people read safety information on airplanes and fire escape information in hotels? The answer, according to research, is that people think it's not "cool" to do so. So next time you fly or stay in a hotel or find yourself in any new environment, forget about "being cool" and take a few seconds to find out where the nearest emergency exit is. It may just save your life.

Tenerife air crash March 27, 1977. The accident led to research into why people sometimes freeze when they need to flee.

2 VOCABULARY feelings

a Look at *How humans behave when the worst thing happens* on page 52 and find adjectives that mean …

1 unable to think clearly or understand what's happening. ______
2 not excited or nervous. ______
3 very surprised by something unpleasant. ______
4 so surprised that you can't move or react. ______

b **p.151 Vocabulary Bank** *Feelings.*

c Look at the pictures. Try to remember an adjective and an idiom to describe how each person feels.

d Choose two adjectives from below and tell your partner why you felt like that.
Can you remember a time when you felt …?

- amazed
- delighted
- exhausted
- furious
- grateful
- homesick
- terrified
- really fed up

3 GRAMMAR unreal conditionals

1 What would you do if your school caught fire?
2 What would you have done if you had been on the Pan Am plane in Tenerife?

a Look at questions 1 and 2 above. Which one refers to a hypothetical situation in the past? Which one refers to a hypothetical situation in the present or future?

b Underline the verb forms in the box above. Which forms are they?

c Without looking back at pages 52 and 53, try to complete 1–4 below.

1 What would do if you __________ (be) in a hotel and the fire alarm went off in the middle of the night?
2 Another 130 people __________ (get out) of the World Trade Center alive if they had tried to leave the building sooner.
3 Many more people would have survived if they __________ (get off) the plane immediately.
4 If a fire alarm went off at work, I __________ (not pay) any attention.

d p138 Grammar Bank 4A. Read the rules and do the exercises.

4 PRONUNCIATION sentence rhythm

a 4.1 Listen and write down the beginning of six sentences. Then match them with the sentence endings A–F.

1 ______________________
2 ______________________
3 ______________________
4 ______________________
5 ______________________
6 ______________________

A I would have died. [5]
B if my husband weren't afraid of flying. [ ]
C if I were you. [ ]
D I wouldn't have acted so quickly. [ ]
E if I'd been in that situation. [ ]
F you wouldn't believe me. [ ]

b 4.2 Listen and check.

c Listen to sentences 1–6 again and underline the stressed words. Practice saying the sentences.

d Write conditional chains. For each chain, write two sentences in the third conditional.

If I hadn't read the safety information, *I wouldn't have known where the emergency exit was.*
If I hadn't known where the emergency exit was, I wouldn't have survived the crash.
1 If I hadn't accepted the invitation, …
2 If I hadn't gotten up so late, …
3 If I had remembered to turn my cell phone on, …
4 If I had known we had a test, …

5 READING & LISTENING

a If you were going to go backpacking in the Amazon rainforest, what do you think would be the biggest dangers?

b Read the beginning of a true survival story and then answer the questions below.

1 What was the three friends' original plan? How did this change?
2 What caused tensions between …?
 a the three men and the guide
 b Kevin and Marcus
3 Why did they finally separate?
4 Which pair would you have chosen to go with? Why?
5 How would you have felt if you'd been in Marcus's situation?

Escape from the Amazon

Four young men went into the jungle on the adventure of a lifetime. Not all of them would come out alive…

THE AMAZONIAN RAINFOREST is roughly the size of Europe or Australia. It is the home of more than half the plant and animal species known to man, many of which are lethal.

In 1981 three friends went backpacking in a remote area of Bolivia: Yossi, 22, and his friends Kevin, 29, and Marcus, 29. They hired an experienced guide, an Austrian named Karl, who promised that he could take them deep into the rainforest to an undiscovered indigenous village. Then they would raft nearly 200 kilometers down river before flying to the capital, La Paz. Karl said that the journey to the village would take them seven or eight days. Before they entered the jungle, the three friends made a promise that they would "go in together and come out together."

The four men set out on their trip from the town of Apolo and soon they had left civilization far behind. But after walking for more than a week, they saw no sign of the village, and tensions began to appear. The three friends began to suspect that Karl, the guide, didn't really know where the indigenous village was. Yossi and Kevin began to get fed up with their friend Marcus because he was complaining about everything, especially his feet, which had become infected and were hurting.

Eventually they decided to abandon the search for the village and just to hike back to Apolo, the way they had come. But Kevin was furious because he thought that it was Marcus's fault that they had had to cut short their adventure. So Kevin decided that he would raft down the river, and he asked Yossi to join him – he didn't want Marcus to come with them. Karl and Marcus agreed to go back to Apolo on foot. The three friends agreed to meet in a hotel in La Paz one week later.

Early next morning the two pairs of travelers said good-bye and set out on their different journeys…

c Now listen to the documentary. When the recording stops, answer the questions with a partner.

4.3

1 What happened to Kevin and Yossi on the raft?
2 Why was Yossi really lucky?
Whose situation would you rather have been in?

4.4

3 How were Kevin and Yossi feeling?
4 What happened to Yossi on his first night alone in the jungle?
What would you have done if you had been in his situation?

4.5

5 Why did Yossi's spirits change from desperate, to optimistic, and then to desperate again?
Do you think you would have given up at this point? What do you think had happened to Kevin?

4.6

6 What had Kevin been doing all this time?
7 Why was he incredibly lucky?
If you had been Kevin, would you have continued to try to look for your friend?

4.7

8 How did Kevin first try to get help?
9 Why was it unsuccessful?
10 What was his last attempt to find his friend?
What do you think had happened to Yossi?

4.8

11 How long had Yossi been alone in the jungle?
12 What did he think the buzzing noise was? What was it?
What do you think might have happened to Marcus and Karl?

d Listen again with the audioscript on page 125. Underline any words that were new for you, or words you knew but didn't recognize.

e Do you think you would have survived if you had been in Kevin or Yossi's situation? Would you have done anything differently?

6 **4.9** **SONG** ♫ *I will survive*

G past modals; *would rather, had better*
V verbs often confused
P reduced form of *have*

4B How I trained my husband

1 GRAMMAR past modals

a **Check what you know.** Look at the photo and then answer the questions using *must be*, *might be*, or *can't be*.

1 What time do you think it is?
 a 2:00 p.m. b 8:00 a.m. c 6:00 a.m.
2 What day of the week do you think it is?
 a Friday b Saturday c Sunday
3 What do you think she is drinking?
 a tea b coffee c soda
4 What do you think the man is looking for?
 a his glasses b his car keys c his briefcase

Any problems? **Workbook p.37**

b 4.10 Listen to check your answers to **a**. What was the problem?

c 4.11 Now listen to two more conversations. What are they arguing about?

d **New grammar.** Listen again to all three conversations and complete the extracts with *must have*, *may / might have*, *couldn't have*, or *should have*.

Conversation 1
1 You ______ left them in your jacket pocket. ☐
2 I ______ put them there – I wasn't wearing a jacket. ☐
3 Someone ______ moved them. ☐

Conversation 2
4 We ______ taken a wrong turn again. ☐
5 We ______ turned left at the last traffic light. ☐
6 OK, I ______ said "right." ☐

Conversation 3
7 Yes, but I think you ______ used less sugar. ☐
8 You ______ read it correctly. ☐

e Look at the extracts in **d** again. In pairs, put A, B, C, or D in the box after each sentence. Which phrases (*may have, couldn't have*, etc.) mean ...?

A you are sure about something that happened or something that somebody did
B you think it's possible that something happened or somebody did something
C you think it's impossible that something happened or somebody did something
D you think somebody did something wrong

f **p.138 Grammar Bank 4B.** Read the rules and do the exercises.

2 PRONUNCIATION reduced form of *have*

a 4.12 Listen to the extracts from the dialogues in **1d** again. Underline the stressed words. How is *have* pronounced?

b 4.13 **Dictation.** Listen and write down six sentences.

c In pairs, complete **B**'s responses with your own ideas. Then practice the dialogues.

1 **A** It was my birthday yesterday!
 B You should have *told me.*
2 **A** I can't find my glasses anywhere.
 B You couldn't have ______
3 **A** I gave Peter a map, but he hasn't arrived yet.
 B He may have ______
4 **A** I have a terrible stomachache.
 B You shouldn't have ______
5 **A** I thought the meeting was this morning, but no one came.
 B ______
6 **A** I failed my math test.
 B ______
7 **A** I was in a restaurant with Jane and she suddenly walked out.
 B ______
8 **A** Mary didn't come to the party last night.
 B ______
9 **A** We're going to be late. There's so much traffic.
 B ______

3 READING

a You're going to read an article by Amy Sutherland, a writer who wanted to cure her husband of some irritating habits. What do you think they might have been?

b Read the article paragraph by paragraph, using the glossary to help you. After each paragraph, stop and answer the questions with a partner.

1 What did Amy use to do when her husband couldn't find his keys? What does she do now?
2 Why and how did she learn about animal training? What idea occurred to her? What is the main principle of animal training?
3 What is the technique called "approximations"? How did she apply it to her husband?
4 What behavior did the bird trainer want to stop? How did he do it? How did she apply this technique to her husband?
5 What did she learn from the dolphin trainer? How did she apply this to her husband?
6 What sometimes happens when animals learn a technique? What technique did her husband use on her, and how?

c What do you think of the author's approach to changing her husband's behavior and improving their relationship? Is there anyone you would like to "train"? What technique do you think would work best?

Glossary

(1) **snarl** make an angry noise, like an animal does
(1) **faucet** the thing you turn to let water come out
(1) **join the hunt** take part in looking for sth (i.e., her husband's keys)
(2) **rapt** so interested that you don't pay attention to anything else
(2) **reward** give sth to sb because they have done sth well, e.g., worked hard
(2) **nag** talk to sb continuously in a complaining or critical way
(3) **hamper** basket for dirty clothes
(3) **praise** say sth positive about sb
(4) **African crested cranes** tall thin birds with very long legs
(4) **parsley** a herb commonly used in cooking
(5) **fuel** (v) increase sth, make sth stronger
(5) **mackerel** a kind of oily fish
(6) **be up to sth** pv be doing sth, often secretly
(6) **braces** metal wires worn on the teeth to correct dental problems
(6) **excruciating** very painful
(6) **tirade** a long angry speech
(6) **acknowledge my rant** show that he heard my angry words
(6) **do the trick** succeed

How I trained my husband

When nagging failed, Amy Sutherland tried a new strategy…

1 As I wash dishes at the kitchen sink, my husband, Scott, paces behind me, irritated. "Have you seen my keys?" he snarls and stomps from the room with our dog, Dixie, at his heels. In the past, I would have turned off the faucet and joined the hunt while trying to soothe my husband. But that only made him angrier, and a simple case of missing keys soon would become a full-blown drama starring the two of us and our poor nervous dog. Now, I focus on the wet dish in my hands. I don't turn around. I don't say a word. I'm using a technique I learned from a dolphin trainer.

2 For a book I was writing about a school for exotic animal trainers, I started spending my days watching students do the seemingly impossible: teaching hyenas to pirouette on command and chimps to skateboard. I listened, rapt, as professional trainers explained how they taught dolphins to flip and elephants to paint. Eventually it hit me that the same techniques might work on that stubborn but lovable species, the American husband. The central lesson I learned is that I should reward behavior I like and ignore behavior I don't. After all, you don't get a sea lion to balance a ball on the end of its nose by nagging. The same goes for the American husband.

3 I began thanking Scott if he threw one dirty shirt into the hamper. If he threw in two, I'd kiss him. I was using what trainers call "approximations," rewarding the small steps toward learning a whole new behavior. You can't expect a baboon to learn to flip on command in one session, just as you can't expect an American husband to begin regularly picking up his dirty socks by praising him once for picking up a single sock. With the baboon you first reward a hop, then a bigger hop, then an even bigger hop. With Scott the husband, I began to praise every small act every time: if he drove just a mile an hour slower, tossed one pair of shorts into the hamper, or was on time for anything.

4 On a field trip with the students, I listened to a professional trainer describe how he had taught African crested cranes to stop landing on his head and shoulders. He did this by training the leggy birds to land on mats on the ground. This, he explained, is what is called an "incompatible behavior," a simple but brilliant concept. Rather than teach the cranes to stop landing on him, the trainer taught the birds something else, a behavior that would make the undesirable behavior impossible. The birds couldn't alight on the mats and his head simultaneously. At home, I came up with incompatible behaviors for Scott to keep him from crowding me while I cooked. I piled up parsley for him to chop or cheese for him to grate at the other end of the kitchen island. Soon I'd done it: no more Scott hovering around me while I cooked.

5 I followed the students to SeaWorld San Diego, where a dolphin trainer introduced me to "least reinforcing scenario" (L. R. S.). When a dolphin does something wrong, the trainer doesn't respond in any way. He stands still for a few beats, careful not to look at the dolphin, and then returns to work. The idea is that any response, positive or negative, fuels a behavior. If a behavior provokes no response, it typically dies away. It was only a matter of time before Scott was again searching for his keys, at which point I said nothing and kept at what I was doing. It took a lot of discipline to maintain my calm, but results were immediate. I felt as if I should throw him a mackerel.

6 Professionals talk of animals that understand training so well they eventually use it back on the trainer. My "animal" did the same. When the training techniques worked so beautifully, I couldn't resist telling my husband what I was up to. He wasn't offended, just amused. Then last fall, firmly in middle age, I learned that I needed braces on my teeth. They were not only humiliating, but also excruciating. One morning, as I launched into yet another tirade about how uncomfortable I was, Scott just looked at me blankly. He didn't say a word or acknowledge my rant in any way, not even with a nod. I started to walk away, then I realized what was happening, and I turned and asked, "Are you giving me an L. R. S.?" Silence. "You are, aren't you?" He finally smiled, but his L. R. S. had already done the trick. He'd begun to train me, the American wife.

Adapted from a newspaper

4 LISTENING

a 4.14 What's the difference between a discussion and an argument? You're going to listen to a psychologist giving some tips to help people when they disagree with somebody about something. Listen once and put a check (✔) next to the six things she suggests.

1 Think carefully about what to say when you begin a discussion.
2 Try to "win" the argument as quickly as you can.
3 Say you're sorry if something really is your fault.
4 Never avoid an argument by refusing to talk.
5 Don't say things that aren't completely true.
6 Don't shout.
7 Don't talk about things that aren't relevant to the argument.
8 Use another person to mediate.
9 Postpone the argument until later, when you have both calmed down.
10 It's a bad thing for a couple to argue.

b Listen again and, with a partner, try to add more detail to the tips you selected in **a**.

c With a partner, decide which two of the psychologist's tips you think are the most useful.

d Look at these sentences and try to figure out what the missing words are.

1 But of course this is **easier said** ______ ______.
2 If you're the person who is ______ ______ **wrong**, just admit it!
3 It is important to ______ **things** ______ **control**.
4 Raising your voice will just make the other person ______ **their temper**, too.
5 Stop for a moment and ______ **a deep breath**.
6 It is also very important to ______ ______ **the point**.
7 There is much more chance that you will be able to ______ **an agreement**.
8 ______ ______ **conflict** is an important part of any relationship.

e 4.15 Listen and check.

5 SPEAKING

a **Communication** *Argument! A p.117 B p.120.* Role-play two arguments with a partner.

b Did you follow any of the psychologist's tips about how to argue? Was there anything you should / shouldn't have done?

6 VOCABULARY verbs often confused

a Circle the correct verb in each pair of sentences.

1 a When I saw my wife's face, I *noticed / realized* that I had bought the wrong size.
  b My husband never *notices / realizes* when I've been to the hairstylist.
2 a The water level in the river is *raising / rising*.
  b Don't *raise / rise* your voice when you are having an argument.
3 a I think we need to *argue / discuss* our new marketing plan.
  b Teenagers often *argue / discuss* with their parents.
4 a There is a new road safety campaign to *avoid / prevent* accidents.
  b We took the freeway to *avoid / prevent* getting stuck in downtown traffic.
5 a Please *remember / remind* to lock the door before you go out.
  b *Remember / Remind* me to call my mother later – it's her birthday.
6 a I *expect / hope* she'll come to the party. I'd really like to see her.
  b My driving test is next week, but I'm not *expecting / hoping* to pass – I've only had a few lessons.
7 a Mandy didn't invite me to her party, but I don't *mind / matter*.
  b It doesn't *mind / matter* if we're a little late.
8 a Oh no! Somebody *stole / robbed* my bike!
  b A 40-year-old man has been charged with *robbing / stealing* a bank on Main Street.
9 a I woke up during the night because I *heard / listened to* a noise.
  b If you had *heard / listened to* what I was saying, you'd know what the problem was.
10 a Your brother *seems / looks* exactly like your father – he has the same eyes.
  b When I spoke to him on the phone, I thought he *seemed / looked* very friendly.

b Compare your answers with a partner, and try to explain what the difference is between the verbs in each pair.

c Complete the questions with the correct form of one of the verbs from the corresponding pair in **a**. Then ask and answer with a partner.

1 Do you usually _____ what color eyes people have?
2 What would your boss do if you asked him / her to _____ your salary?
3 Do you often _____ with people in your family? With who? About what?
4 Do you usually _____ going shopping when the stores are crowded?
5 Are you good at _____ people's birthdays?
6 Are you _____ to pass or fail your next English exam?
7 Do you think it _____ if a wife earns more than her husband?
8 Has your car or bike ever been _____?
9 Are women really better at _____ than men?
10 Who do you _____ like in your family?

MINI GRAMMAR *would rather, had better*

a Look at two sentences from the listening. Which of the highlighted phrases means *should*? Which means *would prefer to*? Do you know what *'d* refers to in each case?

I'd rather talk about this tomorrow after we've both calmed down.

I think we'd better take another look at how we divide up the housework.

b Now read the rules for using *had better* and *would rather*.

- Use *had better* with the base form, e.g.,
  You'd better hurry up. Your train leaves in ten minutes.
  You'd better not tell your parents – they'll be furious.
  NOT ~~You hadn't better tell ...~~

⚠ *had better* is stronger and more immediate than *should* and is often used as a warning.

- Use *would rather* with the base form, e.g.,
  I'd rather go on vacation in July this year, not August.
  Would you rather stay in or go out tonight?
  I'd rather not come to the meeting this afternoon. I'm really busy. NOT ~~I'd not rather.~~

c Rewrite the **bold** phrases using *had better (not)* or *would rather (not)*.

1 I think **I should go now**. It's very late.
2 **I'd prefer to go out** on Friday instead of Saturday.
3 **You shouldn't walk home.** It's kind of dangerous here at night.
4 Ana said **she'd prefer to meet** on Thursday afternoon.
5 Jaime **should be careful**. If the boss finds out, he'll fire him.
6 **Would you prefer not to go to the party** if David is going to be there?
7 **You shouldn't leave your bag there** – someone will steal it.
8 **My wife would prefer not to fly**. She had a bad experience once.

4C

G verbs of the senses
V the body
P silent letters

Let your body do the talking

1 GRAMMAR verbs of the senses

a Look at the photo. In pairs, choose the best description of the man.

1 He looks …
a angry. b pained. c depressed.
2 He looks like …
a a teacher. b a bank manager. c a chef.
3 He looks as if …
a he just ate something horrible.
b he just heard some bad news.
c he is listening to something that sounds awful.

b Now read about a book called *In Character: Actors acting* and check your answers.

1 Who is the man in the photo? 2 What's he doing?

In character: actors acting

The photographer Howard Schatz had a very unusual idea for a book. He invited actors into his studio and asked them to "be" certain characters in certain situations, and he then photographed them. For example, he told the actor Christopher Lloyd to be "a violin teacher who is listening to his student massacre a Mozart piece."

c **p.138 Grammar Bank 4C.** Read the rules and do the exercises.

d Look at the photos of Alan Cumming and Michael Cumpsty from the book and describe the actors. Use *looks*, *looks like*, and *looks as if*.

e Match the faces A–D with situations 1–4, and the faces E–H with situations 5–8.

1 You realize you have been betrayed by your best friend. ☐
2 You are a four-year-old child letting the family's pet parrot out of its cage. ☐
3 You are a young man begging your girlfriend to come with you to visit your parents. ☐
4 You are a young child trying not to listen as your mother tells you off. ☐
5 You are a young driver telling a police officer that you haven't had anything to drink. ☐
6 You are a police officer leaning on the car door waiting for a driver to show his license. ☐
7 You are a young driver admitting that you've had maybe a small drink. ☐
8 You are a police officer looking into a car filled with teenagers. ☐

f 4.16 Listen to these sounds. What do you think is happening? Use *It sounds as if …* or *It sounds like …*

g Make pairs of opposites from the adjectives in the list. Do they usually describe how something feels or how something tastes / smells?

hard loose rough /rʌf/ smooth /smuð/ soft sour / bitter strong sweet tight weak

h Use *feels*, *smells*, or *tastes* + an adjective or + *like* + noun, etc. to describe one of the objects below for your partner to guess. Then change roles.

hair that has just been washed
roses
overcooked steak
cabbage being cooked
a full ashtray
a marble statue
a silk scarf
a lemon
a baby after its bath
a cat's tongue
espresso coffee without sugar
a two-day beard
Mexican food
jeans that are too small for you

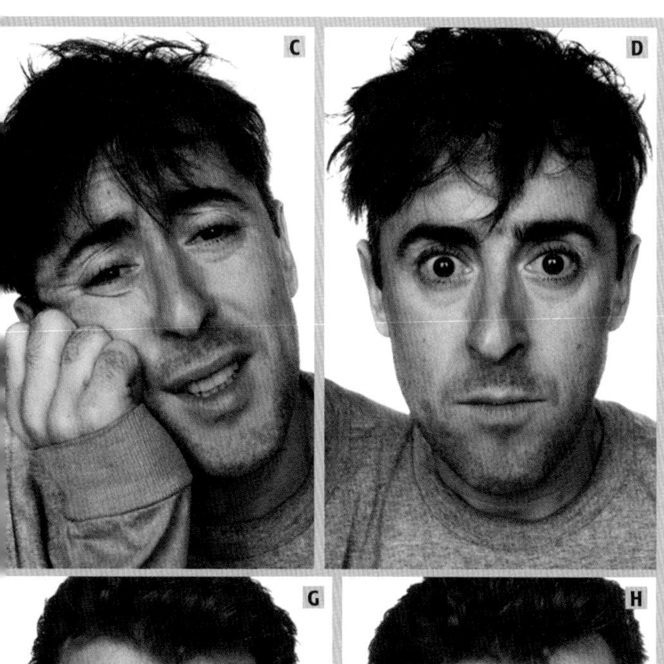

2 LISTENING

a 4.17 You are going to listen to a radio quiz show called *Use Your Senses*, where contestants have to identify a mystery food, a mystery drink, a mystery object, and a mystery sound. Listen once and write what you think the answers are.

1 ________
2 ________
3 ________
4 ________

b Listen again and complete the phrases.

Mystery drink
It smells ________.
It smells a little ________.

Mystery food
It tastes a little bit ________.
It tastes fairly ________.

Mystery object
It feels like ________.
It definitely feels ________.

Mystery sound
It sounds like ________.
It sounds ________.

c Discuss your answers to **a** with a partner.

d 4.18 Now listen to the answers. Were you right?

3 VOCABULARY the body

a Look at a photograph of the actress Judi Dench. Match the words in the list with 1–8 in the photo.

cheek chin eyebrow eyelashes forehead /ˈfɔrhɛd/ lips neck wrinkles /ˈrɪŋklz/

b p.152 Vocabulary Bank *The body.*

c Take the *Body quiz* with a partner.

BODY QUIZ

A Which part of the body?

1 The place where you wear a watch.
2 The two places where you might wear a belt.
3 You can easily twist this when playing sports.
4 These are often red after you've been out in the cold or if you're embarrassed.
5 You use these to breathe.
6 Doctors sometimes listen to this to see if you have a breathing problem.

B Which idiom do you use ...?

1 when you are very nervous (stomach)
2 when you can't quite remember something (tongue)
3 when you can't stop thinking about something, e.g., a particular song (head)
4 when you think a friend is telling you something that isn't true as a joke (leg)
5 when you memorize something (heart)
6 when you have said something that you shouldn't have said because it is a secret or may cause embarrassment (foot)

d 4.19 Listen and mime the action.

4 PRONUNCIATION silent letters

a Cross out the "silent consonant" in these words.

calf wrist palms wrinkles comb kneel thumb

b 4.20 Listen and check.

c Look at some more common words with silent consonants. In pairs, decide which they are and cross them out. Use the phonetic transcriptions to help you.

asthma /ˈæzmə/ castle /ˈkæsl/ doubt /daʊt/ half /hæf/ honest /ˈɑnəst/ island /ˈaɪlənd/ knock /nɑk/ psychologist /saɪˈkɑlədʒɪst/ receipt /rɪˈsit/ sign /saɪn/ whole /hoʊl/ would /wʊd/

d 4.21 Listen and check.

e 4.22 **Dictation.** Listen and write down six sentences.

5 READING

a What do you understand by the phrase "body language"?

b In pairs, look at the pictures below and try to match the body language with the feelings.

A saying something important ☐
B feeling attracted to someone ☐
C feeling defensive ☐
D feeling nervous ☐
E feeling superior ☐
F being honest ☐
G lying ☐
H thinking hard ☐

c Read *Let your body do the talking* and check your answers.

Let your body do the talking

The parts of our body that convey most about how we feel are our hands and arms – and the way we move them. Hand and arm gestures are sometimes deliberate, but most often they occur unconsciously and naturally.

Saying something important Open hands and arms, especially extended and with palms up in front of the body at chest height, indicate that what you are saying is important, and, especially when people are speaking in public, a pointing finger or a hand waving above the shoulders emphasizes an individual point. However, research shows that people often find speakers who point their fingers a lot rather annoying.

Openness or honesty When people want to be open or honest, they will often hold one or both of their palms out to the other person. Soccer players who have just committed a foul often use this gesture to try to convince the referee that they didn't do it.

Nervousness If you put your hand to your mouth, this either indicates that you are hiding something, or that you are nervous. Fidgeting with your hands, for example, tapping the table with your fingers, also shows nervousness, and so does holding a bag or briefcase very tightly in front of the body.

Superiority People who feel superior to you often appear relaxed, with their hands clasped behind their heads. The chin and head is often held high. This gesture is typical of lawyers, accountants, and other professionals who feel they know more than you do. Another gesture of superiority is to put your hands in your pockets with the thumbs protruding.

Feeling defensive Arms folded tightly over the chest is a classic gesture of defensiveness and indicates that you are protecting yourself. It is often seen among strangers standing in lines or in elevators or anywhere where people feel slightly insecure. People also sometimes use this gesture when they are listening to someone, to show that they disagree with what is being said. However, this gesture can simply mean that the person is cold!

Thinking hard A hand-to-cheek gesture, where you bring a hand to your face and extend your index finger along your cheek, with the remaining fingers positioned below the mouth, often shows that you are thinking deeply. When you stroke your chin, you are probably thinking about something important or making a decision.

Attraction If men are attracted to someone, they sometimes play with one of their ear lobes, whereas women will play with a lock of hair or continually tuck their hair behind their ears.

Lying There are many gestures that indicate that someone is lying, and in order to be sure, you would expect a person to show more than one. Gestures include putting your hand in front of your mouth, touching your nose, rubbing your eyes, touching your ear, scratching your neck, pulling at your collar, or putting your finger or fingers in your mouth.

d Focus on the highlighted words, which describe more parts of the body or gestures. In pairs, try to figure out what they mean.

e In pairs, read the article again, paragraph by paragraph, and try to do each of the gestures described. Do you use any of these gestures a lot?

6 SPEAKING

GET IT RIGHT describing pictures

When you are describing the pictures, use these expressions to explain precisely what / who you are referring to:

The woman … on the right / left / in the center of the picture; … in the background / foreground …

Remember you can also use *might be / may be / could be* for speculating, as well as *looks, looks as if*, etc.

Cape Cod Morning (1950) Edward Hopper

a In pairs, look at the painting. Talk about where the woman is, how she is feeling, and what is happening or has happened. Use her body language to help you.

b **Communication** *Two paintings A p.118 B p.120.* Describe your painting for your partner to visualize.

p.157 Phrasal verbs in context *File 4.*

THE INTERVIEW

a You are going to listen to an interview with Trevor White, a Canadian actor. Before you listen, read the glossary and look at how the words are pronounced to help you understand what he says.

Glossary

voice-over /ˈvɔɪsˌoʊvər/ information or comments in a movie or TV program given by a person who you do not see on the screen

fringe theater /ˈfrɪndʒ ˈθiətər/ plays, often by new writers, that are unusual and question the way people think

props /prɑps/ objects used by actors during the performance of a play or movie

rehearsal /rɪˈhərsl/ time that is spent practicing a play or piece of music

Dictaphone /ˈdɪktəˌfoʊn/ a small machine used to record people speaking

oftentimes /ˈɔfənˌtaɪmz/ often

Royal Shakespeare Company A British drama company that specializes in Shakespeare's plays

Coriolanus /kɑrɪəˈleɪnəs/ one of Shakespeare's lesser known plays set in Roman times

feature film /ˈfitʃər fɪlm/ a full-length movie with a story, i.e., not a documentary

sword /sɔrd/ a weapon with a long metal blade

ax /æks/ a weapon with a wooden handle and a heavy metal blade; also a tool for chopping wood

parry /ˈpæri/ to defend yourself by stopping sb from hitting you, e.g., with your arm or with a weapon

b 4.23 Listen to part 1. Answer the questions with a partner.

1 What kinds of acting does he do?
2 How did he become an actor?
3 What does he find most difficult about preparing for a part?
4 How does he learn his lines?
5 What kind of lines are difficult to memorize?

c 4.24 Listen to part 2. Answer the questions with a partner.

What does he say about ...?

1 *Coriolanus*
2 a sword and ax fight
3 the difference between theater acting and film acting
4 the good and bad side about TV and film work
5 being on a red carpet

d 4.25 Listen and complete the phrases. What do you think they mean?

COMMON PHRASES

1 There isn't much I don't do, I guess, ______ ______ as acting goes.
2 You just ______ ______ and you're expected to know all your lines. pv
3 You do it a few times and ______ ______.
4 It's amazing the ______ ______ ______ when the writing is good.
5 I gave the other guy three stitches on his fingers ______ ______ point when he parried in the wrong place.
6 You get to do it ______ and ______ again.

e Listen to the interview again with the audioscript on page 126. Does Trevor make acting sound like an attractive job?

ON THE STREET

a 4.26 Listen to five people talking about acting. Write the number of the speaker next to what they appeared in. How many of them mention feeling nervous?

1 Rachel  2 Josh  3 Kerrie  4 Shelly  5 Juan

commercials   movies   musicals   school / college plays

b Listen again. Who ...?

1 names a musical they have been in
2 found that acting helped them later on
3 did a lot of dancing as well as acting
4 enjoys pretending to be someone else
5 found it difficult to remember the lines

c 4.27 Listen and complete the phrases. What do you think they mean?

COMMON PHRASES

1 It made me feel that I really wasn't ______ to be an actor specifically.
2 ... and commercials as ______ as independent films ...
3 ... so I used to do lots of dancing when I was ______ up. pv
4 I was nervous, at ______, when I got on stage ...
5 ... we just ______ up our own play ... pv

d Listen to the interviews again with the audioscript on page 127. Then answer the same questions with a partner.

Make your home a safer place!

You probably think that your home is the one place where you are safe. That's what I thought until last week. Now I know our apartment is full of accidents waiting to happen. / Next month we're taking care of my niece and nephew while their parents go away for a short break. We asked them to come over and make sure everything was OK. We got a few surprises. We started in the spare bedroom, where the children will sleep. Everybody knows you shouldn't put children's beds under a window in case a child tries to climb out. Everybody except us! Next was the bathroom. We keep our medicines on a shelf above the sink. A terrible idea, as my sister explained. Never leave medicines somewhere children can find them. They might think they are candy. Finally, the kitchen. This is the most dangerous room in the house. Knives should be kept in drawers that children can't reach, and all cleaning liquids in high cabinets. So we have three weeks to make our house safe. It's not difficult... once you know how.

a Look at the three pictures. What do you think the child's parents should / shouldn't have done? Read the article and check.

b This article was originally written in six short paragraphs. Mark (/) where each new paragraph should begin.

c You're going to write an article for a school magazine about how to be safe if you go walking in the country or the mountains. Look at the **Useful language** expressions and make sure you know how to use them.

Useful language

Giving advice

Don't forget to ... / Remember to ...
Make sure you ...
You should ...
Never ...

Reasons

... in case
... so (that)
... because it might ...

PLAN the content in pairs or small groups.

1 Think of a good title and one or two introductory sentences.
2 Write down a few tips, e.g., what to take with you (see picture below for ideas). Then divide the tips into two or three groups and put them into a logical order.

WRITE 120–180 words. Use a neutral or informal style.

CHECK your article for mistakes (grammar, punctuation, and spelling).

4 What do you remember?

GRAMMAR

a Complete the second sentence so that it means the same as the first.

1 They escaped from the jungle because they found the river.
They wouldn't have escaped from the jungle if they ______ ______ the river.

2 I'm sure you left your glasses in the restaurant.
You ______ ______ left your glasses in the restaurant.

3 Why didn't you tell me it was your birthday?
You ______ ______ ______ me it was your birthday!

4 I don't have much time, so I can't go to dance classes.
I would be able to go to dance classes if I ______ more time.

5 I'm sure the backpackers haven't gotten lost. They know the area well.
The backpackers ______ ______ ______ lost. They know the area well.

b Choose a, b, or c.

1 The sky is very dark. It ______ there's going to be a storm.
a looks
b looks like if
c looks as if

2 What ______ do tonight, eat out or stay in?
a would you rather
b had you rather
c do you rather

3 If I hadn't really liked the jacket, I ______ it.
a wouldn't buy
b hadn't bought
c wouldn't have bought

4 What gorgeous material! It ______ silk.
a feels
b feels like
c feels as if

5 Mark is very late. Do you think he ______ forgotten about the dinner?
a couldn't have
b could
c might have

VOCABULARY

a Word groups. Underline the word that is different. Say why.

1 upset	disappointed	relieved	offended
2 amazed	astonished	surprised	anxious
3 palm	calf	wrist	nail
4 kidney	heart	liver	hip
5 nod	wave	clap	point

b Circle the right verb.

1 Please *remind / remember* the children to do their homework.
2 **A** I'm very sorry.
B Don't worry. It doesn't *mind / matter*.
3 The robbers *stole / robbed* $50,000 from the bank.
4 If you know the answer, *raise / rise* your hand; don't shout.
5 Don't *argue / discuss* with your father about it! He doesn't listen.

c Complete with one word.

1 I was jumping ___ joy when I heard I'd passed the exam!
2 You look fed ___. Have you been waiting for a long time?
3 I really put my foot ___ my mouth when I mentioned his ex-wife.
4 Please calm ___. Shouting only makes things worse.
5 My car broke ___ on the highway.

d Write the verbs for the definitions.

1 **ch**______ to bite food into small pieces in your mouth
2 **y**______ to open your mouth wide when you are tired or bored
3 **sc**______ to rub your skin with your nails
4 **f**______ to make a serious, angry, or worried expression
5 **st**______ to look at something / somebody for a long time

PRONUNCIATION

a Underline the word with a different sound.

1	 miserable	realize	notice	rise
2	 devastated	delighted	offended	desperate
3	 blow	homesick	frown	lonely
4	 tongue	lungs	discuss	comb
5	 astonished	shrug	chew	brush

b Underline the stressed syllable.

exhausted prevent expect kidney elbow

What can you do?

CAN YOU UNDERSTAND THIS TEXT?

a Complete the article with a sentence A–F. There is one sentence you don't need.

A The photographs are then put in a drawer and forgotten.
B At the flick of a switch, the manufacturers claim, a woman can lose as much as a dress size.
C "But it did just enough to hide some of the evidence of a few too many good restaurant meals."
D The only victim will be the truth.
E They don't seem to notice that the lost weight seems to have mysteriously returned since the vacation.
F "It worked better than a four-week diet of raw vegetables."

b Look at the highlighted words and phrases. Can you guess what they mean?

Slimline "snapshots" that help vacationers stretch the truth

A chain store, Comet, is selling a new digital camera that will take pictures of you – and make you look thinner.
The HP Photosmart R727 contains a "slimcam" function that " squeezes " the object at the center of the frame without distorting the background. [1] ☐ And a man can develop, if not a flat stomach, then at least a more respectably-proportioned figure for the vacation photograph album.

Comet believes that the photography of self-delusion will become hugely popular in the future. In a culture obsessed with unrealistic ideas of the perfect body, the answer seems to be to show your friends vacation photographs in which you look healthily slim. [2] ☐

"Like many women, I am a size 16, and sometimes my vacation photos are not as flattering as I would like," said Sally Cranham, 24, a professional singer who tried out the camera. "The slimming button certainly trimmed off a little bit where it counts," she said. [3] ☐

People nowadays are used to the doctored images of celebrity magazines, and some users of the camera might worry that the truth of their "slimcam" photography would emerge when friends flipped through the vacation pictures. But Ms. Cranham is convinced that her friends won't realize. "If the camera had made me look like a size 8, then no one would have believed it," she said. [4] ☐

A spokeswoman for Comet said that it brought technology that usually favored only the rich and famous within the grasp of ordinary people. [5] ☐

Adapted from a newspaper

CAN YOU UNDERSTAND THESE PEOPLE?

a 4.28 Listen and circle the correct answer, a, b, or c.

1 What does the speaker think is the most important piece of advice to avoid being bitten by a snake?
  a What you wear.
  b Where you camp.
  c Where you walk.
2 What is the main reason why the captain is talking?
  a To introduce himself.
  b To explain the safety procedures.
  c To talk about what will happen during the flight.
3 What does the man think happened to John?
  a He might have had an accident.
  b He forgot.
  c He'll arrive later.
4 What *doesn't* the man want the woman to do?
  a Spend a lot of money on a dress.
  b Spend more time shopping today.
  c Go shopping again the next day.
5 Who are the people in the painting?
  a A beautiful girl with a sick old man.
  b An ugly child with his grandfather.
  c A young boy with an old man.

b 4.29 You will hear an interview with two young people. Write **C** next to what Caroline says, **B** next to what Ben says, and **N** next to what neither of them says.

1 I didn't think people's English would be so good. ☐
2 I had my credit card stolen. ☐
3 I enjoyed the freedom of choosing my route. ☐
4 My friends and I didn't always agree about what to do. ☐
5 I slept in a tent. ☐

CAN YOU SAY THIS IN ENGLISH?

Can you ...?

☐ talk about what you would do and what you would have done in certain situations
☐ speculate about someone's past actions using *may* / *must* / *couldn't have*, and criticize how someone acted in the past using *should have* / *shouldn't have*
☐ talk about why body language is important and explain what certain gestures indicate

5 A

G gerunds and infinitives
V music
P *ch* and *y*

The psychology of music

1 LISTENING & SPEAKING

a 5.1 Listen to some short pieces of music. How do they make you feel? Would you like to keep on listening?

> **Taking notes**
> We often need to take notes when we are listening, for example, to somebody giving a lecture. If you need to take notes when you are listening to someone speaking in English, try to write down key words or phrases because you won't have time to write complete sentences. After the lecture, you may want to expand your notes into full sentences.

b 5.2 Listen to John Sloboda, a British music psychologist, talking about why we listen to music. Try to complete the notes below by writing key words or phrases. Then with a partner, try to remember as much as you can of what he said.

Why do we listen to music?

1 to make us ...

e.g.:

2 to help us ...

e.g.:

3 to intensify ...

e.g.:

c 5.3 Now listen to John explaining how music can affect the way we feel. Complete the notes below. Then compare with a partner and try to remember what he said.

How does music affect our emotions?

Three important human emotions:

1 happiness

2

3

How we feel affects the way we speak, e.g.:

1 happy – speak faster / higher

2

3

Music copies this, e.g.:

1 fast / high music sounds happy

2

3

Examples:

Music that sounds

1 happy, e.g.:

2 angry, e.g.:

3 sad, e.g.:

This is especially exploited in ...

e.g.:

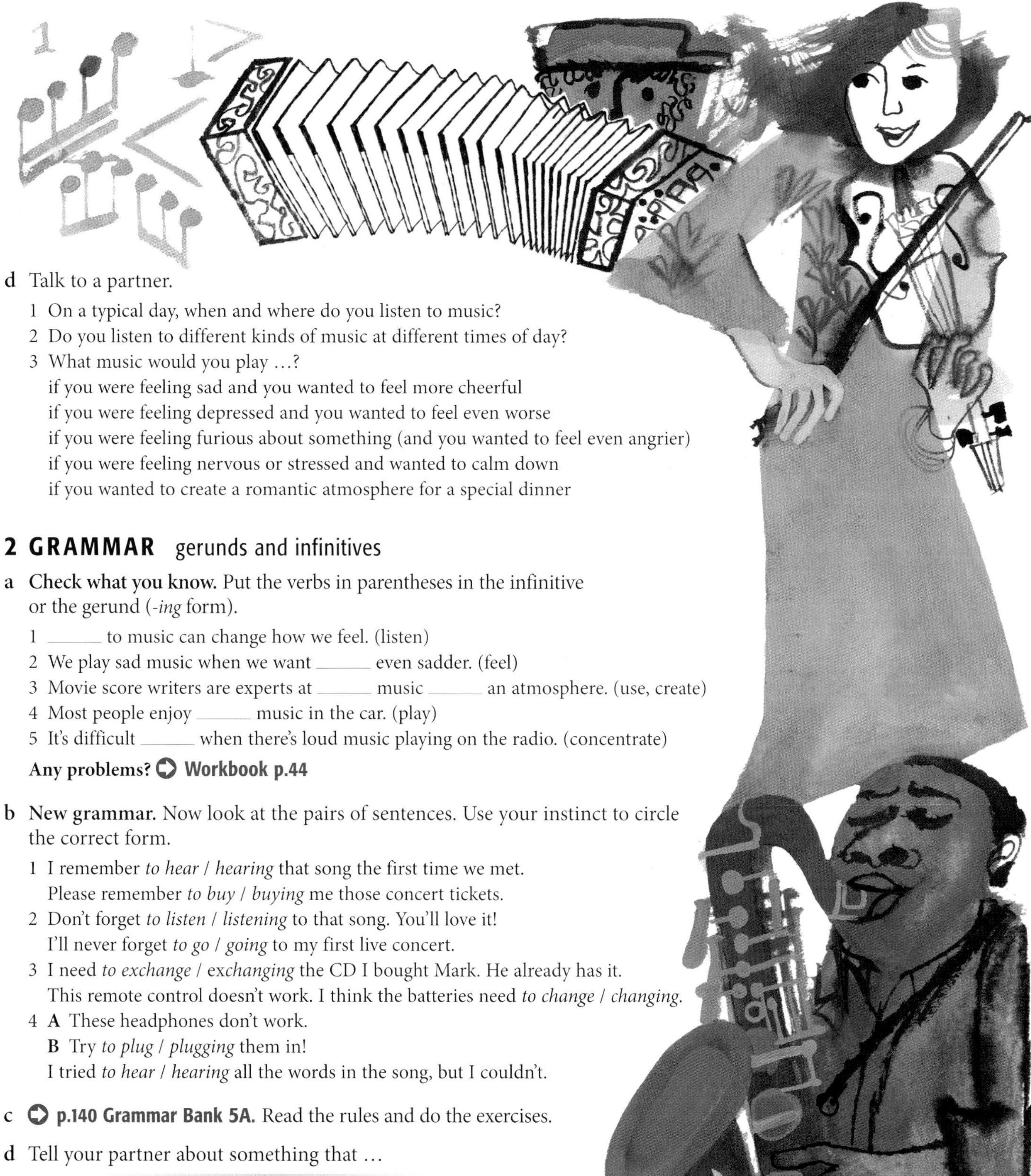

d Talk to a partner.

1 On a typical day, when and where do you listen to music?
2 Do you listen to different kinds of music at different times of day?
3 What music would you play …?
if you were feeling sad and you wanted to feel more cheerful
if you were feeling depressed and you wanted to feel even worse
if you were feeling furious about something (and you wanted to feel even angrier)
if you were feeling nervous or stressed and wanted to calm down
if you wanted to create a romantic atmosphere for a special dinner

2 GRAMMAR gerunds and infinitives

a **Check what you know.** Put the verbs in parentheses in the infinitive or the gerund (*-ing* form).

1 ______ to music can change how we feel. (listen)
2 We play sad music when we want ______ even sadder. (feel)
3 Movie score writers are experts at ______ music ______ an atmosphere. (use, create)
4 Most people enjoy ______ music in the car. (play)
5 It's difficult ______ when there's loud music playing on the radio. (concentrate)

Any problems? ➲ **Workbook p.44**

b **New grammar.** Now look at the pairs of sentences. Use your instinct to circle the correct form.

1 I remember *to hear / hearing* that song the first time we met.
Please remember *to buy / buying* me those concert tickets.
2 Don't forget *to listen / listening* to that song. You'll love it!
I'll never forget *to go / going* to my first live concert.
3 I need *to exchange / exchanging* the CD I bought Mark. He already has it.
This remote control doesn't work. I think the batteries need *to change / changing*.
4 **A** These headphones don't work.
B Try *to plug / plugging* them in!
I tried *to hear / hearing* all the words in the song, but I couldn't.

c ➲ **p.140 Grammar Bank 5A.** Read the rules and do the exercises.

d Tell your partner about something that …

you'll never **forget seeing** for the first time.
you often **forget to do** before you go out.
you **remember doing** when you were less than five years old.
you have to **remember to do** before you go to bed.
needs doing in your house / apartment.
you **need to do** this evening.
you **tried to learn** but couldn't.
you usually **try doing** when you can't sleep at night.

3 VOCABULARY music

a 5.4 Listen and say what instruments you can hear.

b p.153 Vocabulary Bank *Music.*

c 5.5 Listen and say what you can hear, e.g., *a choir singing.*

d With a partner, think of …

- a song with a catchy chorus.
- a singer with a monotonous voice.
- a classical composer.
- a kind of music that has a very strong beat.
- a song or piece of music you find very moving.
- a famous singer-songwriter.
- the lead singer of a well-known band.
- a world-famous tenor.
- a song that has incomprehensible lyrics.

4 PRONUNCIATION *ch* and *y*

a Use your instinct to put these words in the correct columns: *character, chef, research.*

b Read the rules below and check your answers.

The letters *ch*
- are usually pronounced /tʃ/, e.g., *check.*
- are sometimes pronounced /k/, especially in words of Greek origin, e.g., *chemistry, technology.*
- are very occasionally pronounced /ʃ/, especially in words of French origin, e.g., *chauffeur, chef.*

c Use the rules to put some more words in each column.

change cheerful choir choose chorus
machine mustache orchestra psychologist

d 5.6 Listen and check.

e Now read the rules for the letter *y*. Then use them to put the words in the correct columns.

The letter *y*

1 in the middle of a word …
- is usually pronounced /ɪ/ when it is between consonants, e.g., *symptoms, physics.*
- is pronounced /aɪ/ when *y* is followed by a consonant + *e*, e.g., *byte*, or in the prefix *psych-*, e.g., *psychoanalyst.*

2 at the end of a word …
- is pronounced /aɪ/ in words ending *-ify*, e.g., *terrify*, and words where the stress is on the last syllable, e.g., *deny*, and in one-syllable words, e.g., *fly.*
- is pronounced /i/ in all other words ending in *y*, e.g., *melody, windy*, etc.

apply country heavy lifestyle lyrics physical psychiatrist
qualify rhythm shy symphony try type typical

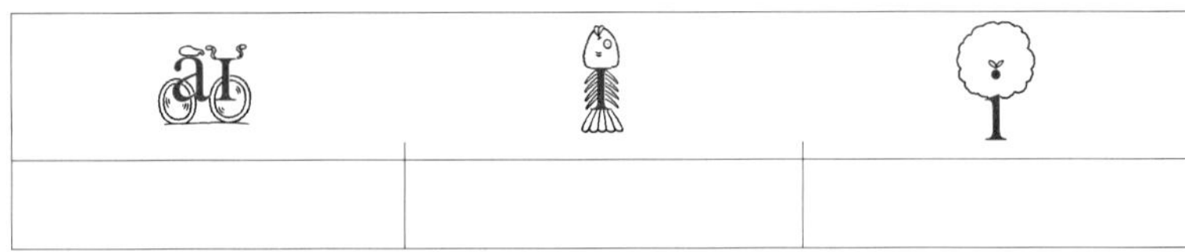

f 5.7 Listen and check.

5 SPEAKING

GET IT RIGHT *the*
Don't use *the* when you are talking in general about kinds of music, e.g., *I love classical music* NOT ~~*the classical music*~~.
Use *the* when you are talking about instruments, e.g., *I play the violin, the guitar*, etc.

Answer the questions with a partner.

What kind of music do you like?

Do you have a favorite …?
band solo artist
song piece of music (symphony, sonata, etc.)
composer soloist conductor

Do you play a musical instrument?

YES
- Have you ever had lessons?
- Can you read music?
- Have you ever played in a band / orchestra?

NO
- Have you ever tried to learn to play an instrument?
- Is there an instrument you would like to learn to play?

What do you think of …?
alternative music classical music
country music dance music electronic music
folk music funk gansta rap heavy metal
hip-hop jazz opera pop music reggae
rock music salsa soul music

Have you ever …?
- sung in a choir
- been in a talent contest
- performed in front of a lot of people

What's the best live concert you've ever been to?

6 READING

a Do you think *What kind of music do you like?* is a good question when you are getting to know somebody? Why?

b Read the introduction to the article. Do you agree with the psychologists?

c Read the rest of the article. Which category(ies) do you fit into best?

What's your soundtrack?

Your taste in music can reveal a lot about you...

The question "What kind of music do you like?" is very revealing. It is the number one topic of conversation among young adults who are getting to know each other, according to psychologists from the universities of Texas and Cambridge. Their research has shown that knowing another person's musical tastes can provide remarkably accurate personality predictions. For most people, music is a very important part of their lives, and psychologists believe that their preferences reveal information about their character and their lifestyle. They think that personality clues are conveyed in the music's tempo, rhythm, and lyrics.

A Upbeat and simple music

Fans of "Top 40" pop, country, and soundtrack music tend to be more conventional and conservative compared with fans of other genres; family and discipline are important life values. They are also typically cheerful, outgoing, and sociable kinds of people who enjoy helping others. In their free time they often enjoy playing or watching sports. They also enjoy watching major Hollywood movies, especially comedies. According to the psychologists, "People who like country and pop try to avoid making their lives unnecessarily complex."

B Energetic and rhythmic music

Hip-hop, funk, rap, soul, dance, and electronic music attracts people who are talkative, outgoing, and romantic and who tend to express their thoughts impulsively. They are the kind of people who love going to parties and for whom friendship and social recognition is very important. They tend to see themselves as physically attractive. When they go to the movies, they typically enjoy watching action movies, science fiction, gangster movies, or comedies.

C Complex and reflective music

Fans of classical, jazz, and other "complex" music typically have above-average intelligence. They tend to be creative and open to new experiences and lovers of classic or foreign films. Regarding lifestyle, fans of this kind of music tend to be politically liberal, are usually rather sophisticated, and often don't like sports. However, compared with other music fans, opera lovers are three times more likely to commit suicide, psychologists say. But don't blame *Madame Butterfly* – people with dramatic personalities, whose moods go up and down a lot, are attracted to opera, not influenced by it.

D Intense and rebellious music

Fans of alternative, heavy metal, rock music, and gangsta rap tend to be people who enjoy taking risks and having thrilling experiences. They are usually physically active. They are typically independent, curious about the world, and rebellious. They're the kind of people who are likely to enjoy watching action, fantasy, war, and horror movies. Parents often worry that this kind of music promotes aggressive behavior in teenagers, but research has found no direct link. In fact, younger fans of gangsta rap or heavy metal are often quieter and shyer than other young people.

d According to the article, what kind of music would these people like best? Write A, B, C, or D.

1 Someone who is fairly vain. ☐
2 Somebody who enjoys dangerous sports. ☐
3 A person who speaks their mind without thinking. ☐
4 Someone who watches subtitled movies. ☐
5 A person who does voluntary work in the community. ☐
6 Somebody who enjoys the simple things in life. ☐
7 A person who might have been quiet as a child. ☐
8 Someone who is intellectual. ☐

e Read the article again and underline five new words or phrases that you would like to learn, and compare with a partner.

f Think about people you know who like each kind of music. Do you agree with what the article says about their personalities?

5 B

G *used to, be used to, get used to*
V sleep
P linking words

Counting sheep

1 GRAMMAR *used to, be used to, get used to*

a Take turns interviewing each other with the questionnaire *Are you sleep deprived?* Ask for and give as much information as you can. Circle the answer that best describes your partner.

b **Communication** *Sleep p.118.* Read the results of the questionnaire and calculate your score. Are you sleep deprived?

c Match the sentence beginnings 1–4 with endings A–D.

1 *I usually* sleep 6 hours a night ☐
2 *I used to* sleep 7 hours a night, ☐
3 *I'm not used to* sleeping only 4 or 5 hours a night, ☐
4 *I'm getting used to* sleeping only 4 or 5 hours a night, ☐

A but now I sleep less.
B so it's new and strange for me.
C so it's becoming less of a problem.
D or more if I can.

d **p.140 Grammar Bank 5B.** Read the rules and do the exercises.

2 PRONUNCIATION linking words

a 5.8 **Dictation.** Listen and write down six sentences. Try to separate the words in your head before you write.

b Practice saying the sentences quickly, trying to link the words.

c Ask and answer the questions with a partner.

When you were a child, did you use to be frightened of the dark?
Did you use to share a room with a brother or sister?
Do you find it difficult to sleep when you're in a bed that you're not used to, for example, in a hotel?
Do you think you could get used to working at night and sleeping during the day?
What do you usually do as soon as you wake up in the morning?
What's the last thing you usually do before going to bed?

Answer these questions and find out.

1 **How long does it usually take you to fall asleep at night?**
a less than 5 minutes b more than 5 minutes

2 **How many hours do you usually sleep?**
a fewer than 7 b 7–8 c more than 8

3 **Did you use to sleep …?**
a more than now b the same amount c less than now

4 **How do you feel about the amount of sleep you get?**
a I think it's OK.
b I probably don't sleep enough, but I'm used to it. It's not a problem.
c I definitely need to sleep more. I usually feel tired.

5 **If you don't sleep enough at night during the week, what do you do?**
a I take short naps during the day.
b I sleep late on the weekend.
c I don't do anything. You get used to not sleeping enough.
d I just get more and more tired.

6 **How do you usually feel during the morning?**
a Wide awake and energetic.
b Awake and able to concentrate, but not at my best.
c Half asleep and unable to concentrate well.

7 **How often do you take a nap on a weekday?**
a Never. I don't need one.
b Always. It's the only way I can get through the day.
c When I need one. Then I always wake up refreshed.
d I'd love to, but I never get the chance.

8 **Do you ever find it difficult to stay awake …?**
(Circle all the ones that apply to you.)
a at work or in class
b on the sofa in the evening
c at the movies
d when you are driving

3 READING & SPEAKING

a Read the introduction of the article. What exactly is the test and what does it show? What does the last sentence mean?

b Work in pairs. A read *So much to do, so little time* and *Going against nature*. B read *Sleepy people* and *SLEEP TIPS*. Then check (✔) the questions that are answered in your paragraphs.

1 How did the invention of the electric light change our sleep habits? ☐
2 Why is it probably better to have an operation during the day than at night? ☐
3 Are naps really useful? ☐
4 How much does the average person sleep? Does it vary according to profession? ☐
5 Why should politicians sleep more? ☐
6 What is our "sleep debt"? ☐
7 What is the world's most popular drug? ☐
8 What's the difference between driving when you are drunk and when you are very tired? ☐
9 Do people sleep more or less than they used to? Why? ☐
10 What should your bedroom *not* be if you want to sleep well? ☐
11 How did lack of sleep cause the Chernobyl nuclear disaster? ☐
12 How much sleep does the average person need? ☐

c Read your two paragraphs again so you can answer the questions in **b**.

d In pairs, explain your answers, giving as much information as you can.

e Now read the parts of the article that you didn't read, to see if your partner left anything out.

f In pairs or small groups, discuss these questions.

1 Do you agree with Paul Martin that we live in a sleep-deprived society?
2 Do you think it's wrong that doctors who are on "night call" sleep so little?
3 Do you think it should be illegal to drive when you are too tired?
4 What do you think are the best three SLEEP TIPS?

Sleepy people – the dangers of sleep deprivation

Take this test tonight when you go to bed. Put a plate on the floor next to your bed. Lie down with one hand hanging over the bed and holding a spoon above the plate. When you fall asleep, the spoon will fall on the plate and should wake you up. If you don't wake up until the next day, it probably means you are "sleep deprived."

We live in a world of tired, sleep-deprived people. This is the theory of behavioral biologist Paul Martin. In his book *Counting Sheep*, he describes a society that is just too busy to sleep and does not give sleeping the importance it deserves. We all know the value of having a healthy diet and exercising, but we don't worry enough about sleeping the hours we need. Paul Martin says: "We might live longer and happier lives if we took our beds as seriously as our running shoes."

So much to do, so little time

Modern society has invented reasons not to sleep. We are now a 24 / 7 society where stores and services must be available at all hours. We spend more time at work than we used to and longer getting to work. Cell phones and e-mail allow us to stay in touch around the clock, and late-night TV and the Internet tempt us away from our beds. When we need more time for work or pleasure, the easy solution is to sleep less. The average adult sleeps only 6.2 hours a night during the week, whereas research shows that most people need eight or even eight and a half hours' sleep to feel their best. Nowadays many people have gotten used to sleeping less than they need and live in an almost permanent state of "sleep debt," owing their bodies perhaps 25–30 hours of sleep.

Hours slept a night	
Lawyers	7.8
Architects	7.5
Social workers	6.9
Teachers	6
Politicians	5.2
Hospital doctors (on call)	4.5

Sleep survey

Going against nature

Until the invention of electric light in 1879, our daily cycle of sleep used to depend on the hours of daylight. People would get up with the sun and go to bed at sundown. But nowadays our hours of sleep are mainly determined by our working hours (or our social life), and most people are woken up artificially by an alarm clock. During the day caffeine, the world's most popular drug, helps keep us awake. Seventy-five percent of the world's population habitually consumes caffeine, which, up to a point, masks the symptoms of sleep deprivation.

Sleepy people

What does a chronic lack of sleep do to us? As well as making us irritable and unhappy, it also reduces our motivation and ability to work. This effect has serious implications for society in general. Doctors, for example, are often chronically sleep deprived, especially when they are on "night call" and may get less than three hours' sleep. Lack of sleep can seriously impair their mood, judgment, and ability to make decisions. Politicians are often "jet-lagged" after crossing time zones. World summit meetings called to deal with a crisis often result in decisions being made after marathon sessions when everyone is severely sleep deprived. Human error caused by tiredness contributed to the worst nuclear accident in history in Chernobyl in 1986, when tired engineers, in the early hours of the morning, made a series of mistakes with catastrophic results. On our streets and highways, lack of sleep kills thousands of people every year. Tests show that a tired driver can be just as dangerous as a drunk driver. However, driving when drunk is against the law while driving when exhausted isn't. As Paul Martin says, it is ironic that we admire people who function on very little sleep instead of criticizing them for being irresponsible. Our world would be a much safer, happier place if everyone, whatever their job, slept eight hours a night.

SLEEP TIPS

1 Give sleep a high priority in your life.
2 Listen to your body. If you feel tired, you probably need more sleep.
3 Pay off your "sleep debt" by going to bed half an hour earlier for a few weeks.
4 Have a regular routine – try to go to bed at roughly the same time every day.
5 Take a nap during the day (ideally after lunch). Research has shown that short naps are very effective in restoring our energy levels and mood.
6 Make sure your bedroom isn't too hot.
7 Don't use your bedroom as an office or for watching TV.

4 VOCABULARY sleep

alarm blankets comforter dreams fall keep you awake insomnia jet-lagged log nap nightmares oversleep pillow set sheets siesta sleeping pills sleepy snore yawn

a **Vocabulary race.** In pairs, write the correct word in the column on the right.

1	Most people start feeling ______ around 11:00 at night.	*sleepy*
2	They often open their mouth and ______.	______
3	They go to bed and ______ their ______ clock.	______, ______
4	They get into bed and put their head on the ______.	______
5	They cover themselves up with a ______, or with ______ and ______.	______, ______, ______
6	Soon they ______ asleep.	______
7	Some people make a loud noise when they breathe. They ______.	______
8	During the night people have ______ or ______.	______, ______
9	If you don't hear your alarm clock in the morning, you might ______.	______
10	If you drink coffee in the evening, it might ______ ______ ______.	______ ______ ______
11	Some people can't sleep because they suffer from ______.	______
12	These people often have to take ______ ______.	______ ______
13	Some people take a ______ or ______ after lunch.	______, ______
14	A person who sleeps well "sleeps like a ______."	______
15	Someone who is tired after flying to another time zone is ______-______.	______-______

b 5.9 Listen to the sentences and check.

c Cover the column of words and test yourself.

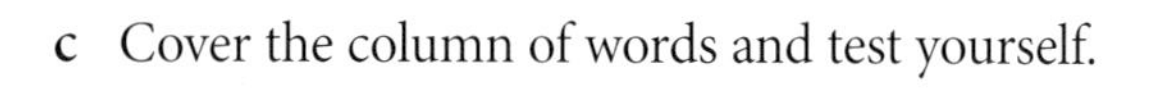

5 SPEAKING

Answer the questions in pairs.
Ask for more information.

Do you sometimes have problems getting to sleep? What do you do?

Have you ever stayed up all night?

Have you ever overslept and missed something important?

Is there any food or drink that keeps you awake or that keeps you from sleeping well?

Are you a light sleeper or do you sleep like a log?

Do you take or have you ever taken sleeping pills? Did they work?

Have you ever been jet-lagged? Where were you going? How long did it take you to recover?

Have you ever fallen asleep at an embarrassing moment, for example, during a class?

Have you ever sleepwalked or do you know anyone who sleepwalks?

Do you usually have nightmares or recurring dreams?

Do you sleep with a comforter or blankets? How many pillows do you like to have?

Do you snore? Have you ever had to share a room with someone who snores? Was this a problem?

Do you remember a time or place where you slept very badly? Why?

6 LISTENING

a Look at the photo and the headline. Why do you think the girl was asleep on the crane? How did she get there?

b 5.10 Listen to the first part of a radio news program and check your answers. What happened next?

c Read a newspaper article about the same incident. The article got eight details wrong. Listen to the news program again and correct the mistakes.

15-year-old girl found asleep on crane

Yesterday a 15-year-old girl was discovered lying on top of a 30-foot-high crane. A passerby saw her in the early evening when he was walking past a construction site in the city and immediately called the fire department. Police and firefighters arrived at 1:30 in the morning. At first, they thought the girl was suicidal, but when a firefighter climbed up the crane, he realized she was drunk. The firefighter crawled along the arm of the crane and carefully put a safety harness on the girl. Then the girl used her cell phone to call her parents, who came quickly to the construction site. The rescue took two hours, and the girl was brought safely down from the crane on a ladder.

After talking to her parents, the police discovered that the girl had been sleepwalking. She had left her house during the night and had been able to get into the construction site because the security guard was asleep. Her parents said that it wasn't the first time that she had sleepwalked and that she had left the house on several other occasions.

d You are going to listen to the second half of the program. Before you listen, work with a partner and discuss whether you think the information in sentences 1–10 is T (true) or F (false).

1 A sleepwalker can drive a car while asleep. ☐
2 It is easy to know if someone is sleepwalking or not. ☐
3 Sleepwalking is not very common. ☐
4 Sleepwalking is most common among young boys. ☐
5 Stress can cause people to sleepwalk. ☐
6 You should never wake up a sleepwalker. ☐
7 Sleepwalkers cannot hurt themselves. ☐
8 People usually sleepwalk for a short time. ☐
9 Sleepwalkers usually don't remember anything afterward. ☐
10 Sleepwalking is no excuse if you commit a crime. ☐

e 5.11 Listen once to check your answers. Then listen again and correct the false statements.

7 5.12 SONG ♫ *I don't want to miss a thing*

5C Breaking news

G reporting verbs; *as*
V the media
P word stress

1 GRAMMAR reporting verbs

a Read the headline of this news story. What do you think it's about? Then read the story. What do you think of Mr. Ivanov?

Man leaves wife at gas station

A Macedonian man drove six hours at the start of his vacation before he noticed that he had forgotten something – his wife. Ljubomir Ivanov left her at a gas station in Italy when he stopped to fill up with gas and didn't realize his mistake until he got a call from the police on his cell phone.

"Are you Ljubomir Ivanov?" they asked.

"Yes, I am," he said. "What's the matter?"

"Where are you?"

"I'm in Germany."

"Well, your wife is waiting for you at a gas station near Pesaro in central Italy."

"I was very tired and not thinking," Ivanov told reporters later. "She usually sits in the back seat, so I didn't notice that she wasn't there."

Mr. Ivanov immediately drove back to Pesaro to pick up his wife so that they could continue their vacation. "I'll have to apologize a lot when I see her," he said.

b **Check what you know.** Read the conversation between the police officer and Ivanov again. Then complete the sentences in reported speech.

1 The police asked the man *if* ______ ______ ______ Ljubomir Ivanov, and he said that ______ ______.
2 Then they asked him ______ ______ ______, and he told ______ that ______ ______ in Germany.
3 He later told the police that he ______ ______ that his wife wasn't there because she usually sat in the back seat.
4 He said that he ______ ______ to apologize a lot when he saw her.

Any problems? ➲ **Workbook p.50**

c **New grammar.** Read four more news stories. Three of them are based on true stories, but one has been invented. Which do think is the invented one?

No, you can't have your ball back!

A British soccer team has threatened to sue a neighbor because he refused to give back their balls. The team has kicked 18 balls over Paul Vose's backyard fence, and the balls are now all locked inside his shed. Gary Ford, the coach of the team, says: "His garden is eight meters from the back of the goal. Some balls are bound to go over the wall." But Vose says, "They should learn to shoot better."

sue take somebody to court, usually to get money from them
shed a small building where people keep tools, etc.
bound to certain to, very likely to
shoot kick a ball toward the goal

Locked out of her life

When Andy Barker, from New Jersey, forgot his wife's birthday for the third year in a row, she decided she had had enough and locked him out of the house. Sue Barker had reminded her husband several times to make reservations for a romantic dinner, and she was hoping for a nice present, too. Andy promised not to forget, but when the day came, it went right out of his head. He was working late and when he got home, the door was locked and a suitcase with his things in it was on the doorstep. Since then Andy has been living in a tent in the backyard. He says, "I'm hoping that if I stay here for a few days, she will forgive me."

Boy glues himself to bed

A Mexican boy glued his hand to his bed so he wouldn't have to return to school after his winter break. "The holidays were such fun," the ten-year-old boy said. His mother found him watching TV in bed with his hand glued to the headboard. After spending two hours trying to unglue him with nail polish remover, she finally gave up. She then called the police and persuaded them to come right over. While paramedics used a spray to try to dissolve the glue, the boy happily watched TV. Eventually, they managed to free him and he got to school only a few hours late. Some people say he was warned by his teacher not to try a trick like that again!

Worker mistaken for jumper

A German construction worker is expecting a big bill after emergency services mistook him for a potential suicide jumper. When the police saw the man on the roof of a five-story building, they closed off a busy street and called the fire department. They then asked negotiators to talk to the man. The negotiators tried to convince him not to jump by shouting to him. But the worker was so busy talking on the phone to his girlfriend that he didn't realize what was happening below, until she asked what the sirens were for. A police spokesperson said that the worker would be given a bill for wasting police time.

sirens the noise made by a police car, fire engine, etc.

d Read the stories again and match sentences A–I with the people who said them. Then underline the words in the text where these ideas are reported.

1 The soccer team *F*
2 The angry neighbor ☐
3 Sue Barker ☐
4 Andy Barker ☐
5 The mother ☐
6 The teacher ☐
7 The police ☐
8 The negotiators ☐

A "Don't jump! It's not worth it."
B "I'm not going to give them back."
C "Please talk to this man."
D "Please come right away. It's urgent!"
E "Don't forget to call the restaurant."
F "We're going to take you to court!"
G "You'd better not do anything like that again."
H "I'll remember this time. I really will."

e **p.140 Grammar Bank 5C.** Read the rules and do the exercises.

2 PRONUNCIATION word stress

a Look at all the two-syllable reporting verbs in the list. All except three are stressed on the second syllable. Circle the three exceptions.

accuse admit advise agree convince deny insist invite
offer persuade promise refuse regret remind suggest threaten

b 5.13 Listen and check.

If a two-syllable verb ends in consonant–vowel–consonant, and is stressed on the **second** syllable, the final consonant is doubled before an *-ed* ending, e.g., *regret* > *regretted*, *admit* > *admitted*.

c Complete the sentences below with the correct reporting verb in the simple past. Practice saying the reported sentences.

1 "You sit down. I'll do it." He *offered* to do it.
2 "No, I won't do it." He ________ to do it.
3 "OK, I'll do it." He ________ to do it.
4 "I'll do it, believe me." He ________ to do it.
5 "Don't forget to do it!" He ________ me to do it.
6 "I think you should do it." He ________ me to do it.
7 "Would you like to do it?" He ________ me to do it.
8 "I didn't do it!" He ________ doing it.
9 "Yes, it was me. I did it." He ________ doing it.
10 "I wish I hadn't done it." He ________ doing it.
11 "Let's do it." He ________ doing it.
12 "You did it!" He ________ him of doing it.

d 5.14 Now listen to the sentences in a different order. Respond with the reported sentence.

3 VOCABULARY the media

news *noun* [u].
1 new information about anything, information previously unknown
2 reports of recent happenings, especially those broadcast, printed in the newspaper, etc.
3 **the news** a regular television or radio broadcast of the latest news

a Look at the dictionary extract for the word *news* above. Then correct the mistakes in sentences 1–3.
1 The news on TV are always depressing.
2 I have a really exciting news for you!
3 It's 9:00. Let's watch news.

b **p.154 Vocabulary Bank** *The media.*

c Talk in small groups about the following.

The media and you

What kind of news stories do you find most / least interesting? Write 1–6 (1 = most interesting).
- celebrity gossip ☐
- politics ☐
- sports ☐
- science /technology ☐
- business ☐
- health ☐

What stories are in the news right now?

How do you usually find out ...?
- what the weather's going to be like
- the sports results
- what's playing at the movies
- the news headlines

Do you ever ...? Where?
- read your horoscope
- do crosswords, sudoku, or other games
- look at cartoons
- read advertisements, e.g., jobs, apartments

Do you have a favorite ...?
- news anchor
- movie critic
- journalist
- sportswriter or sports commentator

Which newspapers / TV channels / radio stations in your country do you think are ...?
- biased
- reliable
- sensational

4 READING & LISTENING

a With a partner discuss what you think would be the good side and bad side of being a theater critic and a sportswriter.

b Now read the articles by two journalists who write for a newspaper and see if your ideas are included.

Irving Wardle, theater critic

The positive side of the job is [1]_______ getting to see a lot of plays and shows, which I love. But the really great thing about being a theater critic is that, as theater is an ongoing thing, something that's going to be repeated night after night for some time, there's also the feeling that you may have a [2]_______ impact on the work. If the producer or the actors read what you've written and agree with you, they might actually change something and improve the performance. That's not something that movie or book critics can do. Some critics also like making friends with the stars and all that – but personally I don't.

For me the worst part of the job is all the traveling. Getting there on time, parking, getting back to the office to write for a nightly deadline. That all gets really stressful. Another awful thing is that editors [3]_______ little pieces from your review without you knowing. You learn as a critic that if you have anything [4]_______, say it right from the start because otherwise it might not get printed. I once wrote a review of a play called *Another Country*. I didn't like it much, but there was a new young actor who I thought was great and who later became a star. That was in the last paragraph and it got cut, so it looked as if I'd never [5]_______ this great new talent.

c Read the two articles again. Choose the best option, a, b, or c, to complete the sentences.

	a	b	c
1	a apparently	b gradually	c obviously
2	a positive	b harmful	c negative
3	a change	b add	c cut
4	a to complain about	b that isn't important	c worth saying
5	a noticed	b spoken to	c criticized
6	a permission	b opportunity	c wish
7	a more exciting	b harder	c easier
8	a vacations	b routine	c unpredictability
9	a drop	b throw	c lose
10	a monotonous	b exciting	c frightening

Pat Gibson, sports journalist

The plus sides – I must have seen some of the most spectacular moments in soccer and other sports over the years. I've also had the [6]_______ to travel to places I wouldn't have seen otherwise, like Australia, South Africa, and the Caribbean. There are much [7]_______ ways to make a living, and it's great to get away from home as much as you can during the winter.

One of the main downsides is the [8]_______. You don't work regular hours – you can spend a couple of days not working, but you never relax because you're waiting for the phone to ring. And then, when a story breaks – it might be on your day off, it might be in the middle of the night – you just have to [9]_______ everything and go. And you never know what time you're going to be home. Another thing is the constant traveling. It's been fantastic visiting the Taj Mahal in India or spending Christmas Day on the beach in Australia, but it does get lonely and it can also be very [10]_______. I've spent a large proportion of the last 40 years driving up and down highways, which I can assure you isn't much fun.

d You're going to listen to Alice, a freelance restaurant critic, and Tim, a war reporter, talking about the good and bad sides of their jobs. Before you listen, predict some of the things they might say.

e 5.15 5.16 Listen and check. Then listen again and mark the sentences T (true) or F (false). Correct the false sentences.

The restaurant critic

1 She sometimes reviews restaurants in other countries.
2 She never orders the most expensive things on the menu.
3 She often misses having company when she's eating out.
4 She used to be slimmer than she is now.
5 She usually goes back to restaurants she has criticized.
6 She never feels like eating out on weekends.

The war reporter

1 Most war reporters would prefer regular hours.
2 They choose the job partly because it's dangerous.
3 The job can be rather lonely.
4 He has problems getting used to normal life when he comes home.
5 Being a war reporter is more dangerous than it used to be.
6 One of his best friends was kidnapped last year.

f From what you've read and heard, which person's job would you most like to have? Which one would you least like to have?

5 SPEAKING

a You are going to debate the following topic in small groups.

> Celebrities have to accept that the media publish stories about their private lives. That is the price they pay for being rich and famous.

- Divide into groups of four, two **A**s and two **B**s.
- The **A**s are going to defend the right of newspapers to publish stories about famous people's private lives.
- The **B**s are going to defend the celebrities' right to keep their private lives private.
- Prepare at least four arguments, and give examples.

b Hold the debate. The **A**s begin, each making two of their points. The **B**s take notes. Then the **B**s speak and the **A**s take notes.

c Now, each side tries to argue against the points made by the other side.

MINI GRAMMAR *as*

It's great to get away from home as much as you can during the winter.

I work as part of a team.

We can use *as* in many different ways:

1 to compare people or things: *She's as tall as I am.*
2 to describe somebody's job or something's function: *She works as a nurse. We had to use a handkerchief as a bandage.*
3 to say that something happened while something else was happening: *As they were leaving, the mail carrier arrived.* (*as* = when)
4 to give a reason: *We didn't go out as it was raining.* (*as* = because)

Decide how *as* is used in each sentence and write 1–4 in the box.

A The review in *The Times* wasn't as good as the one in the *Post*. ☐
B You can use that glass as a vase for the flowers. ☐
C I got to the airport really quickly as there was hardly any traffic. ☐
D As he was driving home, it started to rain. ☐
E My son's hair got darker as he got older. ☐
F He got a job with a TV network as a program researcher. ☐

p.157 Phrasal verbs in context *File 5.*

5 Music festivals

THE INTERVIEW

a You are going to listen to an interview with Sir Nicholas Kenyon, who was the director of a British music festival called the Proms for 12 years. Before you listen, read the glossary and look at how the words are pronounced to help you understand what he says.

Glossary

impresario /ˌɪmprəˈsɑrioʊ/ a person who arranges plays or concerts

the Queen's Hall /kwinz hɔl/ a concert hall in London where the Proms were first held. The Proms were later moved to the Royal Albert Hall.

season tickets /ˈsizn ˈtɪkəts/ tickets that are for many concerts and are cheaper than buying individual tickets

queue /kyu/ (British English) to stand in line

Fauré (1845–1924) a famous French composer

requiem /ˈrɛkwiəm/ a piece of music composed for a person who has recently died

Sir Georg Solti (1912–1997) a famous Hungarian conductor

Verdi (1813–1901) a famous Italian composer

fanfare /ˈfænfɛr/ a short loud piece of music played to celebrate sb / sth important arriving

mobile phone /ˈmoʊbl foʊn/ (British English) a cell phone

The Rite of Spring a famous piece by the Russian composer Stravinsky

bassoon /bəˈsun/ a wind instrument

Simon Rattle a famous British conductor

the stalls /stɔlz/ (British English) the seats in a theater on the ground floor

Radio 4 one of the BBC radio channels in the UK

b 5.17 Listen to part 1. Answer the questions with a partner.

1 What did an impresario want to do in 1895?
2 What was his brilliant idea?
3 Why are the concerts called the Proms?
4 How long do the Proms last?
5 What do people have to do to get the best places on the floor of the hall?
6 What is special about the Proms's audience?

c 5.18 Listen to part 2. Answer the questions with a partner.

What does he say about …?

1 Princess Diana's funeral
2 Sir Georg Solti and the Verdi requiem
3 Colin Davies
4 *Short Ride in a Fast Machine*
5 Simon Rattle and *The Rite of Spring*
6 a radio interview

d 5.19 Listen and complete the phrases. What do you think they mean?

COMMON PHRASES

1 The Promenade Concerts started _____ _____ in 1895.
2 … it basically means that people are able to _____ _____ and stand during the music. pv
3 Very few people attend actually all of them, _____ _____.
4 As it _____ _____, he died just a week later. pv
5 … and so another conductor, Colin Davies, _____ _____ that Verdi requiem … pv
6 Unfortunately, _____ _____, it could have been called absolutely anything …

e Listen to the interview again with the audioscript on page 128. Would you like to go to the Proms? Do you have any similar concerts in your country?

ON THE STREET

a 5.20 Listen to four people talking about music festivals. Write the speaker's number next to the festival(s) they have been to.

1 Savanna

2 Tim

3 Christina

4 Curt

Austin City Limits ☐
EarthFest ☐
Kerrville Folk Festival ☐
Lollapalooza ☐
Sounds of the Underground ☐

b Listen again. Who …?

1 felt old compared to the other people there
2 attended a festival by the water
3 went to some festivals a long time ago
4 mentions the weather

c 5.21 Listen and complete the phrases. What do you think they mean?

COMMON PHRASES

1 The Kerrville Folk Festival is a little bit more _____-_____.
2 It was a lot of _____.
3 And then just _____ out there for the rest of the day. pv
4 … and used to go to a _____ of shows …

d Listen to the interviews again with the audioscript on page 128. Then answer the same questions with a partner.

Study Link MultiROM

A formal letter

270 Dolphin Circle
Orlando, FL 32807
January 9, 2009

Cafe Royale Guest Relations Department
5000 Lake Drive
Orlando, FL 32808

Dear Guest Relations Representative:

[1] *I am writing* to complain about a meal my family and I had at the Cafe Royale restaurant on Lake Drive last Saturday night.

We have eaten at this restaurant [2]__________, and the background music has always been very soft and [3]__________. However, [4]__________ the music was terribly loud, almost deafening. When the waiter took our order, I asked him politely if he could turn the music down, which he did.

However, while we were eating our main course, the music was turned up again and we could hardly hear ourselves speak. This time I asked to see the manager. She spoke to us in [5]__________ and unfriendly manner. She told us that we were the only customers who had ever complained about the music and [6]__________ turn it down. We were so angry we decided to leave without having dessert or coffee.

I have eaten at other locations of Cafe Royale all over the country, but I [7]__________ unless I receive an explanation and apology for the [8]__________ we received.

[9]__________,

Joseph Clements
Joseph Clements

a Read the letter and answer the questions.

1 Who is the letter to?
2 Why is Joseph writing?
3 What does he hope to achieve?

b Complete the letter with the more formal of the two phrases.

1 I'm writing / I am writing
2 lots of times / on many occasions
3 pleasant / nice
4 on this particular evening / when we were there this time
5 a really rude / an extremely rude
6 said she wouldn't / refused to
7 will not do so again / won't go there again
8 unacceptable treatment / awful treatment
9 Best wishes / Sincerely

c Last week you had a bad experience at an expensive hotel. When you get home, you decide to write a letter or e-mail to complain. Look at the **Useful language** expressions and make sure you know how to use them.

Useful language

Typical openings
Dear Customer Service Manager:
Dear Ms. Wong:
I am writing to complain about …
I am writing to express my dissatisfaction with …

Typical endings
I look forward to hearing from you.
Sincerely,

PLAN the content.

1 Decide where you were staying and imagine what problems there might have been. What kind of problem would make you complain?
2 Decide what you would like the hotel to do.

WRITE 120–180 words, organized in three or four paragraphs (reason for writing, details of the problems, conclusion / request for action). Use a formal style (avoid contractions or informal expressions). Use the phrases in **b** and in **Useful language**.

CHECK your letter for mistakes (grammar, punctuation, and spelling).

5 What do you remember?

GRAMMAR

a Complete the second sentence so that it means the same as the first.

1 After being in Australia for a year, I still find driving on the left difficult.
After being in Australia for a year, I still can't get ______ ______ ______ on the left.

2 My hair was very long when I was a teenager.
When I was a teenager, I used ______ ______ long hair.

3 "I think you should talk to a lawyer," he said to us.
He advised ______ ______ ______ to a lawyer.

4 "I didn't kill my husband," the suspect said.
The suspect denied ______ ______ ______.

5 "I'm sorry I'm late," Joana said.
Joana ______ ______ ______ late.

6 My brother is a waiter in a French restaurant.
My brother works ______ ______ ______ in a French restaurant.

b Put the **bold** verb in the gerund or infinitive.

1 I don't remember ______ you before. **meet**
2 The car needs ______. Should I take it to the car wash? **wash**
3 He managed ______ to the airport on time. **get**
4 Please try not ______ late again. **be**

VOCABULARY

a Make nouns for people from the following words. Underline the stressed syllable.

1 conduct ______________
2 violin ______________
3 drums ______________
4 edit ______________
5 compose ______________
6 journal ______________
7 solo ______________
8 report ______________
9 photograph ______________
10 rap ______________

b Complete the missing words.

1 Did you hear the **w**______ **f**______? It's going to rain.
2 Let's not see that movie. It had an awful **r**______ in the paper.
3 This newspaper always supports the government. It's very **b**______.
4 His latest song is really **c**______. Everybody's singing it.
5 I can remember the lyrics, but I can't remember the **t**______.
6 The report was **c**______. He wasn't allowed to say what he wanted to say.
7 Could I have an extra **p**______ for my bed, please?
8 My husband says I **s**______ really loudly when I'm asleep.
9 I didn't get much sleep last night, so I'm going to take a **n**______ this afternoon.
10 He has terrible **i**______. It takes him ages to get to sleep.

PRONUNCIATION

a Underline the word with a different sound.

1	w	whisper	whistle	whole	awake
2	k	choir	conductor	click	convince
3	ɔr	crossword	reporter	snore	keyboard
4	ə	accurate	advise	admit	agree
5	/yu/	refuse	review	accuse	cartoon

b Underline the stressed syllable.

guitarist	orchestra	biased	sensational	critic

What can you do?

CAN YOU UNDERSTAND THIS TEXT?

Read the article and choose a, b, or c to fill in the blanks.

	a	b	c
1	a night	b dawn	c noon
2	a nothing	b medicine	c an injection
3	a asleep	b sick	c well
4	a Because of	b According to	c Thanks to
5	a cooking	b buying	c taking care of
6	a so that	b however	c because
7	a appetite	b sleep	c sleeping pills
8	a so	b even	c although

CAN YOU UNDERSTAND THESE PEOPLE?

a 5.22 You will hear five extracts from a news broadcast. Match each extract with what it is about (A–G). There are two topics you don't need.

- A business ☐
- B crime ☐
- C show business ☐
- D health ☐
- E sports ☐
- F travel ☐
- G weather ☐

b 5.23 Listen to a music expert talking and answer a, b, or c.

1 Music can sound like noise to you if ______.
  a it is the first time you hear it
  b it is sung in a foreign language
  c you don't understand the rules

2 Modern classical music ______.
  a does not have rules
  b can sound like noise
  c is only experimental

3 A lot of young people ______.
  a have negative feelings about some kinds of music
  b only like noisy music
  c never go to classical concerts

4 They changed the music in the shopping mall because ______.
  a the young people complained
  b they knew teenagers wouldn't like it
  c they wanted to attract more customers

5 A lot of older people ______.
  a never listen to pop music
  b associate pop music with crime
  c don't like music with a strong beat

CAN YOU SAY THIS IN ENGLISH?

Can you ...?

- ☐ describe the kind of music you listen to and how it makes you feel
- ☐ describe your sleep habits and any problems with sleeping you have
- ☐ talk about things you used to do and things you have gotten used to doing
- ☐ talk about where you get your news from and compare the different kinds of media in your country

Still awake... after 33 years.

The man who has become the village "alarm clock"

AS BIRDS AWAKEN the early risers at [1]______ on the farm, one person is already up; in fact, he hasn't even been to bed. Sixty-four-year-old Thai Ngoc, from central Quang Nam province in Vietnam, claims that he has not slept for 33 years!

"My insomnia started many years ago after I got a fever. I have tried sleeping pills and Vietnamese traditional medicine, but [2]______ helps, not even to get me to sleep for a few minutes," said Ngoc. But amazingly, despite 11,700 consecutives sleepless nights since then, he has never once been [3]______. "Fortunately, the insomnia doesn't seem to have had a negative impact on my health. I still feel healthy and can farm like other men. I even carry two 50-kilogram bags of fertilizer for four kilometers every day." [4]______ his wife, when Ngoc went for a medical checkup recently, his doctor said he was in perfect health except for a minor decline in liver function.

Ngoc lives with his six children on his farm at the foot of a mountain. He spends the day farming and [5]______ his pigs and chickens, and at night he often does extra farm work or guards his farm to prevent theft. His neighbor Vu said that Ngoc volunteered to help beat a drum during the night and guard the house for the relatives of the dead during funeral ceremonies [6]______ they could take a nap. Vu also said that when the villagers were planting sugar cane, several people asked Ngoc to be their "alarm clock" and wake them up early in the morning to go to work as he was up anyway.

Phan Ngoc Ha, director of the Hoa Khanh Mental Hospital in Danang, said that a chronic lack of [7]______ often causes anorexia, lethargy, and irritability. But, in special cases, some extreme insomniacs can still live and work normally, [8]______ this is a very small minority. Thai Ngoc is obviously one of them.

6 A

G articles
V collocation: word pairs
P sentence stress

Speaking to the world

One small word, one big difference in meaning

1 READING

a What do you know about the first moon landing? Answer the questions with a partner.

1 Who was the first man to set foot on the moon?
a Yuri Gagarin b Buzz Aldrin c Neil Armstrong

2 When did he land on the moon?
a In 1959 b In 1969 c In 1979

3 What was the first thing he said when he landed?
a "Wow! It's so big!"
b "I'm floating in a most peculiar way."
c "That's one small step for man, one giant leap for mankind."

b Read the article and check. What controversy has there been since then about what Neil Armstrong actually said? Why is the missing "a" so important?

c Read the article again. Then, in pairs, say why the following names and numbers are mentioned.

July 20, 1969	*First Man*
6 hours and 40 minutes	James Hansen
500 million	Peter Shann Ford
Buzz Aldrin	

d Cover the article and try to complete the sentences, making words from the words in **bold**. What do they mean?

1 Armstrong made the first human *footprint* on the lunar surface. **foot**
2 His first words were "That's one small step for man, one giant leap for ________." **man**
3 It was the perfect quote for such a ________ occasion. **moment**
4 "One small step for *a* man" would have made it a more ________ sentence. **mean**
5 They were possibly the most ________ words in history. **memory**
6 Armstrong said the "a" so quickly that it was ________ on the recording. **audio**

e 6.1 Listen to the original recording of Armstrong speaking. Can *you* hear the "a"?

As Neil Armstrong became the first man to walk on the moon, a global audience of 500 million people were watching and listening. "That's one small step for man, one giant leap for mankind," they heard him say as he dropped from the ladder of his spacecraft to make the first human footprint on the lunar surface. It was the perfect quote for such a momentous occasion. But from the moment he said it, people have argued about whether the NASA astronaut got his lines wrong.

Armstrong and Buzz Aldrin, who stepped outside a few seconds after him, landed the Apollo 11 spacecraft on the moon on July 20, 1969. In the tense six hours and forty minutes between landing on the moon and stepping out of the capsule, Armstrong wrote what he knew would become some of the most memorable words in history.

Armstrong has always insisted that he wrote "one small step for *a* man, one giant leap for mankind," which would have been a more meaningful and grammatically correct sentence. Without the missing "a," the intended meaning of the sentence is lost. In effect, the line means, "That's one small step for mankind (i.e., humanity), one giant leap for mankind."

But did he really say the sentence incorrectly? Until now Armstrong himself had never been sure if he actually said what he wrote. In his biography *First Man* he told the author James Hansen, "I must admit that it doesn't sound like the word 'a' is there. On the other hand, certainly the 'a' was intended, because that's the only way it makes sense."

But now, after almost four decades, the space explorer has been vindicated. Using high-tech sound analysis techniques, Peter Shann Ford, an Australian computer expert, has discovered that the "a" was spoken by Armstrong, but he said it so quickly that it was inaudible on the recording that was broadcast to the world.

Mr. Ford's findings have been presented to a relieved Mr. Armstrong. James Hansen said, "Neil is a modest guy, but I think it means a lot to him to know that he didn't make a mistake."

Adapted from the newspaper

2 GRAMMAR articles

a Right (✔) or wrong (✘)? Correct the mistakes in the highlighted phrases.

1 Neil Armstrong was born in the US.
2 He was a shy boy, who loved the books and the music.
3 He studied aeronautical engineering in the college.
4 He was the first man who set foot on a moon.
5 His famous words were heard by people all over the world.
6 Before becoming a astronaut, he worked for the US navy.
7 Since 1994, he has refused to give the autographs.
8 In 2005, he was involved in a lawsuit with an ex-barber, who tried to sell some of the Armstrong's hair.

b p.142 Grammar Bank 6A. Read the rules and do the exercises.

c Read three extracts from speeches made by famous people. Use the glossary to help you. Complete the speeches with *a*, *an*, *the*, or (–).

***Winston Churchill** (1874–1965) was the British Prime Minister during World War II. In this extract from a speech given in 1946, the year after the war ended, Churchill first used the phrase "iron curtain" to describe the boundary that ideologically and physically divided the East and the West. This speech marked the beginning of the "Cold War."*

"From Stettin in [1]______ Baltic to [2]______ Trieste in [3]______ Adriatic, [4]______ iron curtain has descended across [5]______ continent. Behind that line lie all [6]______ capitals of [7]______ ancient states of [8]______ Central and Eastern Europe. Warsaw, Berlin, Prague, Vienna, Budapest, Belgrade, Bucharest, and Sofia, all these famous cities and [9]______ populations around them, lie in what I must call [10]______ Soviet sphere."

descend come down	**the continent** Europe (in this text)
ancient very old	**sphere** an area of influence or activity

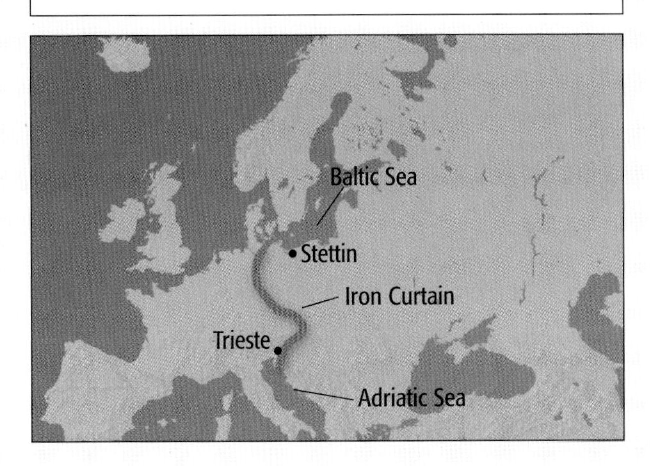

***Martin Luther King, Jr.** (1929–1968) was a leader of the American Civil Rights movement, who was assassinated in Memphis, Tennessee, in April 1968. In this extract from a speech made in 1963, King spoke of his "dream" of a future when all people would be treated equally.*

"I have [1]______ dream that [2]______ my four little children will one day live in [3]______ nation where they will not be judged by [4]______ color of their skin but by [5]______ content of their character."

***Al Gore** (1948–) was Vice President of the United States from 1993 to 2001. Since 2001, Gore has dedicated himself to a campaign against global warming. His 2006 documentary,* An Inconvenient Truth, *which warns against climate change, won him an Oscar and a Nobel Peace Prize. The following is an extract from his Nobel Prize acceptance speech, in which he describes "a planetary emergency."*

"We, [1]______ human species, are confronting [2]______ planetary emergency, [3]______ threat to [4]______ survival of our civilization that is gathering ominous and destructive potential even as we gather here. But there is [5]______ hopeful news as well: we have [6]______ ability to solve this crisis and avoid [7]______ worst – though not all – of its consequences if we act boldly, decisively, and quickly."

species a group of similar animals or plants
planetary concerning the Earth
ominous suggesting that something bad will happen

d 6.2 Now listen to the extracts spoken by the people themselves. Check your answers. Which of the three extracts do you think is the most dramatic?

3 PRONUNCIATION sentence stress

a 6.3 **Dictation.** Listen and write down six sentences.

b Listen again and underline the stressed words. What is the vowel sound in *a*, *an*, and *the* in 1–5? Why is *the* pronounced differently in number 6?

c Practice saying the sentences from **a**. Try to pronounce the reduced forms correctly.

4 6.4 SONG ♫ *Space oddity*

5 LISTENING

a Have you ever had to make a speech or give a talk or presentation in front of a lot of people? When? Where? How did you feel? Was it a success?

b Read part of an article about presentation disasters. Which tip from *Top ten tips* below should the speaker have remembered?

PRESENTATION DISASTERS!

However bad you think your presentation has been, take some comfort from the fact that at least it probably wasn't as bad as these true stories...

A FEW YEARS AGO I had to give a presentation to the Belgian management team of an international IT company. Not wishing to be the "typical American" presenting in English, I had carefully prepared my presentation in French. I intended it as a surprise, so I didn't say anything beforehand. After speaking in French for 45 minutes, I was halfway through my presentation and we had a break for coffee. At this point, the manager of the company came up to me and asked if I would change to speaking in English. "Is my French that bad?" I said. "No," he replied, "it's just that we are all from the Dutch-speaking part of Belgium."

Top ten tips for speaking in public

1. Don't make your presentation too long.
2. Don't have more than four or five main points.
3. Even if something distracting happens, try not to lose your concentration.
4. Be careful about telling jokes – they may not be appropriate.
5. Always be punctual: start on time and try to finish on time.
6. Get to know as much as possible about your audience beforehand.
7. Try not to repeat yourself too much.
8. Be careful not to speak too fast.
9. Practice your presentation beforehand.
10. Make sure the equipment you need is in working order before you start.

c You're going to hear five other people talking about a disastrous presentation. Before you listen, look at pictures A–E. What do you think the problem was?

d 6.5 Listen and number the pictures in the correct order. Did you guess correctly?

e Listen again and write 1–5 in the boxes. Which speaker ...?

A ☐ couldn't understand why nobody found his / her talk interesting
B ☐ felt very relaxed before his / her presentation
C ☐ gave the last part of his / her talk very quickly
D ☐ made the problem he / she had even worse
E ☐ didn't find out he / she had a problem until the end of the talk

f Talk to a partner.

1. Would any of the "top ten tips" have helped some of the speakers? Which ones?
2. Which speaker do you think was the most embarrassed?
3. Have you ever been to a talk or presentation where something went terribly wrong?

6 VOCABULARY collocation: word pairs

Some pairs of words in English that go together always come in a certain order, for example, we always say "Ladies and Gentlemen" and "right or wrong," NOT ~~Gentlemen and Ladies~~, ~~wrong or right~~.

a Read the information in the box. How do you say "Ladies and Gentlemen" and "right or wrong" in your language? Is the order the same?

b Take one word from **A** and match it with another from **B**. Then decide which word comes first. They are all joined with *and*.

A

loud butter thunder knife black breakfast salt quiet

B

fork white peace bed clear pepper bread lightning

c Look at some common word pairs joined with *or*. What is the second word?

right or ______ now or ______ more or ______
sooner or ______ all or ______ once or ______

d 6.6 Listen and check your answers to **b** and **c**. Notice how the phrases are linked and how *and* and *or* are pronounced. Practice saying them.

e Match the word pair idioms with their meanings.

1 I'm sick and tired of hearing you complain. ☐
2 After we cleaned out the garage, only odds and ends were left. ☐
3 I've been having headaches now and then. ☐
4 He's unemployed and down and out. ☐
5 Every relationship needs a little give and take. ☐
6 We've had our ups and downs, but now we get along well. ☐
7 The army was called in to restore law and order. ☐
8 Despite flying through a storm, we arrived safe and sound. ☐

A problems E a situation in which the law is obeyed
B fed up F without problem or injury
C compromise G small things of little importance
D occasionally H without a home or money

f Complete the sentences with a word pair from **b**, **c**, or **e**.

1 He visits us ____________, maybe twice a year.
2 I'm afraid it's your last chance. It's ____________.
3 After lots of adventures, she arrived home____________.
4 Please stop making so much noise. I need some ____________.
5 __________ he'll realize that she's not the woman for him.
6 After the riots, the government sent in soldiers to try to establish ____________.
7 She's ____________ of her husband. She wants to leave him.
8 It was an amazing storm. There was lots of ____________.

7 SPEAKING

a 6.7 When people give a talk, they usually divide what they say into small chunks, with a brief pause between each chunk. Listen to the beginning of a talk and mark (/) the pauses.

Good afternoon, everyone, / and thank you for coming. I'm going to talk to you today about one of my hobbies, collecting comics. Since I was a child, I've been crazy about comics and comic books. I started reading Batman and Superman when I was nine or ten. Later, when I was a teenager, some friends from school introduced me to manga, which are Japanese comics. I've been collecting them for about five years now, and I'm also learning to draw them. ...

b Listen again and underline the stressed words. Practice reading the extract.

c You are going to give a short presentation to other students. You can choose what to talk about, for example:

- **a hobby you have or a sport you play**
- **something you really love doing**
- **an interesting person in your family**
- **a famous person you admire**
- **the good and bad side of your job**

Decide what you are going to talk about and make a plan of what you want to say.

GET IT RIGHT making a presentation

Read through the tips in *Presentation disasters!* again to help you prepare your presentation and give it successfully. When you give your presentation, don't speak too quickly. Remember to pause and take a breath from time to time. This will help the audience follow what you are saying.

d In groups, take turns giving your presentation. While they are listening, the other students should write down at least one question to ask the speaker after the presentation is over. Then have a short question-and-answer session.

6B Bright lights, big city

G uncountable, plural, and collective nouns; *have something done*
V cities and towns
P word stress in multisyllable words

1 READING & SPEAKING

a Look at the photos and read the quote. Do you know who the Amish are? What do you think happens in the television program?

b Read a preview of the TV series and find out. Then discuss the questions with a partner.
1 What is Rumspringa? Do you think it is a good idea?
2 What do you think will be the biggest culture shock for the Amish when they go to Los Angeles?
3 What do you think the majority of the five young Amish will choose to do?

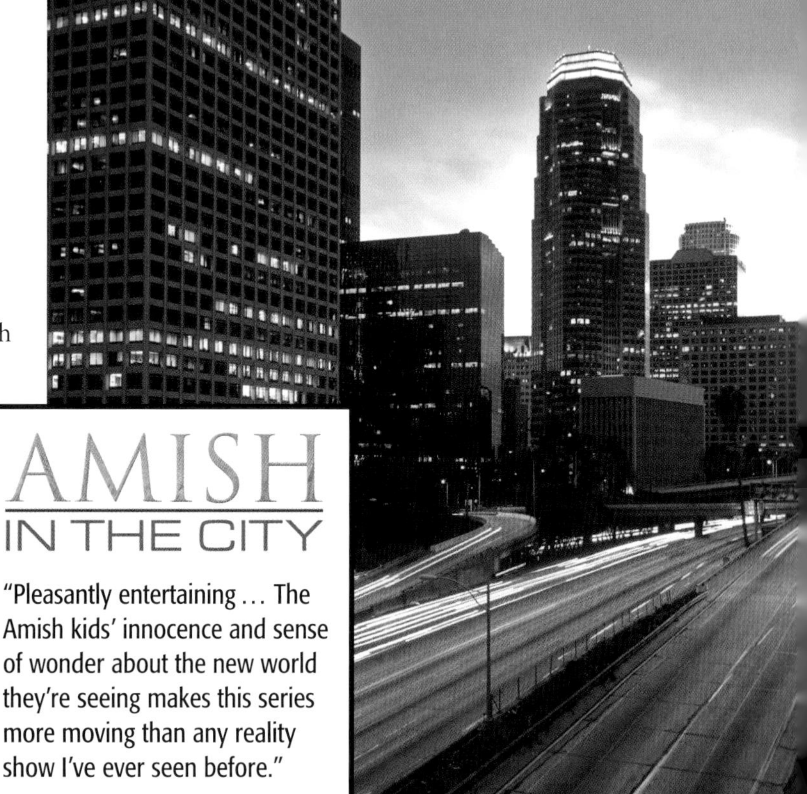

AMISH IN THE CITY

"Pleasantly entertaining ... The Amish kids' innocence and sense of wonder about the new world they're seeing makes this series more moving than any reality show I've ever seen before."

PREVIEW – Tonight's TV

Los Angeles, home to many of the world's most famous movie stars, is known as the entertainment capital of the world, but it is completely unknown to one group of people – the Amish. For 300 years this fascinating group has lived in isolation, working together to grow their own food, make their own clothes, and build their own communities. They reject conveniences like electricity, telephones, and cars, and focus on hard work, religious worship, and family.

However, once Amish people reach their late teens, they are allowed to explore modern society and are given the chance to experience the outside world for the first time. This period is known as "Rumspringa," a time when Amish young people must decide whether to commit to the strict rules of their faith or leave behind the Amish lifestyle and their family forever. Amish teenagers can spend their Rumspringa anywhere, but most of them choose to stay near their homes, venturing only a few miles from their small communities.

But now five of them have chosen to spend their Rumspringa in a way no one has before – living in Los Angeles with six city kids who have no idea that they will be sharing a house with the Amish. For ten weeks they will explore everything the modern world has to offer, with one thing in mind: will they return to the simple life they've always lived, or will they choose to remain "Amish in the City"?

c Now read a review of the program on page 89. Then, without looking back at the text, mark the sentences below T (true) or F (false), and say why the F ones are false.
1 The Amish kids aren't used to seeing such tall buildings.
2 They thought the parking meters were pretty funny.
3 The Amish are very good at painting.
4 Mose thinks that "Reggae" is the name of a singer.
5 The reviewer thinks that the Amish learned a lot from the city kids.
6 Nick felt sorry for the beggar.
7 Most adolescents leave the Amish community after Rumspringa.
8 Mose is not quite sure what he's going to do next.
9 Miriam is planning to travel.
10 The reviewer thinks the program didn't end in a very positive way.

d Answer the questions.
1 Do you think that this kind of television program is a good idea? Why (not)?
2 Do you think Rumspringa really gives Amish teenagers freedom of choice? Why (not)?
3 Do you think that the fact that only one of the Amish went back is a happy ending or a sad ending?

REVIEW – Last night's TV

In the first episode, the five young Amish, three boys (Mose, Jonas, and Randy) and two girls (Miriam and Ruth) are amazed by the height of the skyscrapers, the noise of the traffic in Los Angeles, and the number of cars on the five-lane freeways. They are amused by parking meters – a totally new concept for them – and they love riding in elevators. Even a trip to a grocery store is an adventure. Mose says, "I'm a farmer, but there are so many vegetables here that I've never seen before."

Ruth is entranced by a visit to an art gallery as she has never seen art before. "I didn't know you could make something from boards with paint on them that would look so nice," she explains. "The Amish don't take art in school because they feel it isn't important." Ruth is also as excited as a little child when, for the first time in her life, she sees the ocean.

The Amish are not allowed to use CD players or iPods, and the city kids introduce them to pop music. City girl Megan asks if any of the Amish have heard any reggae at all. "Reggae?" replies Amish boy Mose, "I've never heard of him." As the city kids burst out laughing, he adds, "But he sounds interesting."

But as the program progresses, slowly but surely you feel that the people who are really learning something are the city kids. One evening when they are eating at a sidewalk cafe in a rather run-down neighborhood, a beggar approaches them and asks them for money. City boy Nick ignores him, but Amish girl Miriam offers him a piece of her chicken. "The Amish wouldn't let anyone be homeless," she says. "It just wouldn't happen."

Of course the big question is what happens at the end – what do the young Amish decide to do? Usually, after Rumspringa the vast majority of adolescents choose to stay in the Amish community. However, in the case of *Amish in the City*, the majority decide, at least temporarily, not to go back. Mose decides that big city life is not for him but that he probably won't go back to the Amish either. Jonas and Randy both want to go to college, and Miriam wants to see more of the world. Of the five of them, only Ruth decides to go back to the Amish lifestyle. A sad ending or a happy ending? It depends on your point of view.

2 VOCABULARY cities and towns

a Look at the highlighted words and phrases in the review. Explain in your own words what they mean. Do you have them where you live?

b **p.155 Vocabulary Bank** *Cities and towns.*

c Make nouns from the **bold** words to complete the sentences.

> Typical endings for making a noun from a verb are:
> **-ment**, e.g., *government*, **-ion**, e.g., *congestion*, and **-ation** e.g., *information*.
> Typical endings for making a noun from an adjective are:
> **-ity**, e.g., *reality*, **-ness**, e.g., *darkness*, and **-ence** / **-ance**, e.g., *convenience, entrance*.
> Some nouns from verbs / adjectives are irregular, e.g., *poor>poverty, lose>loss, choose>choice*

1 Los Angeles is well known for its variety of ________. **entertain**
2 ________ is a big problem in many large cities. **homeless**
3 Tourist ________ in Tokyo are often very expensive. **accommodate**
4 There is a large Italian ________ in Buenos Aires. **commune**
5 Vandalism and ________ are often problems in some inner city areas. **violent**
6 The best way to see the ________ of Manhattan is from a ferry around the island. **see**
7 Some museums have free ________ once a week. **admit**
8 The ________ of a typical skyscraper in New York is 500 feet or more. **high**
9 A world-famous violinist is giving a ________ tonight at the Sydney Opera House. **perform**
10 I saw a wonderful ________ at the National Museum of Korea last month. **exhibit**

3 PRONUNCIATION word stress in multisyllable words

a Underline the stressed syllable in these multisyllable words.

accommodations cathedral community cosmopolitan entertainment exhibition
gallery historic homelessness industrial neighborhood overcrowding pedestrian
performance pollution poverty provincial skyscraper synagogue violence

b 6.8 Listen and check. Then practice saying the words.

4 GRAMMAR uncountable, plural, and collective nouns

a Circle the correct form.

1 Amish men can't have *long hair / a long hair.*
2 During Rumspringa the Amish tolerate bad *behavior / behaviors.*
3 There is often *terrible traffic / a terrible traffic* in Los Angeles.
4 A good guidebook will give you *advice / advices* about what to see.
5 We usually have *some bad weather / a bad weather* in April.
6 Walking around cities in the summer can be *hard work / a hard work.*
7 It's best not to take *too much luggage / too many luggages.*
8 I just heard *an interesting news / some interesting news.*

b **p.142 Grammar Bank 6B.** Read the rules and do the exercises.

c Play ***Just a minute***. In small groups, try to talk for a minute about:

modern furniture
good advice you've been given
what's in the news
the traffic in your city / town
the weather you like most
the most beautiful scenery you've seen
politics
chocolate
your family
clothes you love wearing

5 LISTENING

a 6.9 You are going to listen to an interview with a travel writer talking about Chicago. Listen and match the questions with the photos.

1 What advice would you give to someone visiting Chicago for the first time?
2 What's the one thing that someone visiting Chicago should do or see?
3 What's the best place to have your photo taken?
4 What's your favorite landmark?
5 What's the best place to watch the sunset?
6 What would be a good place to go on a scorching hot day?
7 What's your favorite sports venue?
8 What's a good thing to do that is absolutely free?
9 What do you think is the most romantic thing to do in Chicago?

b Listen again and answer the questions.

1 Why does the travel writer suggest taking a boat?
2 What is her suggestion for an indoor activity that visitors to Chicago should do?
3 What is special about the surface of the Cloud Gate sculpture?
4 What does she like about the John Hancock Building?
5 Where should you go to watch the sunset besides the Ferris Wheel?
6 Why does Lake Michigan make Chicago special?
7 Why are most of the Chicago Cubs games sold out?
8 What is the Lincoln Park Zoo famous for?
9 Why was a particular carriage ride memorable for the writer?

c 6.10 Now listen again to five extracts from the interview. Try to fill in the missing words.

1 You can get a great view of the famous buildings and bridges while you're enjoying a ______ down the river.
2 Its surface is like a mirror that reflects the city skyline, and it's ______ on a clear day, a perfect background for a photo.
3 But I am ______ to say I have never been on it.
4 Chicago is ______ in that it's the only big city in the US with a beach right in the heart of the city.
5 In fact, my husband ______ to me on one of those carriage rides!

d Which of the places she mentions would you most like to see? How would you answer the questions in **a** about a city or town that you know well?

6 SPEAKING & WRITING

a Read the questions in *Help me, I'm a tourist!* and decide how you would answer them about your city / town if you were asked by a tourist.

b Work in pairs. **A** is a tourist and **B** is a local person. **A** asks **B** the questions from sections 1–3. **B** tries to answer **A**'s questions as fully as possible. **A** should ask for as much information as possible. Change roles for sections 4–6.

Help me, I'm a tourist!

1 Safety

Is crime a problem in the city? What should I be careful of?

Are there any areas of the city I should avoid ...?

a during the day

b at night

2 Getting around

What's the best way to get around town?

Is it OK to take taxis? Are there many taxi stands?

Can I rent a bicycle? Is it a good city / town for cycling?

Are there any landmarks that will help me know where I am?

3 Sightseeing

If I'm short of time, what *three* sights should I see?

What two galleries or museums should I visit? Do they charge for admission?

Where should I go to get the real atmosphere of the city / town ...?

a by day

b at night

4 Local customs

Are there any dress rules if I go into a place of worship?

Are there any topics of conversation I should avoid if I talk to local people?

How much should I tip ...?

a waiters

b taxi drivers

5 Shopping

What would be a good souvenir to take back with me?

What's the best market to visit?

Is there anyplace where I should bargain?

6 Food and drink

Is the local tap water drinkable?

Is there any food or drink I *must* try?

Is there any food or drink I should avoid or be careful with?

c Now go through the questions again together. Was there anything your partner said that you disagree with?

d Imagine that your school is going to produce a new website giving information about your country for tourists. Write a short description of your city / town for the website. You could use some of the tips you talked about in **b**.

MINI GRAMMAR *have something done*

Where's the best place to have your photo taken?

Use *have (something) done* when you ask or pay another person to do something for you.

Compare:

***I took a photo** of the Great Wall of China.* = I took the photo myself.

***I had my photo taken** on the Great Wall of China.* = I asked someone to take my photo.

Have is the main verb in these sentences, so it changes according to the tense.

***I'm going to have** my hair cut tomorrow.*

***I had** my car repaired after the accident.*

⚠ You can also use *get* instead of *have*.

I'm going to get my hair cut tomorrow.

Complete the sentences with the correct form of *have* and the past participle of a verb from the list.

clean cut paint renew repair service

1 We ________ the walls ________ a new color next week.

2 **A** Your hair looks fantastic!
B Thanks. I ________ it ________ yesterday.

3 My coat is really dirty. I need to ________ it ________.

4 You should ________ your car ________ every 7,500 miles.

5 **A** Our refrigerator is broken.
B Are you going to buy a new one or ________ it ________?

6 I'll need to ________ my passport ________ before my next trip abroad.

6C Eureka!

G quantifiers: *all / every*, etc.
V science
P changing stress in word families

1 LISTENING & SPEAKING

a Read the first paragraph of an article about creative thinking. Do the experiment with a partner.

Eureka! Thinking outside the bath...

Master magician Harry Houdini once amazed the world by making an elephant vanish. You are now going to do the same thing.

LOOK AT THE PICTURES of Houdini's head and an elephant. Now close your left eye and hold the book up at arm's length. Now slowly bring the book toward your face, but make sure that you keep looking at Houdini's head with your right eye. At some point, usually when the book is about eight inches from your face, the elephant will suddenly disappear. This simple illusion works because each of our eyes has a "blind spot," a small area inside the eye that cannot see.

According to Dr. Richard Wiseman, a professor of psychology, most people have psychological "blind spots" that cause us to miss seeing the obvious, simple solution to a problem. The few people who do *not* have these psychological blind spots are people like the Greek mathematician Archimedes, who was taking a bath when he suddenly realized that the volume of an object could be calculated by the amount of water it displaced and cried "Eureka" ("I have found it"), or the English scientist Isaac Newton, who developed the notion of gravity after seeing an apple fall. Dr. Wiseman has studied people who frequently experience this kind of "eureka moment" and thinks that the difference between them and ordinary people is that they think in a different way, which he calls "creative thinking."

Adapted from a newspaper

b Now look at the title of the lesson. Who said it and why? Read the second paragraph and check your answer. What kind of people have "eureka moments"? Why don't most people have them?

c 6.11 You are going to listen to a radio program about creative thinking. First, look at the photo. What do you think is happening? Then listen to the first part of the program and answer the questions.

1 Why don't most people think creatively?
2 What was the gorilla experiment?
3 What happened when Dr. Wiseman tried the experiment on a group of top scientists?

Photo provided by Daniel Simons

This photograph was first published in the article "Gorillas in our midst: Sustained inattentional blindness for dynamic events" by D.J. Simons and C.F. Chabris in *Perception, 28*, pages 1059–1074.

d 6.12 Before you listen to the rest of the program, look at the photos below. In what way do you think these three things were innovative? Then listen and answer the questions.

1 What does the gorilla experiment demonstrate?
2 Why are the three things in the photos examples of creative thinking?
3 What did Dr. Wiseman recommend to the journalists? Why?
4 What was Dr. Wiseman's creative idea?

e Take the quiz below to find out if you are a creative thinker.

Are you a creative thinker?

1 Circle true or false.

a I don't consider myself an especially lucky person.
true **false**

b If I'm working on a problem and I'm not making progress, I usually stop for a while and wait for a solution to present itself.
true **false**

c I like dealing with problems that have clear answers.
true **false**

d I don't like breaking rules.
true **false**

e The best part of working on a problem is solving it.
true **false**

2 Think of a number between 1 and 50 that contains two odd digits but not the same digits.

3 In three minutes, add lines to these boxes to make each one into a different object.

4 Look at this clock and fill in the missing numbers.

f **Communication** *Are you a creative thinker? p.118.* Check the answers.

2 GRAMMAR quantifiers: *all / every*, etc.

a Read these scientific facts. Use your instinct to circle the correct word or phrase.

1 Deciduous trees lose their leaves *every year / all years.*
2 *All living things / All the living things* have cells.
3 *Both / Both of* insects and spiders are invertebrates.
4 If something absorbs *all / every* the colors of the spectrum, it appears black.
5 *All / Everything* is made up of atoms.
6 Without oxygen, neither humans *or / nor* animals can survive.

b **p.142 Grammar Bank 6C.** Read the rules and do the exercises.

c Take the science quiz below with a partner.

How much do you know about science?

Take our quiz and find out.

1 How much of human DNA is the same as chimpanzee DNA?
a Hardly any.
b Some of it.
c Most of it.

2 The air we breathe contains ...
a both nitrogen and carbon dioxide.
b neither nitrogen nor carbon dioxide.
c only carbon dioxide.

3 When we breathe out, how much of that air is oxygen?
a None of it.
b All of it.
c Some of it.

4 While you are asleep, you are in REM sleep (or dreaming sleep) for ...
a all of the night.
b some of the night.
c most of the night.

5 When does a lemon tree produce fruit?
a Nearly all year.
b Nearly every year.
c Some years.

6 If blue-eyed parents have one son and one daughter, who will also have blue eyes?
a Both of them.
b Neither of them.
c One of them.

d **Communication** *How much do you know about science? p.118.* Check the answers.

3 READING

a You are going to find out about how scientists throughout history have suffered while making their discoveries. Read the descriptions and label the illustrations A–D. How many of the scientists actually died as a result of their research?

Suffering for science

Throughout history scientists have risked their health and their lives in their search for the truth...

1 ☐

2 ☐

3 ☐

4 ☐

A Isaac Newton, the seventeenth-century scientist, was a genius, but that didn't stop him from doing some pretty stupid things. In his laboratory in Cambridge, he often did the most bizarre experiments. Once, while investigating how lenses transmit light, he inserted a long needle into his eye, pushed it to the back, and then moved it around just to see what would happen. Miraculously, nothing long-lasting did. On another occasion he stared at the sun for as long as he could bear, to discover what effect this would have on his vision. Again he escaped suffering permanent damage, though he had to spend some days in a darkened room before his eyes recovered.

B In the 1750s the chemist **Karl Scheele** was the first person to find a way to manufacture phosphorus. In fact, he discovered eight more elements, including chlorine, though he didn't get the credit for any of them. He was a brilliant scientist, but his one failing was a curious insistence on tasting a little of every substance he worked with, including mercury and cyanide. This risky practice finally caught up with him, and in 1786 he was found dead in his laboratory surrounded by a large number of toxic chemicals, any of which might have been responsible for his death.

C In the early 1900s **Pierre and Marie Curie** discovered the element radium, leading to their investigation of radioactivity. At the time, nobody realized what a dangerous and deadly phenomenon it was – in fact, most people thought that it was beneficial. There was even a hotel in New York which, in the 1920s, advertised "the therapeutic effect of its radioactive waters." Both Pierre and Marie Curie experienced radiation sickness, and Marie Curie died of leukemia in 1934. Even now, all her papers from the 1890s are too dangerous to touch. Her laboratory books are kept in special lead boxes, and those who view them have to wear protective clothing. Marie's husband, Pierre, however, did not die from radiation – he was run over by a carriage while crossing the street.

D Eugene Shoemaker was a respected geologist. He spent a large part of his life investigating craters on the moon, and how they were formed, and later did research into the comets of the planet Jupiter. In 1997 he and his wife were in the Australian desert, where they went every year to search for places where comets might have hit the earth. While driving in the Tanami desert, normally one of the emptiest places in the world, another vehicle crashed into them and Shoemaker was killed instantly. Some of his ashes were sent to the moon aboard the Lunar Prospector spacecraft and scattered there – he is the only person who has had this honor.

Adapted from *A Short History of Nearly Everything* by Bill Bryson

b Read the descriptions again and answer the questions. Write A–D in the right box.

Which scientist ...?

1 ☐ had a very dangerous way of working with chemicals
2 ☐ was injured twice while he / she was doing experiments
3 ☐ discovered something that slowly killed him / her
4 ☐ was very unlucky to die doing his / her job
5 ☐ needed some time to recover from an experiment
6 ☐ was granted a special honor after his / her death
7 ☐ wasn't recognized for everything he / she discovered
8 ☐ left something behind that is still dangerous today

c 6.13 Look at the highlighted words, which are all related to science. What do they mean? Are they similar in your language? How do you think they are pronounced? Listen and check.

4 VOCABULARY & PRONUNCIATION

science; changing stress in word families

a Match the different kinds of scientists with what they study.

a biologist   a chemist   a geneticist   a geologist   a physicist

1 ______________ natural forces, e.g., light, sound, heat, etc.
2 ______________ living things, e.g., animals and plants
3 ______________ the structure of substances; what happens in different situations or when they are mixed with each other
4 ______________ the parts of cells in living things (genes) that control what a person, animal, or plant is like
5 ______________ rocks and how they are formed

b In pairs, complete the table.

person	adjective	subject
1 scientist	scientific	science
2 chemist		
3 biologist		
4 physicist		
5 geneticist		
6 geologist		

⚠ In some "word families" the stressed syllable changes in the different parts of speech, e.g., *photograph*, *photographer*, *photographic*.

c 6.14 Look at the words in the chart in **b** above and underline the stressed syllable. Listen and check. In which groups does the stress change?

d Practice saying the word families.

e Complete the sentences with the correct form of a verb from the list. Underline the stress in the verbs and also in the **bold** words.

develop   discover   do (x3)   invent   make   prove   volunteer

1 Pierre and Marie Curie ______ **radium** in the early 1900s.
2 Scientists usually ______ **experiments** in a **laboratory**.
3 Archimedes ______ an important **discovery** in his bath.
4 Isaac Newton's experiments ______ his **theory** that gravity existed.
5 The telephone was ______ in the 1870s.
6 **Pharmaceutical** companies try to ______ new drugs to cure illnesses and diseases.
7 Scientists have to ______ a lot of **research** into the possible **side effects** of new drugs.
8 Before a company can sell a new drug, they have to ______ tests and **trials** to make sure it is safe.
9 People can ______ to be **guinea pigs** in clinical trials.

f 6.15 Listen and check. Practice saying the sentences.

5 SPEAKING

Answer the questions with a partner.

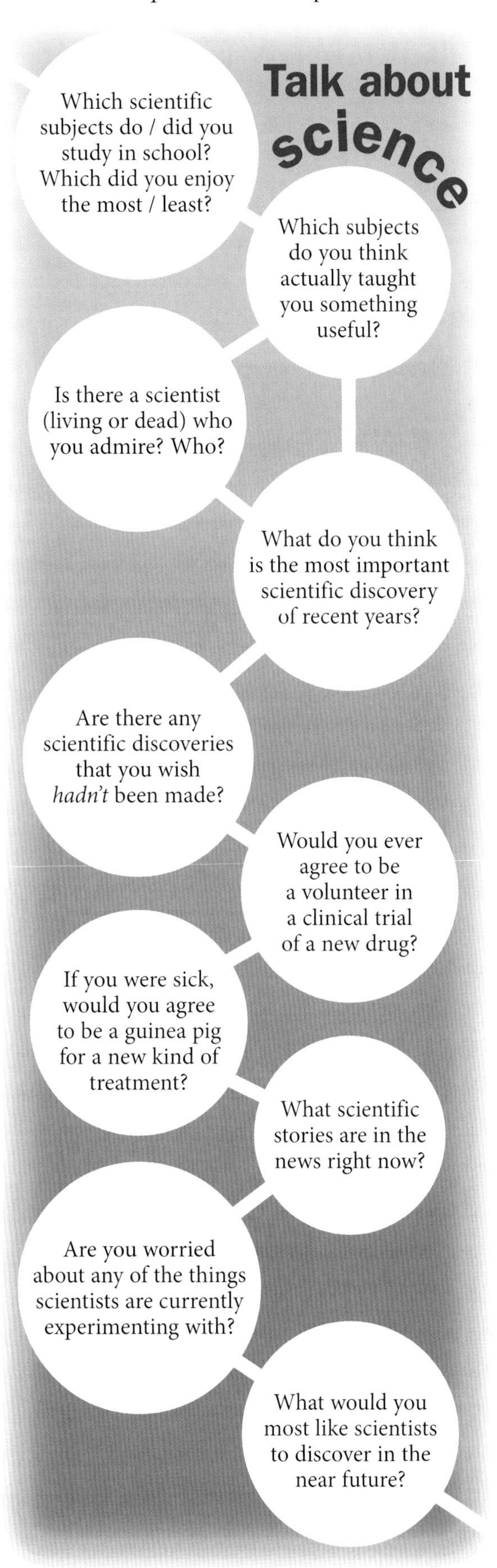

p.157 Phrasal verbs in context *File 6*.

THE INTERVIEW

a You are going to listen to an interview with Graham Bull, a "conDUCKtor" – or a tour guide – for Boston Duck Tours. This company uses "Ducks", renovated World War II vehicles that are amphibious, i.e., they can travel on land and water. Before you listen, read the glossary and look at how the words are pronounced to help you understand what he says.

Glossary

levity /ˈlɛvəti/ humor, fun

Beacon Hill /ˈbikən hɪl/ a historic, upper-class Boston neighborhood

Boston Brahman /ˈbɔstən ˈbrɑmən/ a person of high social status in Boston

Faneuil Hall /ˈfænyəl hɔl/ a meeting hall and marketplace in Boston since 1742

Sam Adams /sæm ˈædəmz/ (1722–1803) a leader in the American Revolution from Massachusetts

roller coaster /ˈroʊlər ˌkoʊstər/ a train track at amusement parks that goes up and down very steep slopes

glee /gli/ joy, delight

shriek /ʃrik/ to give a sudden scream in a high voice

freak out /frik aʊt/ (informal) to have a strong reaction, e.g., fear

Celtics /ˈsɛltɪks/ a professional basketball team based in Boston

the remains of /rɪˈmeɪnz/ the dead body of

rafter /ˈræftər/ a long piece of wood that supports a roof

b 6.16 Listen to part 1. Answer the questions with a partner.

1 What two things make the Duck Tours special?
2 What are the most popular sights on the tour?
3 What is the best thing about Boston for a tourist?
4 What is the worst thing?

c 6.17 Listen to part 2. Answer the questions with a partner.

What does he say about ...?
1 something people are occasionally not aware of during the tour
2 a birthday surprise
3 how the woman felt when the Duck went down the ramp
4 where the new Boston Garden was built
5 some trash found by the janitors
6 what they found when the old building was torn down

d 6.18 Listen and complete the phrases. What do you think they mean?

COMMON PHRASES

1 ... there is a good deal of sense of humor involved, and it _____ _____ very well. pv
2 The worst thing about being a tourist in Boston is, _____ _____, the matter of driving a car.
3 Do not drive a car in Boston unless you live here and know your _____ _____.
4 I _____ _____ she was probably in her seventies.
5 Well, to make a long _____ _____ ...

e Listen to the interview again with the audioscript on page 129. Would you choose a Duck Tour instead of a normal tour? Why (not)?

ON THE STREET

a 6.19 Listen to five people talking about their favorite cities and a city they would like to visit. Write the number of each speaker next to the two cities they mention.

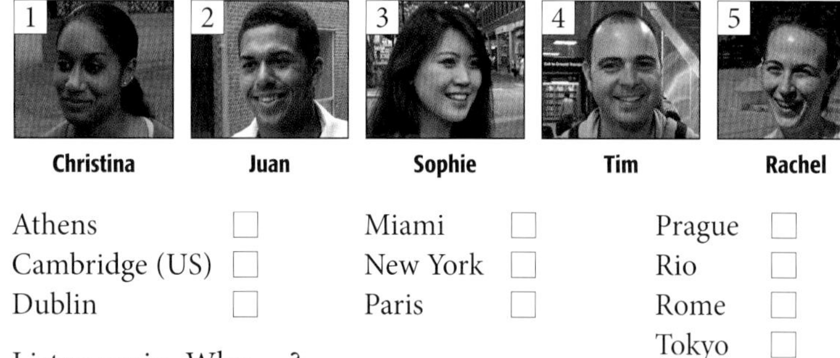

Christina Juan Sophie Tim Rachel

Athens ☐	Miami ☐	Prague ☐
Cambridge (US) ☐	New York ☐	Rio ☐
Dublin ☐	Paris ☐	Rome ☐
		Tokyo ☐

b Listen again. Who ...?

1 went to college in their favorite city
2 didn't like the weather in their favorite city
3 wants to return to a city they visited before
4 has family members in their favorite city
5 thinks their favorite city isn't too big or too small

c 6.20 Listen and complete the phrases. What do you think they mean?

COMMON PHRASES

1 ... the weather could have been better because it rains all the _____ ...
2 My favorite city in the world would _____ to be Miami.
3 ... that was pretty _____, I really enjoyed that.
4 I was there for a day, but didn't get a _____ ...
5 I haven't been to South America at _____.

d Listen to the interviews again with the audioscript on page 130. Then answer the same questions with a partner.

a Read the report on restaurants and think of an appropriate heading for parts 1, 3, and 4.

b Find synonyms in the report for the expressions in **bold**.

Useful language

Talking in general

Most / __________ restaurants in my town ... (part 1)
In general / __________ (part 2)
Cafes **are likely to be** / __________ fairly cheap. (part 2)
Almost always / __________ (part 3)
Usually / __________ (part 4)

c You have been asked to write a report on either entertainment or sports facilities in your city / town for an English language magazine. With a partner, decide what kind of information would be most useful for visitors to your city / town.

PLAN the content.

1 Decide which report you are going to write.
2 Decide what headings you can use to divide up your report.
3 Decide what information to include under each heading.

WRITE 120–180 words, organized in three or four sections, each with a heading. Use a neutral style (avoid contractions and informal expressions).

CHECK your report for mistakes (grammar, punctuation, and spelling).

This report describes various options for students who want to eat out while staying in Chicago.

1 __________

Fast food – The majority of fast-food restaurants are clean and the service is fast, but they are often noisy and crowded, and of course the food is the same all over the world.

Outdoor hot dog stands – You can try a delicious Chicaco-style hot dog with all the condiments. Not much atmosphere, but the food is relatively inexpensive.

2 *When you don't mind spending a little more*

Ethnic restaurants – Chicago has dozens of ethnic neighborhoods from Greektown to Little Italy to Chinatown and more, all packed with restaurants. Generally speaking, these ethnic restaurants are reasonably priced. Enjoy a festive meal at a Mexican restaurant or try a Chicago-style deep-dish pizza at an Italian restaurant or pizzeria. Portions tend to be large, so come hungry.

Sports pubs – At Chicago's lively sports pubs, the main attraction is the people – mostly sports fans – and the vibrant atmosphere. Moderately priced dishes include burgers and sandwiches.

3 __________

There are many options if you want to try somewhere special, but this nearly always means spending a lot of money. Chicago steak houses, among the best in the country, tend to be fairly expensive, so be prepared for an enjoyable, though costly, meal.

4 __________

- Even if you have a limited budget, take advantage of the different restaurants Chicago has to offer.
- Don't make your meal cost more by ordering expensive drinks.
- If you really want to go to a particular restaurant, be sure to make reservations, especially on weekends and holidays.
- Consider having your main meal at lunchtime, when prices are commonly lower than at dinner.

6 What do you remember?

GRAMMAR

Choose a, b, or c.

1 After the robbery, he was in ___ prison for ten years.
  a the
  b –
  c a

2 I now live next door to ___ school I used to go to.
  a the
  b –
  c a

3 ___ Lake Michigan is one of the largest freshwater lakes in the world.
  a The
  b –
  c A

4 He wants to buy ___ inexpensive clothes.
  a a piece of
  b some
  c an

5 Let me give you ___ – don't marry him!
  a some advice
  b an advice
  c some advices

6 I need to buy a new ___.
  a pant
  b pants
  c pair of pants

7 I'm going to the optician. I need to ___.
  a have tested my eyes
  b test my eyes
  c have my eyes tested

8 There's ___ milk. I'll have to buy some.
  a no
  b any
  c none

9 I didn't buy my jeans in that store because ___ were so expensive.
  a everything
  b all
  c all of them

10 They shouldn't go in the boat alone because ___ of them can swim.
  a both
  b either
  c neither

VOCABULARY

a Complete the sentences with the right form of the **bold** word.

1 Gyeongju is a ___ city in Korea. **history**
2 One of the biggest problems in big cities is ___. **poor**
3 The ___ has to do more to protect the environment. **govern**
4 A lot of research is being done into human ___. **genes**
5 Many important ___ discoveries were made in the 19th century. **science**

b Complete the phrases.

1 Please turn the TV down. I need some peace and **q**______.
2 He arrived back from his adventure safe and **s**______.
3 Why have you taken only black and **w**______ photos?
4 I don't know him very well. I've only met him once or **t**______.
5 We've moved almost everything to the new office. There are just a few odds and **e**______ left.

c Circle the correct verb.

1 Scientists usually *do* / *make* experiments in a laboratory.
2 Archimedes *did* / *made* an important discovery in his bath.
3 Drug companies have to *make* / *do* a lot of research into possible side effects.
4 These pills are *made* / *done* in Puerto Rico.
5 Before a company can sell a new medicine, it has to *make* / *do* tests and trials using volunteers.

d Word groups. Underline the word that is different. Say why.

1	cathedral	synagogue	harbor	mosque
2	taxi stand	cable car	bus station	airport
3	suburb	district	landmark	neighborhood
4	square	skyscraper	town hall	courthouse
5	chemist	scientist	physicist	genetics

PRONUNCIATION

a Underline the word with a different sound.

1	aɪ	height	vibrant	science	neighborhood
2	ʌ	government	prove	slums	discovery
3	ɪr	volunteer	theory	research	souvenir
4	ð	breathe	both	neither	the
5	dʒ	geologist	synagogue	genes	biology

b Underline the stressed syllable.

biological physicist cosmopolitan outskirts industrial

CAN YOU UNDERSTAND THIS TEXT?

a Complete the article with a sentence A–F.

A For most of us the idea of having the weaknesses of our speech exposed is scary.

B I talk for two minutes on four topics: a happy memory, a sad memory, something that makes me angry, and a neutral work-related topic.

C The idea is that when you are tempted to say "um," you simply remain silent.

D Mr. Grant receives a report on the results and, armed with that information, he and his associates coach me to use my voice more effectively.

E On the other hand, I do not vary my pitch much, which means I have a monotonous voice.

F Voice coaching, once only for actors, is now commonly used by politicians and business people.

b Look at the highlighted words and phrases. Can you guess what they mean?

Loud and clear: the message sent by your voice

I am sitting in an office having my voice recorded. 1☐ The reason? I am about to have my voice analyzed, and expressing these feelings provides a balanced view of the voice's emotional content.

2☐ A badly delivered speech can have a devastating impact on the public image of a politician. For chief executives, an unconvincing speech can damage the company's standing with employees, customers, or investors.

When I am finished, the man who has been listening to me, Alastair Grant of presentation analysts Grant Pearson Brown, sends the recording to Branka Zei, a Swiss psychologist who specializes in linguistics. Using software, Ms. Zei measures the recording against an "ideal" voice, whose pitch, articulation, and fluency, among other things, are derived by analyzing the voices of hundreds of good speakers. 3☐

So, what does my analysis show? The good news is that my median pitch is 158.25Hz compared with the standard reference for a woman of 200Hz – another way of saying that my voice is fairly deep. "Deeper voices carry more authority than high-pitched voices," says Mr. Grant. My loudness level and range are perfect. 4☐ Also my articulation is not clear enough because I sometimes have difficulty pronouncing the letter "r." Last, I use "disfluencies," which means that I overuse terms such as "um" and "uh." The best news, however, is that my "vocal indicators" point to a balanced personality, with no clear tendency toward introversion or extroversion.

If Mr. Grant were to work with me further, he would get me to read from a script and pause after each phrase. 5☐ "If people are comfortable with silence, then they don't have to put in those filler words." To counteract my problem of sounding monotonous, he would ask me to imagine myself telling a story to a child, as this very naturally makes people vary their pitch.

6☐ But for those brave enough to try it, voice analysis offers the chance of really improving the way we speak in everyday life and when we are on the podium.

Adapted from a newspaper

CAN YOU UNDERSTAND THESE PEOPLE?

a 6.21 Listen and circle the correct answer, a, b, or c.

1 What does the woman offer to do?
 a Get a technician.
 b Fix the projector.
 c Make the room darker.

2 Which of these problems *doesn't* the man mention?
 a Too many people.
 b A lot of crime.
 c Too much traffic.

3 What does the tour guide recommend the tourists do?
 a Visit the Roman room.
 b Plan their own tour of the museum.
 c Buy postcards in the gift shop.

4 What is the teacher going to show the children?
 a How to use a microscope.
 b How to look at something closely without a microscope.
 c How to know which tree a leaf comes from.

5 Which of the following is true about Newton?
 a He was not a very healthy baby.
 b He was brought up by his father's mother.
 c His father was a poor farmer.

b 6.22 You will hear an interview with a woman who moved from the city to the country. Mark the sentences T (true) or F (false).

1 Her friends thought she would miss her job.
2 She sees friends more often than before.
3 She gets along well with the people in the village.
4 She often gets takeout for dinner.
5 The bus service is good.

CAN YOU SAY THIS IN ENGLISH?

Can you ...?

- ☐ give a short presentation on a subject you know about
- ☐ give advice about how to speak in public successfully
- ☐ describe a big city you know well and its attractions or problems
- ☐ talk about famous scientists and their discoveries

G structures after *wish*
V *-ed* / *-ing* adjectives and related verbs; expressions with *go*
P sentence rhythm

I wish you wouldn't ...!

1 SPEAKING

GET IT RIGHT expressing annoyance

When you talk about things that annoy you, you can use these expressions:

It really annoys me when ... *It drives me crazy / nuts when ...* *It drives me up the wall when ...* *It really gets on my nerves when ...*	*people shout into cell phones.*
People who shout into cell phones ...	*really annoy me,* etc.

a Read through the list of annoying things (A–O) in the magazine article. With a partner, say which of these things annoy you, too. Choose your top three "pet peeves."

b Think of three other things that annoy you. Then compare your three things with other students.

2 GRAMMAR *wish* + simple past and *would / could*

a 7.1 Listen to four conversations. Which of the irritating things (A–O) in the magazine article do they refer to?

1 ☐ 2 ☐ 3 ☐ 4 ☐

b Listen again and complete the sentences.

1 I wish ___ ___ ___ that!
2 I wish ___ ___ a dollar for every time I picked the *one* broken one.
3 I wish ___ ___, but it depends on the traffic.
4 I wish ___ ___ ___ in the street.

c Which speakers would like *somebody else* to change their behavior?

d **p.144 Grammar Bank 7A.** Read the rules for *wish* + simple past and *wish* + *would / could.* Do exercise **a**.

e Complete the sentences so that they are true for you. Compare with a partner.

About me
I wish I could __________. (ability)
I wish I were more __________. (adjective of personality)
I wish I weren't so __________. (adjective of personality)
I wish I had __________. (personal possession)
I wish __________.

Things people do that annoy me
I wish my __________ wouldn't __________. (brother, sister, friend)
I wish __________ would / wouldn't __________. (drivers / cyclists)
I wish young people today would / wouldn't __________.
I wish there were a law against people who __________.

Things that really annoy us

– we asked people around the world ...

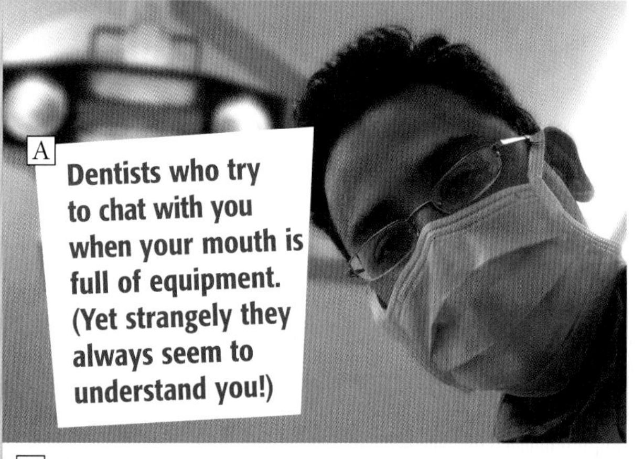

A Dentists who try to chat with you when your mouth is full of equipment. (Yet strangely they always seem to understand you!)

B People who criticize politicians and the government but then don't vote in the elections.

C I get into the shower, and then either the water goes cold or there's no shower gel left.

D Cyclists who ride on the sidewalk and nearly knock you down.

E When I'm traveling on a plane or train, and a child sitting behind me keeps kicking my seat.

F People reading over your shoulder in a public place.

G TV or radio news programs with a male and female presenter, who each speak only a couple of lines at a time.

H When I'm standing in line for a train ticket and the person in front of me can't make up their mind what kind of ticket they want.

I When you want to buy something in a store, and you have to wait for the salesperson to finish a telephone conversation with a friend.

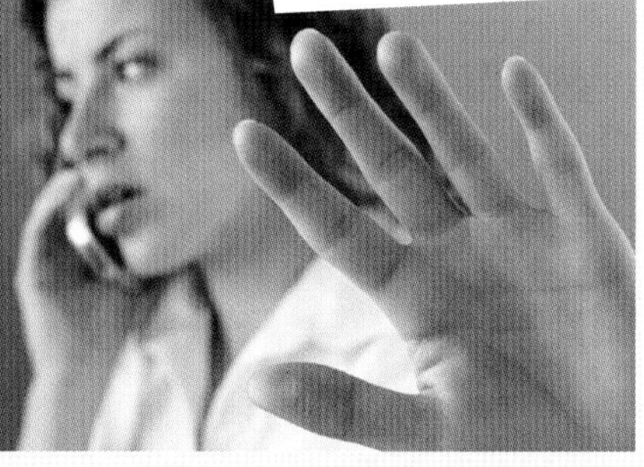

J When you get a cart in a supermarket and one of the wheels is broken.

K When you get in a taxi, and the driver asks you the best way to go.

L I'm talking on the phone and I need a pen quickly, but I can't find one that works.

M Drivers who double park on a busy street and then put their emergency lights on (as if that makes it OK).

N People who wear sunglasses indoors.

O Telemarketers that call you during the evening, trying to sell you something.

3 VOCABULARY *-ed / -ing* adjectives and related verbs

We often talk about feelings in three different ways, either by using a verb (e.g., *annoy*) or by using the *-ed* or *-ing* adjective (e.g., *annoying, annoyed*).

It really annoys me. (verb)

That noise is really annoying. / Jane is so annoying.
(*-ing* adjectives describe the thing or person that produces a feeling)

I'm really annoyed about last night.
(*-ed* adjectives describe how a person feels)

a Complete the sentences with the correct form of the word in **bold**.

1. I get very ____________ when I speak Spanish and people don't understand me. **frustrate**
2. It's ____________ when you can't remember someone's name. **embarrass**
3. It really ____________ me when people are late. **irritate**
4. I wish the sun would come out. I find these gray days so ____________. **depress**
5. We were ____________ when the plane suddenly began to lose height. **terrify**
6. The trip had been very ____________, so she decided to go to bed early. **tire**
7. I wish he'd come home! It ____________ me when he's out late at night. **worry**
8. Jack wasn't very ____________ when we made fun of his new tie. **amuse**
9. The end of the movie really ____________ me. It was totally unbelievable. **disappoint**
10. It was a ____________ game! Our team won 3-2 with a goal in the last minute. **thrill**
11. She really ____________ her parents when she told them she was getting divorced. **shock**
12. What an ____________ day! I need to relax and put my feet up. **exhaust**

b A few "feeling" verbs have an *-ed* adjective, but not the *-ing* form. Complete the adjectives in the sentences below.

1. I was delight**ed** to meet her. She was a *delightful* person.
2. I was scar**ed** during the movie. The movie was very ________.
3. We were extremely impress**ed** by your résumé. Your résumé was extremely ________.
4. I'm very stress**ed** by my job. My job is very ________.
5. I was really offend**ed** by what you said. What you said was really ________.

c In pairs, talk about some of these:

- something in the news recently that shocked you
- a movie you found really disappointing
- something that frustrates you about learning English
- the kind of weather that makes you feel depressed
- an embarrassing mistake you once made
- an area of your town / city that is scary at night

4 READING

a Look at the photos of actress Paula Wilcox as she is today and in the TV series that made her famous, *Man About the House*. How old do you think she is in each photo? How has she changed?

b Read a magazine article where Paula talks about things she regrets. In which paragraph does she talk about ...?

A ☐ a time when she misjudged other people
B ☐ a time when she didn't want to seem different from other people
C ☐ her insecurity about her appearance
D ☐ how she regrets not taking more risks
E ☐ situations when she shouldn't have talked so much
F ☐ advice she should have listened to

c Read the article again carefully. Find words or phrases that mean:

1 ____________ it makes me remember (1)
2 ____________ very beautiful (1)
3 ____________ a missed opportunity (1)
4 ____________ having a leading role (2)
5 ____________ amusing and intelligent (3)
6 ____________ the most amusing and interesting person (3)
7 ____________ kind, soft (4)
8 ____________ things that are new or difficult, but stimulating (6)

d Use your own words to summarize the advice she gives in each paragraph to younger people. What do you think of her advice?

5 GRAMMAR *wish* + past perfect

a Underline the seven sentences in the article with *wish*. What tense is the verb after *wish*? Are they wishes about the present, the past, or the future?

b **p.144 Grammar Bank 7A.** Read the rules for *wish* + past perfect. Do exercise **b**.

c What regrets do you think these people might have? Make sentences with *I wish ...* + past perfect.

1 John has always been extravagant and never has much money in the bank. Now he really wants to buy an expensive car, but he can't afford it.
2 Annie has just been to the hairstylist. She isn't very happy with her new look.
3 Claudia was offered a job in San Francisco but didn't take it because she didn't think her English was good enough.
4 Mark got really angry with his girlfriend last night. They had an argument and she left him.

I wish I'd saved part of my salary. I wish I hadn't spent so much money on that vacation...

Regrets, I've had a few...

Actress Paula Wilcox, now in her fifties, was best known for her role in the TV series *Man About the House*, which she starred in when she was only 19. Here she talks about things she wishes she had known then...

1 Now when I look in the mirror and think, "Oh boy, I'm getting older," it reminds me that I used to do the same thing when I was 19 and 20. I used to look at myself and think I looked awful. I wish I'd known what I was going to look like 30 years later, because then I might have realized how gorgeous I was then. I looked great but I didn't appreciate it – what a waste!

2 I now understand that it's OK to be successful. When I was 19, I was starring on TV and making lots of money, but most of my friends were college students. I felt embarrassed and used to walk around with my hands in front of my face so as not to be recognized. I wish I'd known that it's possible to enjoy the good things about fame and that you can keep your friendships in spite of it.

3 I wish I had learned sooner how to listen to people better. I used to think I had to be intelligent and witty in social situations. If I'd known how much people appreciate being listened to, I wouldn't have tried so hard to be the life and soul of the party.

4 Life has taught me that sometimes when people behave badly with you, it is because of some unhappiness that they are carrying around with them, a problem that has nothing to do with you. I wish I had been more gentle with people in that situation and not reacted so angrily. Once you find out what's really going on, the whole relationship can change.

5 My dad always used to say, "Learn what you can while you are young and in school because when you are older, you either won't have enough time or won't have enough money to pay for lessons." That was good advice, and I wish I'd spent more time on my piano lessons.

6 Finally, I wish I had always said yes to challenges. I'd say to young people today, if you are offered the opportunity to do something you have never done before, go for it. You might feel a little nervous, but say yes anyway.

Adapted from a newspaper

6 PRONUNCIATION sentence rhythm

a 7.2 **Dictation.** Listen and write down six sentences with *wish*.

b Listen again and underline the stressed words.

c Match each sentence from the dictation with a sentence below. In pairs, practice the dialogues.

A ☐ Do you want me to call and make an excuse?
B ☐ I thought you said we were in a hurry!
C ☐ So do I. I didn't bring an umbrella today.
D ☐ Well, it's not *my* fault. You have no self-control!
E ☐ Why don't you go back to the store and see if they still have it?
F ☐ I'm sorry, but it is. And I'm getting hungry.

7 LISTENING & SPEAKING

a 7.3 Listen to five people and match the speakers with the regrets. Who ...?

A wasted time when he / she could have been doing something else ☐
B wishes he / she had said something to someone ☐
C missed an opportunity because he / she wasn't independent ☐
D wasn't old enough to take advantage of a situation ☐
E regretted trying to change his / her appearance ☐

b Listen again. Why do the speakers mention or say the following?

1 "Mercedes" and "Bosch" "It would have opened doors for me."
2 "The top and skirt I wore were really skimpy."
3 "The Russian revolution." "Old letters."
4 "I really liked him." "Now it's too late."
5 "I just did the bare minimum." "This was a unique opportunity."

c Read about the research below. Do you identify with any of the regrets?

Psychologists have researched things that people regret about their lives. Here are some of the things people wrote:

Family

- I regret arguing with my parents yesterday.
- I wish I'd listened to my sister when she had problems.
- I regret not visiting my grandfather more when he was in the hospital.

Lifestyle

- I wish I hadn't eaten so much last night.
- I wish I hadn't had my hair cut short last month.
- I regret not buying some really cheap shoes when I first saw them on sale – when I came back an hour later, they were gone.
- I wish I had been brave enough to go up to the top floor of the Eiffel Tower when I was in Paris.

Education, work, etc.

- I wish I'd studied more for my final exams last year.
- I wish I'd saved more money when I was earning a good salary.
- I regret not learning to play the guitar when I was younger.

d Think of three regrets (big or small) that you would add to the lists. Compare with a partner and ask for more information.

8 VOCABULARY expressions with *go*

Once you find out what's really going on, the whole relationship can change.

If you are offered the opportunity to do something you have never done before, go for it.

a Look at the highlighted phrasal verbs with *go* from the article about Paula Wilcox on page 102. What do you think they mean?

b Complete the questions with the correct word.

back on far for off on over sleep with without wrong

1 Do you usually **go** ______ your notes after class?
2 What do you usually do when something **goes** ______ with your computer?
3 Have you ever promised someone something important and then **gone** ______ your word?
4 Do you think you could **go** ______ food for 24 hours?
5 Do you usually choose shoes that **go** ______ the clothes you're wearing?
6 How long does it usually take you to **go to** ______ at night?
7 Do you think that speaking English will help you **go** ______ professionally?
8 I woke up immediately when my alarm clock **went** ______ this morning.
9 If you were offered a job abroad, would you **go** ______ **it**?
10 What's **going** ______ in the celebrity world in your country these days?

c Now ask and answer the questions in pairs.

9 7.4 SONG ♫ *If I could turn back time*

G clauses of contrast and purpose; *whatever, whenever*, etc.
V business and advertising
P changing stress in nouns and verbs

7B A test of honesty

1 READING & LISTENING

a Look at the title of the article below and the photos. Try to guess what the article is about.

b Read *Honest workers or thieves?* and check. Then, in pairs, cover the article and say what you can remember about ...
1 Paul Feldman's original job.
2 the incident that made him decide to change his job.
3 how the "bagel habit" started, and what it involved.
4 why he started asking for money, and the proportion of people who paid.
5 his friends' and family's reaction to his change of job.
6 how his business progressed.
7 the economic experiment he (unintentionally) designed.

c You are going to hear an economist talking about Paul Feldman's experiment. Before you listen, in pairs, predict the answers to the questions.
1 What do you think the average payment rate was?
a 70–80% b 80–90% c 90–100%
2 Were smaller offices more or less honest than big ones?
3 How often has the cash basket been stolen?
4 Did people "cheat" more during good or bad weather?
5 Did people "cheat" more or less before Christmas? Why?
6 Who "cheated" more, executives or lower-level employees?

d 7.5 Listen and check your answers to c.

e Listen again and choose a, b, or c.
1 More people paid in Feldman's own office ...
a after he caught somebody stealing.
b because he asked them personally for the money.
c because the people were his coworkers.
2 Feldman eventually stopped selling bagels to ...
a a company where less than 80% paid for their bagels.
b a company where the money basket got stolen.
c a company where less than 90% paid for their bagels.
3 People are more honest in smaller companies because ...
a they are more likely to get caught.
b they would be more embarrassed about being caught.
c there is more control from the management.
4 People "cheat" more ...
a after a day off.
b before all public holidays.
c before some public holidays.
5 Which of these people is most likely to pay?
a An employee who doesn't like the boss.
b An executive who is very popular with the staff.
c An employee who likes the company where he / she works.

Honest workers or thieves? Take the bagel test.

Once upon a time, Paul Feldman dreamed big dreams. Trained as an agricultural economist, he wanted to tackle world hunger. Instead, he took a job in Washington, analyzing weapons expenditures for the US Navy. He held senior-level jobs and earned good money, but he wasn't always recognized for his best work. At the office Christmas party, colleagues would introduce him to their wives not as "the head of the public research group" (which he was) but as "the guy who brings in the bagels."

The bagels had begun as a casual gesture: a boss treating his employees whenever they won a research contract. Then he made it a habit. Every Friday, he would bring in some bagels, a serrated knife, and cream cheese. When employees from neighboring floors heard about the bagels, they wanted some too. Eventually he was bringing in 15 dozen bagels a week. In order to recoup his costs, he set out a cash basket and a sign with the suggested price. His collection rate was about 95 percent; he attributed the underpayment to oversight, not fraud.

When his research institute fell under new management, Feldman decided to quit his job and sell bagels. His economist friends thought he had lost his mind, but his wife supported him.

Driving around the office parks that encircle Washington, he solicited customers with a simple pitch: early in the morning, he would deliver some bagels and a cash basket to a company's snack room; he would return before lunch to pick up the money and the leftovers. Within a few years, Feldman was delivering 8,400 bagels a week to 140 companies and earning as much as he had ever made as a research analyst.

He had also, quite without meaning to, designed a beautiful economic experiment. By measuring the money collected against the bagels taken, he found it possible to tell, down to the penny, just how honest his customers were. Did they steal from him? If so, what were the characteristics of a company that stole versus a company that did not? Under what circumstances did people tend to steal more, or less?

From *Freakonomics*

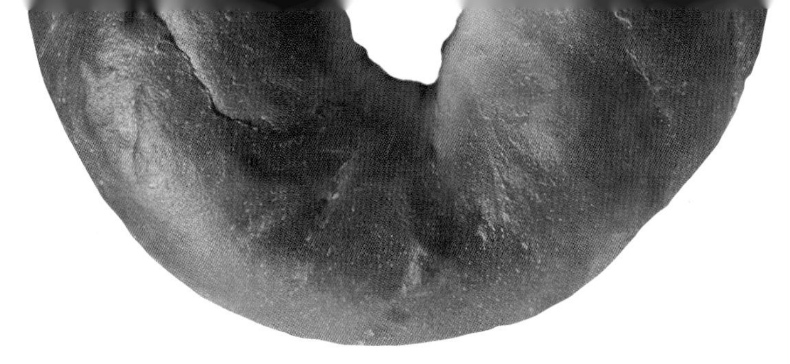

f How do you feel about people ...?
- downloading music and movies from the Internet without paying
- buying pirate DVDs / CDs
- photocopying a book
- taking home pens, paper, etc. from the office or school
- keeping a library book
- buying designer goods that they know are fakes
- not saying anything when a salesperson gives back too much change

2 VOCABULARY business and advertising

a Look at the *Honest workers or thieves?* article again and find words that mean ...

1 __________ the person who is in charge of a group or department in an organization (paragraph 1)
2 __________ an employer or manager (paragraph 2)
3 __________ people who work for somebody (paragraph 2)
4 __________ people who buy a product from a store or company (paragraph 5)

b **p.156 Vocabulary Bank** *Business and advertising.*

c Take the business quiz with a partner.

What's the difference between ...?

1 an employer / an employee
2 a customer / a client
3 the boss / the staff
4 set up a company / take over a company
5 export a product / import a product

Name a business or company in your town / city that ...

1 is part of a well-known chain.
2 belongs to a multinational.
3 started as a small family business and then became much bigger.
4 was taken over by another company.
5 spends a lot of money on advertising.

3 PRONUNCIATION changing stress in nouns and verbs

Some words change their stress depending on whether they are nouns or verbs. As nouns, they are usually stressed on the first syllable, e.g., *a project, a record*. As verbs, they are often stressed on the second syllable, e.g., *to project, to record*. Words like this include: *convert, object, present, produce, progress, reject*. Sometimes the vowel sounds change, too.

a Read the information in the box and practice saying each word both ways: as a noun with the stress on the first syllable, and as a verb with the stress on the second syllable.

b Underline the stressed syllable on the highlighted word.

1 We're making good progress with the report.
2 The new building is progressing well.
3 Home sales are recorded at the courthouse.
4 Sales of hybrid cars have reached a new record.
5 Half the applicants for the job were rejected.
6 Rejects are sold at a reduced price.
7 The demand for organic produce is growing.
8 Most toys are produced in China nowadays.
9 My boss objects to people dressing casually at work.
10 Making a profit is the company's main object.

c 7.6 Listen and check. Practice saying the sentences.

MINI GRAMMAR
whatever, whenever, etc.

The bagels had begun as a "thank you" to his employees whenever they won a research project.

We use *whenever* to mean "at any time" or "it doesn't matter when," e.g., *Come and see me* ***whenever*** *you like.*

We can also use:

whatever (= any thing), *whichever* (= any thing, from a limited number), *whoever* (= any person), *however* (= it doesn't matter how), *wherever* (= any place).
They also have the meaning *it doesn't matter what / which / who / how / where*, etc.

Complete the sentences with *whatever, whichever, whoever, whenever, however,* or *wherever.*

1 Please sit __________ you like.
2 There is a prize for __________ can answer the question first.
3 __________ she opens her mouth, she says something stupid.
4 I'm going to buy it, __________ expensive it is!
5 __________ I give him, it's always the wrong thing.
6 I'll go by bus or train, __________ is cheaper.

4 GRAMMAR clauses of contrast and purpose

a Read the ad below. Would you try *Pumavite*? Why (not)?

"I slept my way to fitness"

No exercise – but now Simon has muscles to die for!

Simon Sloth had never been one for exercise. With three children and a busy job, he had very little time for the gym.

But then Simon discovered PUMAVITE tablets, an exclusive product marketed by Cure Everything Pharmaceuticals. A three-month course of the tablets has transformed him!

"You take it at night," explains Simon, "and its special secret ingredient gets to work immediately." **PUMAVITE** contains plant extracts from the Andes and complex vitamins. Together these produce exactly the same effect as a two-hour workout at the gym or swimming pool.

"Pumavite is absolutely fantastic and a miracle cure for people like me. It is guaranteed to work and is the best investment I have ever made," says Simon. "I slept my way to fitness!"

Only $799 for a three-month supply Limited supplies – offer ends on March 31st!

Adapted from a website

b Read the magazine article. Put a check (✔) next to the "tricks" that the *Pumavite* ad uses.

How advertisers win our hearts and minds... and get our money

There's no such thing as a free lunch

"Get a free camera when you subscribe to our magazine for two years." There's something about the word "free" that immediately attracts us – something for nothing – I want it! The idea makes us feel clever, as if we got the better of the company. But that camera (which will probably break as soon as you get it out of the box) wasn't a gift at all. In spite of [1]__________, its price was really included in the magazine subscription.

Buy now while supplies last!

"There are only a few left! And after they're sold, there won't be any more available." What happens when we read or hear these words? Even though [2]__________, maybe don't even like them, we immediately want to be among the lucky few who have them. But no manufactured products are ever scarce. Do you really think the manufacturers of that "limited edition" DVD couldn't produce a few more if they thought they could sell them?

Just sign your name here – and give us your address

"Just fill out this form for [3]__________." Do you think companies really want to spend their money on sending you a free brochure? It costs them to produce it and to mail it. In fact, these kinds of ads are really produced so as to [4]__________. From then on, they will bombard you with more direct advertising and probably pass on your name and address to other companies, too.

c Read the article again with the glossary on page 107 and complete it with the phrases below.

A free information
B the actress is holding the product in the photo
C get us to believe it
D get your personal information
E we can't fail to get the message
F demonstrate the amazing effects of their product
G we don't really need the products
H the ad saying it was free

d Look at the eight phrases again, and the highlighted word(s) immediately before them. Which ones express a contrast? Which ones express a purpose?

e p.144 Grammar Bank 7B. Read the rules and do the exercises.

Everybody's doing it

And everybody can't be wrong, so the product must be fantastic. In order to [5] ___________, they use expressions like "It's the new sensation sweeping the country," "People just can't get enough of them," "Record sales," "Unbelievable response!" and combine this with a photograph of a large group of people, so that [6] ___________. But don't be fooled. Even if everybody is doing it (and they may not be), everybody can be wrong.

The camera never lies, or does it?

Ads frequently use "real people" to [7] ___________ on our health or fitness. But of course the person in the ad or TV commercial is a gym-toned model!

Trust me, I'm a doctor (or a celebrity)

If a celebrity is using the product, it must be fantastic. If a doctor recommends it, it must work. The bigger the authority, the more powerful the advertising message is. But be careful. Although [8] ___________, do you really think she colors her hair with it at home? Do the authorities mentioned really exist? "My dog biscuits are recommended by the International Association of Dog Nutritionists" (an organization I started last week). "A recent study found that my lemonade tastes better than any other brand" (my mother liked it better).

Glossary

subscribe pay money regularly in order to receive sth
get the better of to defeat sb / sth or gain an advantage
available that you can buy or get
be scarce there is not much of it
bombard "attack" sb with, e.g., too many questions, too much information
be fooled be tricked

f **Sentence race.** Try to complete all the sentences in two minutes.

1. The customer took the shoes back to the store to …
2. Even though I was really late, my boss …
3. She applied for a job with a company in Miami so that …
4. He got promoted to branch manager despite …
5. Most of the employees don't like the new CEO, although …
6. He left the company he used to work for in order to …
7. Although John was the hardest worker in the company, …
8. In spite of a huge marketing campaign, …
9. I went to our headquarters in New York for …
10. I think the advertising of cigarettes and alcohol should be banned so as not to …

5 SPEAKING

GET IT RIGHT **stress in word families**

- Underline the stressed syllable in this word family. Be careful – the stress is different on one of the words:
  product *production* *producer*

Talk in small groups.

1. Are there any products that you have bought recently …
   a because of the ads?
   b in spite of the ads?
2. Have you bought something recently that wasn't as good as the advertisement made you think?
3. Are there any ads that make you *not* want to ever buy the product? Why do they have this effect on you?
4. Do you think people should be allowed to advertise the following? Why (not)?
   - alcoholic drinks
   - expensive children's toys
   - junk food
   - political parties
5. How successful do you think the following forms of marketing are?
   - cold-calling
   - leaflets / brochures in your mailbox
   - junk e-mails
   - website pop-ups
   - sports sponsorships
6. Think of ads and commercials that use the following to sell a product:
   - a celebrity
   - an authority (e.g., a doctor)
   - a catchy song
   - something free
   - humor
   - a good slogan
   - a story
   - animals or nature
7. Which of the above marketing techniques might influence you to buy the product?

7 C Tingo

G relative clauses
V prefixes
P word stress

1 GRAMMAR relative clauses

a English has borrowed many words and phrases from other languages. In pairs, try to match the words with the languages they come from. Do you use any of these words (or very similar ones) in your language?

1	robot /'roʊbɑt/	☐	A Arabic
2	igloo /'ɪglu/	☐	B Chinese
3	chauffeur /ʃoʊ'fər/	☐	C Czech
4	shampoo /ʃæm'pu/	☐	D French
5	algebra /'ældʒəbrə/	☐	E Hindi
6	tea /ti/	☐	F Inuit
7	macho /'mɑtʃoʊ/	☐	G Italian
8	tycoon /taɪ'kun/	☐	H Japanese
9	graffiti /grə'fiti/	☐	I Spanish
10	yogurt /'yoʊgərt/	☐	J Turkish

b **Check what you know.** Complete definitions 1–6 with *that*, *who*, or *whose* and write the correct word from **a**.

1 ___*tea*___ a drink ___*that*___ is made by pouring hot water over dried leaves
2 ________ a house ________ walls and ceilings are made of hard snow
3 ________ a machine ________ can perform a complicated series of tasks automatically
4 ________ a person ________ is successful in business or industry
5 ________ a person ________ job is to drive a car, especially for somebody rich or important
6 ________ writing or drawings ________ people make on a public wall or building

c What word could you use instead of *who*? Instead of *that*?

d How would you define the other four words in **a**?

Any problems? ➲ **Workbook p.70**

e **New grammar.** Read about the book **THE MEANING OF Tingo** on page 109. Do you have words for any of these concepts in your language?

f Now complete the definitions with *who* (x6), *that* (x4), *whose* (x2), *which* (x1), or *whom* (x1).

g Look at the completed definitions on page 109. Answer the questions below with a partner.

1 Which two sentences contain non-defining relative clauses (ones that add extra information to a sentence)?
2 In which sentences could you change a word to *that*?
3 In which sentences can you leave out the relative pronoun altogether?
4 Look at the definitions for *puntare* and *rujuk*. How does the position of the preposition affect the relative pronoun?

h ➲ **p.144 Grammar Bank 7C.** Read the rules and do the exercises.

i ➲ **Communication** *What's the word? A p.118 B p.120.* Define more foreign words that English has borrowed, and ask your partner to guess what they are.

2 SPEAKING

GET IT RIGHT giving examples

If you want to give examples when you are speaking English, you can use these phrases: *for example*, *for instance*, or *such as*.

English has borrowed many words from other languages, such as "shampoo" and "yogurt."

Work in groups of three or four. Discuss the questions, giving as many examples as you can.

- Which *three* of the words defined on page 109 would you choose to add to your language? Why?
- Think of *five* words or phrases that your language has borrowed from English.
  Have these words been borrowed because there wasn't an existing word for this concept in your language?
  If not, why do you think this word or phrase is being used in your language?
- How do you feel about these borrowed English words?
- Can you think of any words / phrases that have been borrowed from other languages besides English?
- Can you think of *two* English words or phrases that don't have an exact translation in your language? Why do you think that is?
- Do you know of any words in your language that don't have an exact translation in English?
- Do you have any favorite words in English? Why do you like them?

THE MEANING OF Tingo

In this book, Adam Jacot de Boinod, [1]__________ works as a researcher for TV quiz shows, has collected words from all over the world that do not exist in English, but that he thinks perhaps English ought to incorporate into the language. The title of the book comes from one of his favorites. "Tingo," [2]__________ is a word from the language spoken on Easter Island in the Pacific Ocean, means to borrow things from a neighbor's house one by one until there is nothing left!

Bakkushan (Japanese) A woman [3]__________ you think is pretty when you see her from behind but is not when you see her from the front.

Drachenfutter (German) The presents [4]__________ guilty husbands give their wives (literally "dragon's food").

Fucha (Polish) A job [5]__________ you do in your free time without paying any tax.

Lampadato (Italian) An adjective to describe a person [6]__________ skin has been tanned too much by a sun lamp.

Neko neko (Indonesian) To have a creative idea [7]__________ only makes thing worse.

Puntare (Italian) To stare intensely at a person [8]__________ you are attracted to.

Rujuk (Indonesian) To remarry a woman to [9]__________ you had been married before.

Seigneur-terrasse (French) A person [10]__________ spends a lot of time but very little money in a cafe.

Fshes (Albanian) A long mustache [11]__________ looks like a broom.

Aviador (Spanish) A government employee [12]__________ only shows up on payday.

Zechpreller (German) Someone [13]__________ leaves without paying the bill.

Zhengron (Chinese) A person [14]__________ looks have been improved by plastic surgery.

From *The Meaning of Tingo*

3 READING & LISTENING

a Read about the origin of ten English words. Can you guess what any of them are? Use the pictures to help you.

The story behind the words

1 ________ Comes from two Old Norse words (the language spoken by the Vikings) that mean "house" and "owner." The word originally had nothing to do with marital status, except for the fact that home ownership made these men extremely desirable marriage partners.

2 ________ From "cabrioler," a French word that means "jump like a goat." The first carriages for public rental bounced up and down so much that they reminded people of goats jumping on a hillside.

3 ________ From the Italian "To arms!"– which was what soldiers shouted when they saw that the enemy was attacking.

4 ________ Genoa, called "Gene" by sixteenth-century Europeans, was the first city to make denim cloth. The pants were named after the city.

5 ________ In Latin, this means "without your cape." The ancient Romans would often avoid capture by throwing off their capes when fleeing so that they could run more quickly.

6 ________ It is believed that this term originated from a man's last name. The man, whose first name was Patrick, terrorized a section of London with his family in the 1890s.

7 ________ Many banks in post-Renaissance Europe issued small, porcelain "borrower's tiles" to their customers. Like credit cards, these tiles were imprinted with the owner's name and credit limit, and the name of the bank. In order to borrow money, the customer had to present the tile to the bank teller, who would compare the imprinted credit limit with how much the customer had already borrowed. If the borrower was over the limit, the teller broke the tile on the spot.

8 ________ From the Latin, originally meant "placed on the knees." In Ancient Rome, a father legally claimed his newborn child by sitting in front of his family and placing the child on his knee.

9 ________ The popular explanation of the origin of this word is that it is an acronym meaning "To Insure Promptness," that is, to make sure the service in, e.g., a restaurant, is fast. This is incorrect. The word was underworld slang from the early 1600s, meaning "to pass on a small sum of money."

10 ________ This was the Latin name for a slave given to Roman soldiers to reward them for performance in battle. Eventually, this term was applied to anyone who was a slave to anything, e.g., a drug.

Glossary

bounce (paragraph 2) move up and down like a ball

cape (5) a piece of clothing with no sleeves worn around your shoulders

tile (7) flat, square piece, usually of baked clay

acronym (9) a short word that is made using the first letters of a group of words, e.g., PIN = personal identification number

promptness (9) quickness

slang (9) very informal words and expressions

b Now complete 1–10 with the words below. Did you guess any of them?

addict alarm broke (adj = having no money) cab (= taxi)
escape genuine jeans hooligan husband tip

c Read the article again carefully. Underline any words you don't know and try to guess their meaning from the context. Check with your teacher or a dictionary.

d Now cover the article and focus on the words in the list in **b**. In pairs, try to remember the origin of each word.

e 7.7 You're going to listen to a language expert talking on the radio about the origins of the words below.

• ketchup • orange • tennis

1 Which word's origin is related to a legend?
2 Which word changed its form because the original word was hard for the English to say?
3 Which word originated from the way the English pronounced a foreign word?

f Listen again and complete the summaries with one or more words.

Ketchup

The original sauce was invented by [1]__________. *It was made from* [2]__________. *British explorers first tried it in the* [3]__________ *century and really liked it. Later, some* [4]__________ *mixed* [5]__________ *into it, and it became the sauce it is today.*

Orange

This word, and also the word for orange in [6]__________ *and* [7]__________, *doesn't come from* [8]__________; *it comes from ancient Sanskrit. The Sanskrit word, "narangah," may come from "naga ranga," which means* [9]__________. *The story is that an* [10]__________ *once ate so many that he* [11]__________, *and some orange trees grew from his* [12]__________.

Tennis

The sport started in [13]__________. *It was* [14]__________ *called "tenez," which means* [15]__________. *The sport lost* [16]__________ *there and became popular in* [17]__________. *But the "tenez" sounded more like "tennis" when it was said with an* [18]__________.

4 VOCABULARY & PRONUNCIATION
prefixes and word stress

One way of making new words is by adding a prefix at the beginning of a word, e.g., *over-*, *under-*, *mis-*, etc. These prefixes change the meaning of a word. They are usually used without a hyphen but sometimes need one.

a Look at the words in the list. Then match the **bold** prefixes with their meanings.

antisocial **auto**graph **bi**annual **ex**-husband **micro**scopic **mis**spell **mono**syllable **multi**national **over**worked **post**graduate **pre**conceived **re**wind **semi**finals **under**paid

1	after	______	8	many	______
2	again or back	______	9	not enough	______
3	against	______	10	of or by oneself	______
4	badly / wrongly	______	11	one	______
5	before	______	12	small	______
6	former	______	13	too much	______
7	half	______	14	twice	______

⚠ Unlike suffixes (which aren't stressed), prefixes are often stressed, so a word with a prefix may have two stressed syllables, the main stress on the base word and the secondary stress on the prefix, e.g., *antisocial*).

b 7.8 Listen and underline two stressed syllables in each word in **a**.

c Which prefix(es) could you add to the words below to describe ...?

biography circle cooked impressionists sleep understand

1 food that tastes a little bit raw in places
2 when you wake up later than you had planned to
3 the story of someone's life, written by that person
4 the artists who came after Monet, Van Gogh, etc.
5 what happens if you don't understand something correctly
6 the shape of a half moon

d Ask and answer the questions with a partner. Ask for more information.

- Are there any professions that you think are **overpaid**?
- How often do you take **antibiotics**?
- Have you ever asked a celebrity for an **autograph**?
- Do you know any **ex-smokers**?
- Do you know any people who are **bilingual**?
- Are there any English words you sometimes **mispronounce**?
- Who do you think is better at **multitasking**, men or women?
- How often do you buy **precooked** meals?
- When was the last time you **redecorated** your room or apartment?

p.157 Phrasal verbs in context *File 7.*

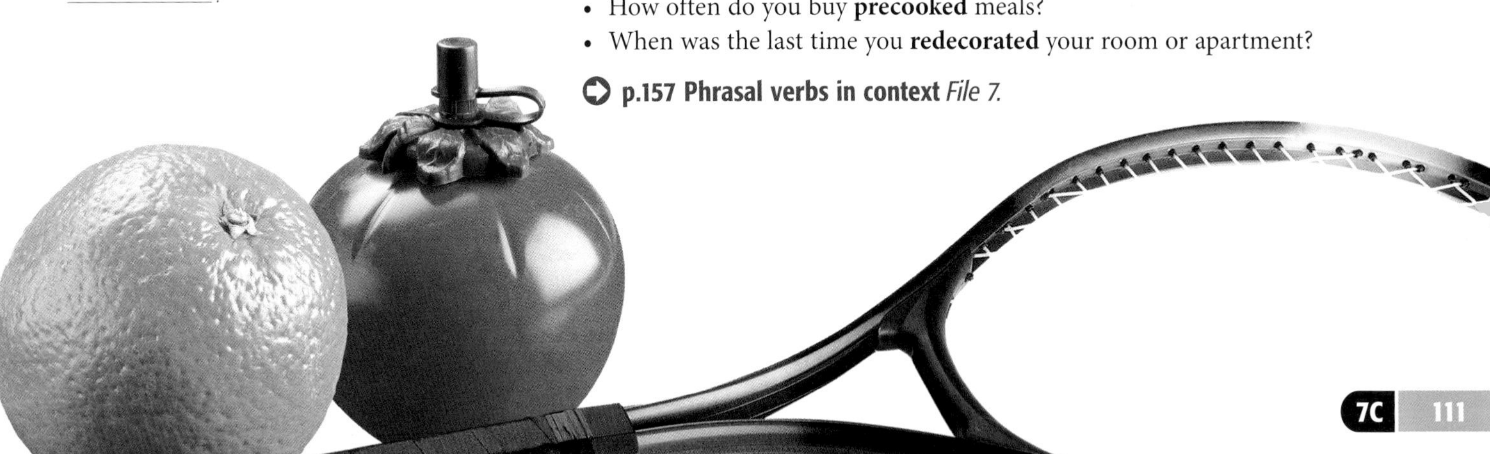

THE INTERVIEW

a You are going to listen to an interview with Jesse Sheidlower, a lexicographer and one of the main editors of the *Oxford English Dictionary*. Before you listen, read the glossary and look at how the words are pronounced to help you understand what he says.

Glossary

coin *v* **(a word or phrase)** /kɔɪn/ to invent (a new word or phrase)

podcasting /ˈpɒdkæstɪŋ/ broadcasting a program for downloading over the Internet

ubiquitous /yuˈbɪkwətəs/ being everywhere at the same time

shift *v* /ʃɪft/ to move or change

on behalf of as another person's representative

appendectomy /ˌæpɛnˈdɛktəmi/ to have the appendix removed surgically

appendicitis /əˌpɛndəˈsaɪtəs/ a swelling of the appendix (a small organ attached to the intestines inside the body)

coronation /ˌkɔrəˈneɪʃn/ a formal ceremony when a crown is first placed on the head of a new king or queen

King Edward VII (1841–1910) King of Great Britain and Ireland from 1901 to 1910

b 7.9 Listen to part 1. Answer the questions with a partner.

1 How many new words go into the *Oxford English Dictionary* each year?
2 Why do some terms go into the dictionary faster than others?
3 Why did *podcasting* enter the dictionary very quickly?
4 What other example does he give of a word that came into the language quickly?

c 7.10 Listen to part 2. Answer the questions with a partner.

What does she say about …?
1 *hang time* and *time-shift*
2 *hawala* and *ki*
3 *appendectomy* and *appendicitis*

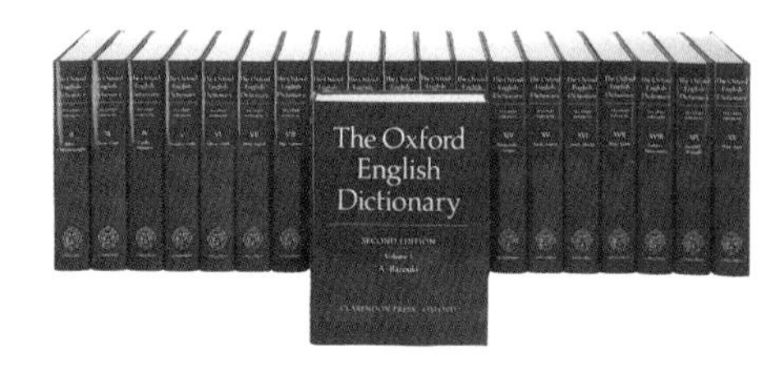

d 7.11 Listen and complete the phrases. What do you think they mean?

COMMON PHRASES

1 There are going to be words that come in very briefly, but no one really _____ _____ to …
2 … this is clearly such a big thing that it has to go in _____ away.
3 There are a _____ _____ different ways that words can be formed in English.
4 And the editor of the OED at _____ _____ actually wrote to a consultant …
5 These are too technical. You can _____ _____ out. pv
6 Well, you don't have these words in. What's _____ _____ you?

e Listen to the interview again with the audioscript on page 131. Can you think of any new words that have come into your language recently?

ON THE STREET

a 7.12 Listen to four speakers talking about English words used in their language. Who is the most positive about using English words? Who is the most negative?

1 Mateusz

2 Victoria

3 Matandra

4 Volke

b Listen again. Who …?
1 says that their own language is dominant in one particular field
2 mentions a language that doesn't use English words for many modern inventions
3 talks about an "English word" that isn't really English
4 mentions two words connected with food

c 7.13 Listen and complete the phrases. What do you think they mean?

COMMON PHRASES

1 It is used, I think, _____.
2 … which actually doesn't _____ sense in English.
3 … everything to _____ with technology … pv
4 Most people just _____ with *downloadare*. pv
5 And if there are new inventions or _____ like that, we don't invent new words.

d Listen to the interview again with the audioscript on page 131. Then answer the same questions with a partner.

Which is better, working for someone else or being your own boss?

More and more people are choosing to give up their jobs and follow their dream of setting up their own company.

Being your own boss has many obvious advantages. 1__________ is that you are in charge. You have the opportunity to do something you really believe in, 2__________ offering a new product or providing a new service. 3__________ is that you do not have a boss watching over you, which gives you more freedom to do things your way. Finally, the greatest advantage of all for some people, you could 4__________ become extremely rich if your company becomes successful.

This all seems very tempting, but 5__________, there are a number of disadvantages. You have to make a lot of big decisions, 6__________, whether to expand, or whether to employ new staff. This is often very stressful. 7__________ you are the boss and in theory can decide what time you finish work, you might find that instead of finishing early, you have to work all night 8__________ an important deadline. Finally, there is an element of risk. If the company fails, you could lose not only your job, but also your home and your life savings.

9__________, owning a business has both advantages and disadvantages. Whether it would be the right move for you or not depends on your skills, your personality, and your family circumstances.

a Complete the composition with linking expressions from the list. Use capital letters where necessary.

also although another advantage because of for example on the other hand such as the main advantage to sum up

b Put the linking expressions in the correct spaces below.

Useful language

To list advantages / disadvantages

____

____

To add more points to the same argument

In addition, ...
Furthermore, ...

____

To introduce an example

For instance, ...

____

____

To make contrasting points

However, ...
In spite of (the fact that) ...

____

____

To give a reason

Because (+ clause) ...
__________ (+ noun) ...

To introduce the conclusion

In conclusion, ...

____

c You are going to write a composition titled *What are the advantages and disadvantages of being famous?*

PLAN the content.

1 Decide what you could say about how people today are interested in famous people or want to be famous themselves. This will give you material for the introduction.
2 List two or three advantages and disadvantages, and number them in order of importance.
3 Decide if you think on balance there are more advantages than disadvantages.

WRITE 120–180 words, organized in four paragraphs: introduction, advantages, disadvantages (or disadvantages and then advantages), and conclusion. Use a formal style (avoid contractions and informal expressions). Use the linking expressions in **Useful language**.

CHECK your report for mistakes (grammar, punctuation, and spelling).

7 What do you remember?

GRAMMAR

a Complete the second sentence so that it means the same as the first.

1 I don't have a car, but I would like one.
I wish ______ ______ a car.

2 Please stop whistling. I'm trying to concentrate.
I wish ______ ______ stop whistling. I'm trying to concentrate.

3 I regret not speaking to her before she left.
I wish I ______ ______ to her before she left.

4 He got a good job, although he didn't have the right skills.
He got a good job, despite ______ ______ the right skills.

5 That's the man for whom I used to work.
That's the man I used ______ ______ ______.

b Choose a, b, or c.

1 I opened the door quietly ______ my father up.
a to not wake
b so that I don't wake
c so as not to wake

2 He still works, ______ he won ten million dollars in the lottery last year.
a in spite of
b despite
c even though

3 That's the house in ______ Shakespeare was born.
a which
b that
c where

4 My aunt Amy, ______ was the CEO of an important company, just retired.
a that
b who
c which

5 That dog follows me ______ I go.
a wherever
b however
c whatever

VOCABULARY

a Circle the right word.

1 That walk was *exhausted / exhausting*. I need a good rest now.
2 I was really *shocked / shocking* when I read the e-mail.
3 This company has 40 *employees / employers*.
4 Do you *do /make* business with many foreign companies?
5 That lawyer must be very successful – he has so many *customers / clients*.

b Complete the missing words.

1 Will the company make a **p**________ this year?
2 The **s**________ for their new advertising campaign is "You'll never find a better one."
3 He works for a **m**________ company with offices in Asia and Europe.
4 We are planning to **l**________ our new product in September.
5 The bank has **br**________ all over the country.

c Complete the sentences with one word.

1 He set ______ a new company that makes software.
2 Our local grocery store was taken ______ by a big supermarket chain.
3 They missed the last bus, so I ended ______ driving them home.
4 There are many different kinds of pasta, such ______ *fettucine*.
5 Many English words come from French, ______ example, *royal*.

d Complete the sentences using the **bold** word and a prefix.

1 This word is very difficult to say. I always ________ it. **pronounce**
2 After I graduate from college, I want to get a ________ degree. **graduate**
3 The city was completely ________ after the war. **built**
4 We are really ________. We can hardly survive on our salary. **paid**
5 The actress wrote her ________ after she retired. **biography**

PRONUNCIATION

a Underline the word with a different sound.

1		amusing	business	whose	misunderstand
2	ar	cart	alarm	scary	market
3	oʊ	profit	logo	though	owner
4	aɪ	client	biannual	irritate	tiring
5	ʌ	company	shocked	money	become

b Underline the stressed syllable.

disappointed record (verb) produce (noun) expand manufacture

What can you do?

CAN YOU UNDERSTAND THIS TEXT?

a Read the article and choose a, b, or c.

1 Over the centuries the Pirahã tribe has ____.
  a not decreased in numbers
  b kept its customs
  c communicated without words

2 Their language is unusual because ____.
  a some concepts don't exist
  b men and women use different vocabulary
  c there is no grammar

3 When the Pirahã women speak together, they ____.
  a can't be understood by men
  b usually whistle to each other
  c sound as if they are just making noises

4 When Everett tried to teach them arithmetic, ____.
  a he quickly gave up
  b he eventually realized it was impossible
  c they didn't want to learn

5 Chomsky's Theory of Universal Grammar maintains that ____.
  a children can learn a language quickly
  b all languages have some rules in common
  c all languages count in the same way

b Look at the highlighted words and phrases. Can you guess what they mean?

A world without time or number

The Pirahã are an isolated Amazonian tribe of hunter-gatherers who live deep in the Brazilian rainforest. The tribe has survived, their culture intact, for centuries, although there are now only around 200 left. The Pirahã, who communicate mainly through hums and whistles, have fascinated ethnologists for years, mainly because they have almost no words for numbers. They use only three words to count: *one*, *two*, and *many*.

We know about the Pirahã thanks to an ex-hippy and former missionary, Dan Everett, now a professor of phonetics, who spent seven years with the tribe in the 1970s and 1980s. Everett discovered a world without numbers, without time, without words for colors, without subordinate clauses, and without a past tense. Their language, he found, was not just simple grammatically; it was restricted in its range of sounds and differed between the sexes. For the men, it has just eight consonants and three vowels; for the women, who have the smallest number of speech sounds in the world, only seven consonants and three vowels. To the untrained ear, the language sounds more like humming than speech. The Pirahã can also whistle their language, which is how men communicate when hunting.

Their culture is similarly constrained. The Pirahã can't write, have little collective memory, and no concept of decorative art. In 1980 Everett tried to teach them to count: he explained basic arithmetic to an enthusiastic group eager to learn the skills needed to trade with other tribes. After eight months, not one could count to ten; even one plus one was beyond them. The experiment seemed to confirm Everett's theory: the tribe just couldn't understand the concept of number.

The Pirahã's inability to count is important because it seems to disprove linguist Noam Chomsky's influential Theory of Universal Grammar, which holds that the human mind has a natural capacity for language, and that all languages share a basic rule structure, which enables children to understand abstract concepts such as number. One of Chomsky's collaborators has recently gone on an expedition with Everett to study the tribe. We do not yet know if the Pirahã have persuaded him to change his theory.

CAN YOU UNDERSTAND THESE PEOPLE?

a 7.14 Listen and circle the correct answer, a, b, or c.

1 What does the woman find irritating?
  a The man never does the dishes.
  b The man leaves dirty dishes on the table.
  c The man eats so slowly.

2 Why does the man regret not going to college?
  a He would have been able to get a more interesting job.
  b He would be earning much more money.
  c He would have enjoyed the experience.

3 Everybody who buys the fitness program ______.
  a can work out with a personal trainer
  b gets a free set of weights
  c can consult a trainer if necessary

4 How much profit did the company make this year?
  a 132 billion dollars.
  b 43 billion yen.
  c 1.2 billion dollars.

5 What is the woman's new boss like?
  a She's rather arrogant.
  b She's very friendly.
  c She makes people feel inferior.

b 7.15 You will hear part of a radio program about a book called *The Professor and the Madman*. Listen and answer the questions.

1 What is the book's subtitle?
2 Who was W. C. Minor?
3 What did he help create?
4 What happened when Murray, the editor, went to meet him?
5 What crime had Minor committed?

CAN YOU SAY THIS IN ENGLISH?

Can you ...?

- ☐ describe things that irritate you and that you would like people to stop doing, using *I wish*
- ☐ talk about things you regret in life
- ☐ talk about advertisements you like or dislike and explain whether they make you want to buy the products
- ☐ talk about foreign words that are used in your language and how you feel about them

1B You're psychic, aren't you? **Student A**

a Imagine you're a psychic. Make guesses and complete the sentences below about B.

1 Your favorite color is ________, ...?
2 You really like ________, (a sport or hobby) ...?
3 You went to ________ last weekend, ...?
4 You haven't been to ________ (a country), ...?
5 You were born in ________ (place), ...?
6 You'd like to be able to ________, ...?
7 You can't ________ very well, ...?
8 You're very good at ________, ...?

b Check if your guesses are true, by saying the sentences to B and checking with a tag question, e.g., *Your favorite color is pink, isn't it?* Try to use a falling intonation.

c Now B will check his / her guesses about you. Respond with a short answer. If the guess is wrong, tell B the real answer.

d Count your correct guesses. Who was the better psychic?

1C You're the doc! **Students A + B**

Check your answers.

1 *c* The correct treatment is to pinch the soft part of the nose. This will usually stop a nosebleed if you do it for five minutes. If not, repeat for ten minutes, and if that still doesn't work, go to your nearest hospital.

2 *a* The correct treatment is first to pour cold water on the burn for at least ten minutes and then to cover it with a loose bandage. If you don't have a bandage, you can use a clean plastic bag or plastic wrap. Do not break blisters and don't put any sunscreen or other cream on the burn.

2A Clothes quiz **Student A**

a Ask B the questions (the answers are in *italics*).

1 What's the opposite of ...?
- These pants are too tight. (*These pants are too loose.*)
- trendy clothes (*old-fashioned clothes*)
- get dressed (*get undressed*)

2 What material are the following usually made of?
- a sweater (*wool*)
- cycling shorts (*spandex*)
- a tie (*silk*)

3 What does it mean if you say "These shoes don't fit me"? (*They're too big or too small.*)

4 When do people usually ...?
- try clothes on (*in a store before they buy them*)
- get dressed up (*for a party, a wedding, etc.*)

5 What does it mean if you say "Paula's dressed to kill tonight"? (*People will admire her because of her clothes.*)

b Answer B's questions.

2B Flight stories **Student A**

a You're going to read a newspaper article and then tell your partner about it. Read the article and write down ten words that will help you remember the story.

Lovesick violinist grounds plane

Nuala Ni Chanainn, an Irish violinist, had been traveling around San Francisco as part of a theater group. When the tour was over, she went to the airport and boarded the plane that would take her back home to Ireland. She was in her seat, waiting for the plane to take off, when she suddenly decided not to go after all. She rushed off the plane at the last minute, leaving airline officials thinking that perhaps she had planted a bomb on the plane and escaped. The plane and all the luggage were thoroughly searched by a bomb-sniffing dog. Meanwhile, the airport authorities stopped Nuala and took her away to be questioned. However, after extensive questioning, she managed to convince them that she hadn't planted a bomb: she simply couldn't bear to leave her new boyfriend! The plane was allowed to depart nearly four hours later, minus the love-struck violinist, who then spent another two weeks in the US with the boyfriend.

b Close your book and tell B your story in your own words, e.g., *There was a woman named Nuala who was a violinist from Ireland ...*

c Now listen to B's story, and ask your partner to clarify or rephrase if there's anything you don't understand.

2C Reading habits **Students A + B**

a Answer the questions in the reading questionnaire below with a partner.

b How similar are your reading habits?

The press	Books	Online
national newspapers	novels	web pages
local papers	classics	blogs
sports publications	short stories	chat rooms and forums
magazines	nonfiction, e.g., biographies, history	academic / work-related texts
comics	textbooks	news websites
academic journals	manuals	song lyrics

The reading questionnaire

General reading

Which of the above do you read? How often?
Do you ever read any of them in English?
Do you read anything specifically to improve your English?
Do you enjoy reading on screen?
Do you read more or less than you used to?

If you read books ...

What was the last book you read?
Why did you choose to read it?
What are you reading now?
Do you have a favorite author or authors?
What's the best book you've read recently?

If you don't read books ...

Why don't you read books?
If you had more time, would you read more?
Did you use to read books when you were younger?
What's your favorite way to relax?

3A There's only one place burglars won't look... **Students A + B**

Read and check your answers.

Fifty professional burglars described their working methods to researchers who visited them in jail. Their research revealed:

1 **b** An experienced burglar searches a house in 20 minutes and usually takes $3,000 worth of goods.

2 **a** Favorite items to steal are expensive goods that are fairly easy to transport, including digital cameras and flat screen TVs.

3 **a** The criminals unanimously considered a barking dog more of a deterrent than a burglar alarm.

4 **a**, **b**, **d** However, ten of the fifty burglars said they actually preferred homes to be occupied, as there was less risk of being disturbed by returning residents.

5 **b** The burglars' favorite method was dismantling windows or patio doors.

6 Burglars search rooms in this order: **1** the main bedroom, **2** the living room, **3** the dining room, **4** the office, **5** the kitchen, **6** a child's bedroom.

So if you want a tip from the professionals, hide your jewelry in the children's bedroom and leave the dog at home when you go out!

4B Argument! **Student A**

Read the situations and role-play the arguments.

1 It's your birthday today. Your spouse (B) had promised to come home early so that you could go out for dinner. You have been dropping hints for the past month about what you really want for your birthday as your spouse is usually very unimaginative about choosing presents. Last year for your birthday, your spouse bought you some DVDs, which you didn't particularly like. He / She arrives home late, and produces a box of chocolates (you're on a diet, and he / she knows this), which looks as if it came from a drugstore.

You start. B has just given you the chocolates.

2 You're in your first year of college, studying engineering. You haven't enjoyed it at all and have just failed all your final exams. In fact, you never really wanted to study engineering, but your parents are both engineers, and you feel they pushed you into it. You would like to change your major and study journalism, which you think would be a better fit. You want to try to convince your mother / father, although you know they're not very pleased with your final exam results.

B will start.

Communication

4C Two paintings **Student A**

The Hotel Lobby (1943) Edward Hopper

a Look carefully at your painting. Then describe it in detail to B, focusing especially on the people and their body language. Say who you think they are and what you think they're doing.

b Show your picture to B and see if he / she agrees with you.

c Listen to B describe another painting. Try to visualize it.

d B will now show you the picture to see if you agree with his / her description and interpretation.

5B Sleep **Students A + B**

Read the results of the questionnaire and calculate your score. The higher your score, the more sleep deprived you are. The maximum is 14.

1 a 0	b 1		
2 a 1	b 0	c 0	
3 a 1	b 0	c 0	
4 a 0	b 1	c 2	
5 a 0	b 1	c 2	d 2
6 a 0	b 1	c 2	
7 a 0	b 1	c 0	d 1

8 1 point for each one you circle

6C How much do you know about science? **Students A + B**

Check your answers to the quiz.

1 c	4 b
2 a	5 a
3 c	6 a

6C Are you a creative thinker? **Students A + B**

Check your answers to the test.

Are you a creative thinker?

1 The more times you circled false, the more creative you are and the higher your "eureka potential".

2 The vast majority of people choose either 35 or 37. However, truly creative people usually come up with a different number, e.g., 17 or 31.

3 The more boxes you were able to fill, the more creative you are. The following are some of the more creative ideas that people have come up with:

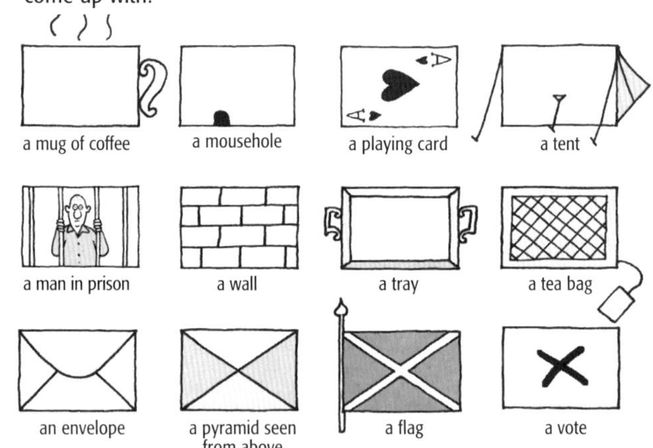

4 The important question concerns how you represented the number 4. In Roman numerals the number 4 is always represented as "IV." However, on almost all clocks and watches with Roman numerals, except for Big Ben in London, the number is represented as "IIII." If you filled it in as "IV," that means that, although you have probably seen clocks and watches with Roman numerals hundreds of times, you have not really seen or remembered what is right in front of your eyes.

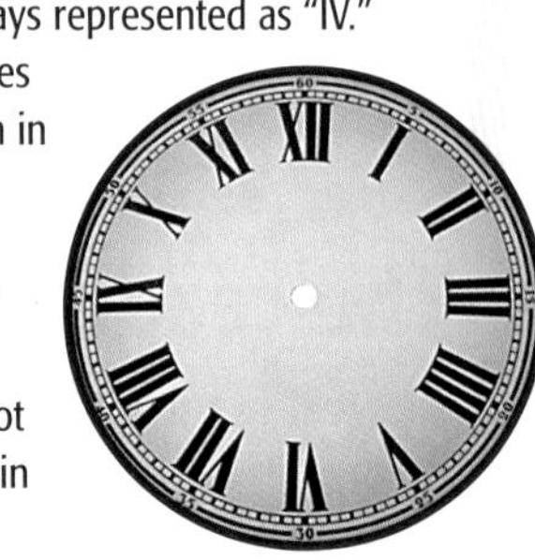

7C What's the word? **Student A**

a Check that you know what your list of words below mean. Then define them to B, saying which language they come from.

1 **caravan** /ˈkærəvæn/ (Persian)
2 **blanket** /ˈblæŋkət/ (French)
3 **embarrassed** /ɪmˈbærəst/ (French)
4 **tsunami** /tsuˈnɑmi/ (Japanese)
5 **soprano** /səˈprænoʊ/ (Italian)
6 **massage** /məˈsɑʒ/ (Arabic)
7 **mosquito** /məˈskitoʊ/ (Spanish)
8 **fog** /fɔg/ (Danish)

b Listen to **B's** definitions and say what the word is.

c Has your language "borrowed" any of these words?

1B You're psychic, aren't you? **Student B**

a Imagine you're a psychic. Make guesses and complete the sentences below about A.

1 You're going to ________ tonight, ...?
2 You don't like ________, (a kind of music) ...?
3 You've seen ________ (a movie), ...?
4 You didn't ________ last night, ...?
5 You were born in ________ (month), ...?
6 You wouldn't like to be a / an ________ (a job), ...?
7 Your favorite season is ________, ...?
8 You can speak ________, ...?

b A is going to make some guesses about you. Respond with a short answer. If the guess is wrong, tell A the real answer.

c Now check if your guesses about A are true by saying the sentences and checking with a tag question, e.g., *You're going to see a movie tonight, aren't you?* Try to use a falling intonation.

d Count your correct guesses. Who was the better psychic?

2A Clothes quiz **Student B**

a Answer A's questions.

b Ask B the questions (the answers are in *italics*).

1 What's the opposite of ...?
   - He looks stylish. (*He looks scruffy.*)
   - a short-sleeved T-shirt (*a long-sleeved T-shirt*)
   - put your shoes on (*take your shoes off*)
2 What material are the following usually made of?
   - stockings (*nylon*)
   - shoes (*leather*)
   - jeans (*denim*)
3 What does it mean if you say "Those shorts aren't very flattering on you"? (*They don't look good on you.*)
4 When do people usually ...?
   - hang clothes up (*after they iron them or after they take them off, e.g., in the evening*)
   - change clothes (*to go to the gym, when they get home from work*)
5 What does it mean if you say "Please keep our conversation under your hat"? (*Don't tell anyone about our conversation.*)

2B Flight stories **Student B**

a You're going to read a newspaper article and then tell your partner about it. Read the article and write down ten words that will help you remember the story.

Tourist stranded at airport for five months

When student Sheridan Gregorio arrived at Fortaleza airport in Brazil, he was planning to fly home to Holland. He had had a great vacation, but unfortunately he had spent all his money. All he had was his airline ticket back to Amsterdam. But when he checked in, the airline employees at the airport told him that he would have to pay airport tax before he could leave the country. Even though Sheridan explained that he was completely broke, he wasn't allowed to fly, so he missed his flight home. His ticket was nonrefundable, so now he needed to buy a new ticket *and* pay the airport tax.

Since he had no money, Sheridan's only option was to sleep in the airport and work in restaurants in exchange for food and some money. After working for five months, he had saved enough for the airport tax, and the Brazilian police persuaded the airline to let him use his old ticket to go home. Sheridan told a reporter from the Brazilian news program *Jornal da Globo*, "The Brazilian people were really nice to me, they treated me very well." Sheridan finally arrived home safe and sound last week.

b Listen to A's story, and ask your partner to clarify or rephrase if there's anything you don't understand.

c Close your book and tell A your story in your own words, e.g., *There was a Dutch tourist who was on vacation in Brazil ...*

Communication

4B Argument! **Student B**

Read the situations and role-play the arguments.

1 It's your spouse's birthday today. You know that he / she wants a specific present, but you have been very busy at work and haven't had time to go shopping. You had intended to finish work early and go shopping today, but you couldn't, so you stopped at a drugstore on the way home and bought some chocolates that you know he / she usually likes.

A is your partner. He / She will start.

2 Your son / daughter is in his / her first year of college studying engineering. You yourself are an engineer, and you really encouraged your child to follow in your footsteps. He / She was good at math in school, and you think he / she would make an excellent engineer. He / She was interested in studying journalism, but you think that this is a "lazy option" and that it's very difficult to get a good job in journalism nowadays. So you were very relieved when he / she agreed to study engineering. Although he / she worked hard in high school, this year in college he / she seems to go out with friends all the time and spends a lot less time studying than you did at the same age. You have just discovered that he / she failed all the final exams.

You start.

4C Two paintings **Student B**

Nighthawks (1942) Edward Hopper Photography © The Art Institute of Chicago

a Look carefully at your painting, which you're going to describe to **A**.

b Listen to **A** describe another painting. Try to visualize it. **A** will now show you the picture to see if you agree with his / her description and interpretation.

c Now describe your painting to **A**. Focus especially on the people and their body language. Say who you think they are and what you think they're doing.

d Show your picture to **A** and see if he / she agrees with you.

7C What's the word? **Student B**

a Check that you know what your list of words below mean. You're going to define them to **A**.

1 **bungalow** /ˈbʌŋgəloʊ/ (Hindi)
2 **monsoon** /ˌmɑnˈsun/ (Arabic)
3 **lottery** /ˈlɑtəri/ (Dutch)
4 **poodle** /ˈpudl/ (German)
5 **bonsai** /ˈbɑnsaɪ/ (Japanese)
6 **parasol** /ˈpærəsɔl/ (Italian)
7 **kidnap** /ˈkɪdnæp/ (Danish)
8 **iceberg** /ˈaɪsbərg/ (Dutch)

b Listen to **A's** definitions and say what each word is.

c Now define your words to **A**, saying which language they come from.

d Has your language "borrowed" any of these words?

Audioscripts

1.3 **Interviewer** … and Emily and Alex are here with me. Emily, what kind of questions did you ask?
Emily Well, the organizers of the event suggested a list of topics, you know, sort of pre-prepared questions, but I thought that they were very… um… artificial, you know, strange. So I asked fairly common questions like, "Why did you come tonight?" or… um… "Have you tried speed dating before?" or "What do you like doing in your free time?" I found that the conversation ran more smoothly when I asked people these kinds of everyday questions.
Interviewer How about you, Alex?
Alex Yes, same as Emily, really. I also asked typical questions like, "What do you do? Have you ever done this before? Do you enjoy living in this city?" Things like that.
Interviewer Did other people ask *you* interesting questions?
Alex Yeah, some were pretty interesting. The ones I can remember are, "If you were an animal, what would you be?" Or, "If you had to choose a different career from the one you have now, what would it be?" One woman even said, "I heard that you were in prison once – is that true?" I don't know where she got that from!
Interviewer And you, Emily? Were you asked anything unusual?
Emily Not really! The most common question was "Where are you from?" The second most common was, "Why do you live in this city?" Although one person did ask me, "If you could be invisible for a day, what would you do?"
Interviewer How did you answer that?
Emily I said I'd go to work and play tricks on my coworkers in the office, like hiding things!
Interviewer How many matches did you get?
Emily I chose six men that I thought I would like to see again, and of those six, four of them chose me too, so I got four matches.
Alex I got three.
Interviewer Did you go out with any of the people?
Emily Yes, I went on one date with a guy who teaches at a university. It was kind of a disaster though, because earlier that morning I'd been to the dentist, and I'd had an injection. So, by the time that we met for coffee, I had a terrible toothache and I was in agony. I had to go home after half an hour. We've exchanged a few e-mails since then, but we haven't managed to meet. We're both very busy. Also, to be honest, I don't think he's really my type. He seems to be really anxious to get married and have children right away, and I'm not.
Interviewer What about the other three matches?
Emily The second man contacted me right after the event and invited me to dinner. But then he sent me a text message the next day and canceled. He said that he had met someone else. The other two have been in touch, but we haven't been able to meet yet. But, in fact, I've decided that, for now, I'm actually happy being single. So, I don't think I'll be speed dating again any time soon.
Interviewer How about you, Alex?
Alex I e-mailed one of the matches, a woman I really liked, and we met in a cafe. At the speed dating event, she seemed really bubbly and fun. But after spending a few minutes with her at the cafe, I realized that we had *nothing* in common. The atmosphere was awful, and it became very awkward. I think she felt the same way, so we just finished our coffees and left. We didn't contact each other again.
Then I arranged to meet another one of my matches. We really got along well at the speed dating, so I was excited about meeting her. Unfortunately, that morning I found out that I'd lost my job, and I was really worried that I wouldn't make a good impression. After all, I was feeling really unhappy about my work situation. But Susanna made me forget everything in no time, and we had a great evening. Then we got together the next day and went for a long walk. And, well, to make a long story short, six months later I proposed, and two months ago we got married!
Emily Aaaah!
Interviewer So it was a real success story for you then?
Alex Absolutely!

1.6 **Jane** When I arrived, I was shown into Sally's office – which was much more normal than I'd expected. Sally looks like a kind and sincere woman. She says that she inherited from her grandmother the ability to "see" the past and future of other people. First, she asked me a few basic questions – was I married, did I have children, and so on. However, her next questions surprised me…
Sally Who's Caroline?
Jane I don't know. I don't know anybody named Caroline.
Sally Well, somebody named Caroline is going to have a powerful and positive effect on your finances… Australia is very important in your life.
Jane It is? I've never been to Australia.
Sally Well, you'll be going there very soon.

1.7 **Sally** Another place that's very important in your life is Ireland.
Jane Yes, that's true. Ireland *does* play a big role in my life. In fact, I grew up there.
Sally Ireland is a place where you will find answers to a lot of your problems. Look for the Irish connection. I'm very, very optimistic that an Irish man is going to be "the one for you."
Jane Ah, very interesting! What does he look like?
Sally He's very tall.
Jane That's good – I'm five-foot-ten myself.
Sally And he's highly intelligent. In fact, it's his brain that will really attract you to him. He's a distinguished public figure – maybe a professor?
Jane So, when am I going to meet him?
Sally Actually, you already know him. You just don't think of him in that way.
Jane I immediately started thinking about all the people I know, but, to be honest, I couldn't think of anyone who fit the description.

1.8 **Jane** I decided to ask Sally some questions myself.
Jane What about my health?
Sally Let's see, your mother suffers from headaches, doesn't she?
Jane Yes, she does, as a matter of fact. She gets bad headaches.
Sally Well, you'll need to watch out for headaches, and so will your mother, because hers are going to get worse. But in general, you're a healthy woman, and you'll have a long life without any major illnesses… but you must *never* be tempted to have plastic surgery – if you do, it will go horribly wrong.
Jane So far it was all very positive, but I wasn't really convinced. It was only when she started talking about my children that I really started listening.
Sally Your son, Conor, is a lot like you. He's good with language, and he may end up working with words, maybe a poet or a songwriter.
Jane In fact, he *does* like words and writing, and last week he won a poetry prize at school.
Sally But your daughter, Clara, is more like your ex-husband. She's not good with words at all.
Jane It's true! They're both dyslexic.
This was beginning to make me wonder…

1.9 **Jane** I left Sally's office feeling very positive. She gave me a recording of our conversation on a CD because she said I needed to listen to everything she had told me a few times. When I got home, I put on the CD. When I listened again, I realized that for each thing that Sally got right, she got several things wrong. I came to the conclusion then that Sally *doesn't* have any paranormal abilities. She is just very good at judging people's character and makes good guesses about their lives from the information she gets from them. But strangely enough, I've recently started seeing a lot more of an old friend of mine who is a professor. He's not Irish, but he just invited me to join him on a lecture tour… of Australia.

1.15 When I saw the lady's face, I knew it was really serious. Her face was starting to turn blue. I put my arms around her waist, and I pulled hard in and up three times, and the piece of steak came out. Then I just put my arm around the lady and gave her a hug. I knew exactly what to do because before I started to work as a television presenter, I used to be a flight attendant. We were taught a lot about first aid. The technique I used is called the Heimlich maneuver, and it's what you should do when someone is choking. I must admit I was a little bit embarrassed by all the attention I got in the restaurant, and then the next day the story was in all the newspapers. But I'm very glad I was there to help. And maybe this story will make people think about learning first aid. I really think it's something that should be taught in school. It's so important!

1.16 I knew I was hurting Peter, but I kept on pushing my fingers down his throat. I managed to touch the tomato with two of my fingers and I was able to move it a little. That was enough – Peter started coughing, and the tomato came out.
But I was very lucky. Afterwards, I found out that my ignorance of first aid had nearly killed my son! Hitting Peter on the back was OK, but putting my fingers down his throat was a big mistake. I could have pushed the tomato even further down his throat, and he could have died. I made every mistake possible and nearly killed him because of my ignorance. I should have called 9-1-1 right away because I don't know first aid, and the emergency operator would have told me exactly what to do… and what *not* to do.

1.18 **Interviewer** Joyce Levine is an astrologer and author of books on astrology. What does an astrologer do?
Joyce What an astrologer does is give people a better understanding of themselves – why they are the way they are and what they can do with that in life.
Interviewer What kind of knowledge does an astrologer need to have?
Joyce There's really a wide body of knowledge that you have to learn to… to be able to interpret what the planets mean. So you have to know the meanings of the planets in terms of how they affect human nature.
Interviewer And what skills do you have to have?
Joyce One, you have to be good with people. When a person walks in my door, I've never seen them before and in two hours I'm going to tell them very personal things about themselves. So I have to be able to establish a rapport, I have to be not intimidating, because some of the… some of the information that I give them may be hard to listen to. And so you need a sense of compassion, you need counseling skills. And if you're going to be self-employed, you need business skills.
Interviewer What do you do when somebody comes to see you?
Joyce Before I see someone, I calculate their chart, which is based on their date, their time, and their place of birth. And then when they come in for an appointment, what we do is basically go over what that means.
Interviewer What can a birth chart or horoscope tell you about a person?
Joyce A person's chart shows their temperament, their personality, their character, their family background, how they're likely to work or spend money, the kind of people they are attracted to in life, what their relationships are like and, you know, what their aspirations are.
Interviewer Can a person's chart predict their future?
Joyce Within a range, yes. Life is cycles, and those cycles are predictable. And there's an intersection between fate and free will. So your chart is what you're like. Now, you have a range of possibilities – you can be the best of yourself or the worst

of yourself. The cycles themselves are basically predictable and then human beings have a choice in terms of what they do with them.

1.19 **Interviewer** Why do people usually come to see you?

Joyce Typically, the first time someone comes in they have some kind of problem or they've hit some kind of obstacle. People don't usually come in the first time because they're happy or they're curious. They've either lost a job or they want to make a change and they're not sure what to do. Or they're having some kind of relationship difficulty and they want to understand what's going on in their life, how they got there and basically what they can do about it.

Interviewer What kind of people come to see you?

Joyce The clients I have really are a wide range of people. On one hand, you know, I work... I work with individuals, I work with couples, I work with families, and I work with businesses. And so a mother might call me because a baby was just born and she wants to have the baby's chart done. For relationship consultations, a couple might come in and say, you know, "We're having difficulties." And I can work with businesses, you know – Are you more likely to make money this year? Are there going to be... Will you have problems with employees? When's a good time for hiring?...

Interviewer If you saw on someone's chart something bad about their future, would you tell them?

Joyce If I saw something that could be a serious problem, I would tell someone, but I would tell them in such a way, ideally, that is not going to particularly frighten them. So I would say, you know, "Maybe, given your cycles, this is probably a good time for a checkup. You know, you want to make sure that your health is OK." Or... "There could be some health problems in the family, you know. You might want to spend more time with your mother," or something like that. Ideally, I wouldn't scare them, but they'd get the message

Interviewer Do you ever look at your own future?

Joyce Of course, you can't help it! It's... I mean, I always know where the planets are, and so I always know what's affecting me.

1.21 **Interviewer** What's your star sign?

Duey My star sign is Aquarius.

Interviewer Do you ever read your horoscope?

Duey I do, actually. I start most of my mornings with my horoscope surprisingly.

Interviewer Do you think someone's star sign has an influence on their personality?

Duey I think it's what you read into it. I mean, it's fun stuff, so it's entertaining. I don't think you should take it too seriously.

Interviewer What's your star sign?

Dennis My what?

Interviewer Your star sign.

Dennis Leo.

Interviewer Do you ever read your horoscope?

Dennis I do every once in a while, but I don't really like to listen to what it says 'cause it's usually crazy.

Interviewer Do you think someone's star sign has an influence on their personality?

Dennis Um, maybe. If that's something they grow up reading a lot, I might... I think it might kind of influence you if... if you read it and maybe that would influence you by reading it often, so...

Interviewer What's your star sign?

Fern Sagittarius.

Interviewer Do you ever read your horoscope?

Fern No, hardly.

Interviewer Do you think someone's star sign has an influence on their personality?

Fern Um, I guess it might do. But I would say probably where you grow up and the people you talk to have a bigger influence on how you turn out.

Interviewer What's your star sign?

Curt Um, I'm a Cancer – the moody emotional sign.

Interviewer Do you ever read your horoscope?

Curt Once in a while, uh, not too often... If I'm flipping through a magazine and it has them, I'll read it, but, you know, I don't go out of my way every day to find my horoscope and read it, no.

Interviewer Do you think someone's star sign has an influence on their personality?

Curt Yeah, I do. Uh... Yeah, I don't necessarily want to admit that, but yeah, I do.

Interviewer What is your star sign?

Tiffany I'm a Taurus.

Interviewer Do you ever read your horoscope?

Tiffany No, I don't ever read my horoscope because I once took a course in psychology and, um, we kind of got a little bit of insight into how horoscopes are developed and how generalizable they are to different people. So often you read them and they do apply. However, they might apply to several other people as well.

Interviewer Do you think someone's star sign has any influence on their personality?

Tiffany Um... From things that I've read about astrology, a lot of times you can find things that, you know, relate to people's, like, personality characteristics that relate to their sign. However, I personally think, again, it's more like a generalizable sort of thing.

2.1

1 I'd say we're a down-to-earth people, friendly and hospitable. We believe in working hard, but we really enjoy our leisure time, when we usually socialize around a barbie – a barbecue, that is – or sport, and this is where we make our friends. Men talk about having a mate, like a buddy or friend, and you stand by your mates no matter what. We're also known for being extremely outgoing and having a good sense of humor. We treat others as equals, irrespective of their profession or standing in society. On the other hand, we tend to "knock down tall poppies." That means we criticize people who try to stand out from the crowd, by distinguishing themselves through money, intellect, or skill. In some ways, I suppose I *am* typical – I'm down-to-earth and friendly, but I'm not as outgoing as others are perceived to be.

2 I think overall we're strong individualists. We like making our own decisions and dislike being controlled by someone else, whether it's the government or a boss. I think individualism is a good quality because it encourages self-expression and often leads to success in life... We're also very hardworking. People here want to provide for their families, but work is also valued for its own sake. Even the rich like to work! We're also very optimistic; we think that if we work hard, we can achieve anything. On the negative side, I think we're a little bit too materialistic. Some of us are overly concerned with having "things" – possessions, I mean. Personally, I think I've inherited the typical optimism and drive, and I'm also an individualist because I don't always follow the crowd, so I think I'm probably fairly typical, but I hope I'm not as materialistic as some of my countrymen seem to be.

3 It's difficult to generalize about us as a people, especially as our big cities now have such a multiethnic population, but I would say that we're basically very tolerant and open-minded. We're not nearly as insular as we used to be. We defend the things that we believe in – when we have to – and we avoid taking extreme positions, which I think is another strength. One of our main weaknesses, though, is that we can be quite self-satisfied and arrogant towards foreigners. Just think of our inability, or our unwillingness, to learn foreign languages! I'd also say that we can be lazy, and we're a bit careless about the way we dress, and also we drink too much. I don't think I'm very typical, though I do definitely have one of the weaknesses – but I'm not going to say which!

4 People in this country are thought of as very polite, nice, and friendly, and we think of ourselves that way, too. Also, we're extremely tolerant people. It's a very multicultural society here, so we try to accept everyone's culture and welcome their customs, their food, their traditions. And, of course, we're a great hockey-loving nation! On the negative side, maybe we're a little too reserved. Even though we're thought of as polite and friendly, we're physically reserved, compared to other cultures that might have more touching or hugging or kissing. We save that for people we're close with. We keep a bigger space around ourselves and don't touch people unless we know them very well, and that can be seen as a little cold... Maybe it's because our weather is so cold! I think I'm pretty typical; I like to think of myself as polite and friendly and helpful, and yes, maybe a little reserved. But I can't say that I'm a hockey lover!

2.6 **Interviewer** With me in the studio today are two pilots, Richard and Steven, who are going to answer some of the most frequently asked questions about flying and air travel. Welcome to both of you.

Pilots Thank you... Nice to be here.

Interviewer Now, the first question is: what weather conditions are the most dangerous when flying a plane?

Steven Probably the most dangerous weather conditions are when the wind changes direction very suddenly. This tends to happen during thunderstorms and typhoons, and it's especially dangerous during takeoff and landing. But it's rather unusual – I've been flying for 37 years now, and I've only experienced this three or four times.

Interviewer Is all turbulence dangerous?

Steven No, in fact, it's not usually dangerous. Pilots know when to expect turbulence, and we try to avoid it by changing routes or flight levels.

Interviewer Which is more dangerous, takeoff or landing?

Richard Both takeoff and landing can be dangerous. They're the most critical moments of a flight. Pilots talk about the "critical eight minutes" – the three minutes after takeoff and the five minutes before landing. Most accidents happen in this period.

Steven I would say takeoff is probably slightly more dangerous than landing. There is a critical moment just before takeoff when the plane is accelerating, but it hasn't yet reached the speed to be able to fly. If the pilot has a problem with the plane at this point, he has very little time – maybe only a second – to abort the takeoff.

Richard That's true.

Interviewer Passengers often think that putting on seat belts in a plane is really a waste of time. Is that true?

Richard Not at all. When the plane is moving on the ground, and the pilot suddenly puts the brakes on, passengers can be thrown out of their seats, just like in a car. But more importantly, during the flight, if there is sudden and severe turbulence, you could be thrown all over the cabin if you aren't wearing your seat belt. That's why airlines usually recommend you wear your belt even when the seat belt light is off.

Interviewer Do we really need to listen to the safety information?

Steven It's definitely worth listening to the information about emergency exits. If there's a fire on a plane, it may be dark and the plane will be full of smoke and fumes. So listening to where the exits are and knowing which one is the nearest exit to you might save your life. Most airline crew members can even tell you where the emergency exits are in the hotels where they stay.

Interviewer What about life jackets?

Richard Fortunately, planes very rarely have to land in water but, to be honest, the chances of surviving if your plane did crash into the ocean are not high.

Interviewer Are some airports more dangerous than others?

Steven Yes, some are – particularly airports with high mountains around them and airports in countries with older or more basic navigation equipment.

Richard For some difficult airports like, let's say Kathmandu, they only allow very experienced pilots to land there. And for some of these airports pilots have to practice on a simulator first before they are given permission to land a plane there.

Interviewer How important is it for pilots and air-traffic controllers to speak good clear English?

Steven It's the official language of the air, so obviously it's crucial for pilots and air-traffic controllers to speak good English. To be honest, it doesn't always happen.
Richard And besides people's English not being good, some countries don't respect the convention and don't force their pilots to speak in English. But most of them do, fortunately.

2.7 **Interviewer** Have you ever had a problem with a famous person as a passenger?
Richard I've carried a lot of famous people, and they are usually very well behaved. But I remember once I had the actor Steven Seagal as a passenger – and the cabin crew told me that he had just gotten on board, and he was carrying an enormous samurai sword. Weapons aren't allowed on board, of course, so I had to go and speak to him. He looked very imposing standing in the cabin. He was about six and a half feet tall, dressed completely in black, carrying a sword, and he is – as you probably know – a martial arts expert. But, in fact, he was perfectly willing to give us the sword, which was gold and had been given to him as a present in Bali.
Interviewer What's your most frightening experience as a pilot?
Steven Crossing the street outside the airport terminal! That's certainly the most dangerous thing I do. Probably in connection with flying, my most frightening experience would have to be a near miss I had when I was flying a Boeing 747 at night. A small airplane passed in the opposite direction just 50 feet below my plane. Just after this happened, a flight attendant brought us some hot snacks, and I distinctly remember how good they tasted!
Interviewer Have you ever become ill during a flight?
Richard Once I was flying from Hong Kong to Toronto, that's a 15-hour flight, and I got food poisoning after six hours. I felt terrible – incapable of doing anything at all for the rest of the flight. Luckily, though, the rest of the crew was fine, because on all flights the crew members are given different meals, just in case. So, because my copilots had eaten a different meal and felt fine, the flight was able to continue safely.

2.15 "No!" Peter shouted.
The windshield cracked and popped out as the fire engine hit the floor... broken. Peter hadn't even played with it once, and his second-best Christmas present was broken.
Later, when Mommy came into the living room, she didn't thank Peter for picking up all the wrapping paper. Instead, she scooped up Little Brother™ and turned him on again.
He trembled and screeched louder than ever.
"My God! How long has he been off?" Peter's mother demanded.
"I don't like him!"
"Peter, it scares him! Listen to him!"
"I hate him! Take him back!"
"You are not to turn him off again. Ever!"
"He's mine!" Peter shouted. "He's mine and I can do what I want with him! He broke my fire engine!"
"He's a baby!"
"He's stupid! I hate him! Take him back!"
"You are going to learn to be nice with him."
"I'll turn him off if you don't take him back. I'll turn him off and hide him someplace where you can't find him!"
"Peter!" Mommy said, and she was angry. She was angrier than he'd ever seen her before. She put Little Brother™ down and took a step toward Peter. She would punish him. Peter didn't care. He was angry, too.
"I'll do it!" he yelled. "I'll turn him off and hide him someplace dark!"
"You'll do no such thing!" Mommy said. She grabbed his arm and spun him around. The spanking would come next.
But it didn't. Instead, he felt her fingers searching for something at the back of his neck.

2.16 **Interviewer** Heidi Evans is a flight attendant for JetBlue, a discount airline. What made you want to be a flight attendant?
Heidi I actually saw a movie about a flight attendant, and it looked like something I could do. It looked very exciting, traveling around the world, meeting new people, going to different destinations.
Interviewer What kind of training did you have?
Heidi We had an extensive training, four weeks down in Orlando. We did a lot of work on the cabin simulators, we did a lot of emergency situations, a lot of safety drills to make sure we were prepared if something ever would occur that we would need to use our emergency situation skills for. We learn how to deal with many different situations... safety related, we learn CPR, we learn how to use a defibrillator. We learn how to deal with situations where people are afraid to fly, where people don't want to be on the airplane anymore, or they are sick.
Interviewer What kind of person do you think the airlines are looking for?
Heidi Someone who is happy, energetic, loves to fly, loves to be at their job. They don't really want to hire somebody that's going to be cranky and doesn't want to be there. They're looking for someone with good customer service skills. They're looking for someone who is patient, someone who is willing to go the extra mile, someone who is willing to work with other people.
Interviewer What are the good sides of being a flight attendant?
Heidi There are a lot of good perks being a flight attendant! You get to travel for free, you can go visit the country – which I take advantage of, many times. There's no office. There is an office – it's the plane – but it changes every day. My destinations change, the people on the plane change, which is exciting because I get to meet a whole slew of people that are new, that's different – and it's great! That's the great perk for me.
Interviewer And what are the bad sides?
Heidi There aren't that many bad sides. The few you could think of probably would be the delays, the sitting, waiting. But that doesn't happen as much as people think. There's also red-eye flights, which is flying throughout the night, through the whole night, and you're up all night and you have to get in and you get very exhausted. It takes a toll on your body, so you pretty much sleep the rest of the day when you get home.

2.17 **Interviewer** What tips do you have for someone going on a long flight?
Heidi Before you go on a long haul, red-eye flight through the night, I suggest you sleep in the morning before, make sure you get plenty of rest, drink lots of water. Always a good thing to do is exercise before and, actually, while you're on the flight, take walks through the aisle, stretch your legs, stretch your calves, drink plenty, plenty, plenty of water.
Interviewer You must come into contact with a lot of passengers who are afraid of flying. How do you deal with this?
Heidi We just ask "Are you okay? Do you have a question? Do you need something?" And usually it's, "What's that noise? What's that bump? What's going on?" And we calm them down, talk to them, and they usually... once they get their questions answered, they're usually pretty good.
Interviewer How can you tell if someone's scared?
Heidi You can see it in their face. You can see them clenching their fists onto the arm rests, their eyes are shut tightly, they're making a scared face.
Interviewer Have you ever been in a dangerous situation?
Heidi Yes, I have. We were taking off out of New York, and as we were taking off, we started to smell smoke. We looked around, and you could actually see little bits of smoke coming through the cabin, and at that moment we called the captain, we told him, "We smell smoke. There's smoke in the cabin." And at that point he got on the phone with the ground people to make an emergency landing. The flight attendants got up. We walked through the cabin, we looked, calmed the people down, we told them, "Everything is going to be fine." We got back in our seats, we landed the plane, got the people off the plane safely. Everyone worked together, nobody got hurt, thankfully, and that was that. We ended up getting in another plane, taking off, and landing at our destination just fine.

2.19 **Interviewer** How do you feel when you fly?
Shelly I feel pretty good once I'm in the air. Taking off and landing is sometimes a little nerve-wracking, but otherwise, fine.
Interviewer What do you least like about flying?
Shelly Uh... probably my least favorite part about flying is waiting in long lines, whether it's for the bathroom, or check-in, or luggage.
Interviewer Have you ever had a frustrating experience when you were flying?
Shelly Yes, certainly. And I think we all have. There was a time in Chicago when I had to wait on the runway for about four hours, and they kept telling us that we'd be taking off any moment and that never happened and finally we got sent to a hotel and didn't get out until the next day.
Interviewer How do you feel when you fly?
Sophie When I fly? I love to fly. I think it's so exciting.
Interviewer What do you least like about flying?
Sophie Uh... I get bored after, like, in the third hour. Towards then I start getting bored.
Interviewer Have you ever had a frustrating experience when you were flying?
Sophie Um, oh geez, off the top of my head that's pretty hard, I don't know.
Interviewer How do you feel when you fly?
Tiffany Um, I'm not the easiest flyer. I feel a little bit nervous, especially about takeoff and landing
Interviewer What do you least like about flying?
Tiffany Landing. I tend to feel a little bit sick when I land – so, you know, nausea and kind of being uncomfortable and wanting to get off the plane right away.
Interviewer Have you ever had a frustrating experience when you were flying?
Tiffany Flying? Hmm... I can't think of anything offhand, but there's been a time... there have been times before where we've been stuck waiting to get off the plane for over an hour and a half without being able to get off, so... That was pretty frustrating, but aside from that, no.
Interviewer How do you feel when you fly?
Juan I get kind of nervous when I'm flying on planes. It's one of my fears.
Interviewer What do you least like about flying?
Juan Flying?... Uh... the turbulence, it's one of the scariest things. And just the stuff you see on the news, planes crashing, it's not something you want to do.
Interviewer Have you ever had a frustrating experience when you were flying?
Juan Uh... I had one bad experience when I was flying. We were going to Puerto Rico, I was about 12 years old, uh, the weather was terrible, the turbulence was awful, the plane dropped about 60 feet and... I... I just started bawling my eyes out. I had my younger brother right next to me, about four years old and telling me, "It's going to be all right." And here I am, the big guy, the oldest in the family, uh, crying my eyes out.

3.1 **Interviewer** How did you become the pickpocket consultant for *Oliver Twist*?
Consultant Well, I'm the director of a company that supplies magicians for live events and for TV and movies. The director of the movie was looking for someone to train the actors – the young boys – to teach them to be pickpockets. He wanted them to be able to pick pockets so fast and so skillfully that it would look like they'd been doing it for years, so that they would look like professional pickpockets. So, anyway, the movie company got in touch with my company, and then I flew to Prague, where they were shooting the movie, to meet the director.

Interviewer What happened when you met him?
Consultant Well, he didn't give me an ordinary interview. He just asked me to steal his watch, without him noticing.
Interviewer And did you?
Consultant Yes, I did. So he gave me the job!
Interviewer How long did it take the boys to learn to pick pockets?
Consultant Not very long. They learned really quickly. To be a good pickpocket, you need confidence, and children have that confidence. In the end, they got so good that they were stealing from everybody on the movie set, even from me. I started to feel a little bit like Fagin myself.
Interviewer For our listeners who aren't familiar with the story of *Oliver Twist*, Fagin is the master thief who trains the young boys to be pickpockets. So, what's the trick of being a pickpocket?
Consultant The real trick is to make people notice some things but not others. Some magicians call it "misdirection," but I call it "direction" – you have to direct people *toward* what you *want* them to see, and of course *away* from what you *don't want* them to see. Let me show you. What do you have in your jeans pockets?
Interviewer Uh… just keys.
Consultant Can you show them to me?
Interviewer Wow! That's amazing! You just stole my wallet… and my pen. I really didn't notice a thing…
Consultant That's the trick, you see. All I had to do was direct your attention to your jeans pocket and your keys, and you forgot about your jacket pocket and your wallet.
Interviewer That's incredible. I mean, I was expecting it – I knew you were going to try to steal from me. And I still didn't see you. So, if someone weren't expecting it, it would be even easier!
Consultant That's right. If you know where people are looking, you also know where they're *not* looking. So, for example, if someone comes up to you on the street with a map and asks you where something is, they make you look at the map, and maybe while you're doing that, they're stealing your wallet or your phone from your back pocket.
Interviewer Uh-huh… Tourists are especially at risk from pickpockets, aren't they?
Consultant Yes, and that's because pickpockets know exactly what they're going to look at, which is usually a building or a monument. For example, take tourists in New York. When they come out of a subway station in the city, the first thing people do is look up at the tall buildings. And when they look up, it's easy for pickpockets to do their work. And of course, thieves *love* the posters in the subway that warn people to be careful with their belongings – you know, the ones that say things like "Watch out for pickpockets!" As soon as men read that, they immediately put their hand on the pocket that their wallet is in, to make sure it's still there. The pickpockets see that, and so they know exactly where it is.
Interviewer Well, I'm sure that information will be very helpful to everyone, and especially to tourists. Thank you very much for talking to us this afternoon.
Consultant Sure. You're welcome.

3.6 I was at work when I heard the news on TV. It had been pouring rain for several days, and I could see that the River Vltava was swollen. Now it appeared that there was a real danger that the river would overflow. All of us who lived or worked near the river were being advised to get out and move to a safe place. My office is in the center of Prague, only a hundred yards from the river bank, and I live in an apartment in a small town just a few miles north of Prague, right on the banks of the River Vltava, so I was in danger both at work and at home.

My wife and baby were at my apartment, so I did the sensible thing and went home immediately. I put my wife and my child into the car, and I drove them to her parents' house. They would be completely safe there. So far, so good! But then I stopped being sensible, and I jumped back into the car and went back to our apartment. Why did I do that? I told myself that it was because I was afraid of looters breaking into our apartment and stealing things, but the truth was that I sort of felt that I wanted to be in the middle of things, to be involved in what was happening.

I stayed up all night watching the TV bulletins. They were giving regular reports on how fast the water level was rising at various places throughout the Czech Republic. There was a journalist reporting from just down the street from where I was, north of Prague, so I could sit in my living room and watch the danger increase as the minutes passed, but I still didn't move. I suppose I had a kind of perverse desire to be the last person to leave our apartment building. I could hear cars starting up and driving away all evening, and from time to time I looked out at our parking lot, and I could see that it was almost empty.

At about three in the morning, my car was the only one left in the parking lot, and my nerves gave out – or maybe I just came to my senses, because I finally decided to get into the car and escape. The roads toward Prague were flooded, so I decided to try to get to a relative's house, which was a few miles away in the opposite direction, away from the river. I tried various escape routes, but even these roads were impassable now. I was about to give up – I thought I'd waited too long. On my last attempt, I drove until I met another car, which was blocking the road. The road ahead was flooded, but the driver of the other car was wading into the water to see how deep it was. He said he thought he could make it, so I decided to follow him. The water was rising quickly now, but he drove really, really slowly through the water, and I felt kind of impatient. Anyway, he managed to get through the water safely. I followed him, but I went much more quickly. Water was coming into the car under the door, and the engine made a funny noise like a cough a couple of times, but I got through and finally arrived safely at my relative's house.

I was one of the lucky ones. My office escaped the flood, and my apartment wasn't damaged at all as it's on the third floor. But the poor people who lived on the first floor – their apartments were very badly damaged. They had been completely under water.

3.8 More and more of us are trying to do our part for the environment. But would you go as far as Barbara Haddrill did?

Six years ago, Barbara, who comes from Britain, decided to make big changes to her lifestyle because she was worried about climate change, especially about the amount of carbon dioxide emissions that she herself was producing. So she stopped driving, and she started buying organic food from local stores and using a wood fire to heat her home. But then Barbara was invited to be a bridesmaid at her best friend's wedding in Australia.

The flight to Australia takes 24 hours and produces a huge amount of carbon dioxide emissions. But she really wanted to go to the wedding. So now she had a terrible dilemma. To fly or not to fly?

Instead of flying, Barbara decided to travel to Australia over land and sea! She traveled by train and bus through Russia, China, Vietnam, Thailand, then by boat to Singapore, and finally to Australia. The epic journey took her nearly two months. Fortunately, Barbara works part-time at the Center for Alternative Technology, and they were willing to give her such a long vacation.

3.9 But… how much has Barbara *really* done to help the planet? Let's compare the two trips. Barbara's trip cost her about $4,000. She traveled 14,004 miles, and it took her 51 days. The total amount of CO2 emissions her trip produced was 1.65 metric tons. If she'd traveled by plane, it would have cost her about a quarter of the price, only $900, she would have traveled 10,273 miles, and it would have taken her just 25 hours. But the CO2 emissions would have been nearly 2.7 metric tons.

So, yes, Barbara's journey overland and by sea did produce less carbon dioxide. On the other hand, of course, if she hadn't gone at all, she wouldn't have produced any emissions. So, what do you think of Barbara's trip? We would be very interested in hearing your comments. You can e-mail us at…

3.10 We spend a lot of time in our cars. The average driver spends nearly an hour and a half a day in the car, so obviously the risks involved in driving are something we should take very seriously.

Driving gets a lot of bad publicity, and there are a lot of myths about how dangerous it is – but the fact is that, mile for mile, it's riskier to be a pedestrian or a jogger than to drive a car, or ride a motorcycle, for that matter. We're also more likely to be injured at work or at home than we are when we're driving a car.

But accidents *do* happen, and the reason why a lot of them happen is because people break the rules. In fact, 50 percent of all fatal accidents occur because someone breaks the law. The most frequent reason is exceeding the speed limit, and the second most frequent is drunk driving. The third cause of fatal accidents is when drivers fall asleep, a surprising 10 percent.

When we drive is also a significant factor in assessing our risk of having an accident. Driving at night, for example, is four times as dangerous as during the day. This is mainly because visibility is so much worse at night. By day, a driver's visibility is roughly 550 yards, but at night, driving with headlights, it is much worse, maybe as little as 130 yards.

What are the most dangerous times and days to be on the road? Well, between 2:00 and 3:00 a.m. on a Saturday morning is the most dangerous time of the week, when you're most likely to have a *fatal* accident. So, if possible, try to stay off the road then.

The time when you are most likely to have a *nonfatal* accident is Friday afternoon between 4:00 and 6:00 p.m. This is when people are finishing work for the week, and it's a time when drivers need to concentrate especially hard. Strangely, Tuesday is the safest day of the week to be on the road.

Which brings us to *where* accidents happen. Most fatal accidents happen on country roads, so highways or freeways are much safer. Also 70 percent of fatal accidents happen within 20 or 25 miles of where we live. Why is that? The answer seems to be that we concentrate less when we're in familiar territory.

And finally, let's look at *who* has accidents. Another myth about driving is that women are worse drivers than men. While it's true that mile for mile women have more *minor* accidents than men, a man is *twice* as likely to be killed in a car accident. In general, men take too many unnecessary risks when they're driving. Women are generally more careful and cautious drivers.

But the most important factor of all is age. A driver aged between 17 and 24 has double the risk of an older driver. Which is why a lot of people would like to see the age limit for having a driver's license raised to 21.

3.12 **Interviewer** And this afternoon on *Schools Around the World*, we are visiting an unusual little preschool in a village in southern England. What makes this preschool different is that whatever the weather is like, the 20 children spend most of their day not in a classroom, but playing outside. Sue Palmer is the director of the preschool. Hello, Sue.
Sue Hello.
Interviewer Sue, do the children *really* spend all day outside?
Sue Yes, even in the winter, and even if it's raining. They only come inside for breaks, so they probably spend about 90 percent of their day outside. We think this is a much better way of teaching children than by shutting them up in classrooms all day.
Interviewer What kind of things do children learn from being outside?
Sue They can learn about the world by doing things. We have a large field next to the school, so they're in the field all day – playing, exploring, experimenting. They learn about how plants and trees grow, and they can learn about insects. They can learn about the danger of fire by sitting around a real fire. They can climb trees and walk on logs…

Interviewer And don't you think this is a little bit dangerous for young children? They might easily fall down, have accidents.

Sue Oh, no, no, not at all. I think that today's children are totally overprotected; they don't have enough freedom. People have forgotten just how important it is to give our children some freedom. They need to be allowed to take risks during play. Our children know which plants can hurt them. And they know that fire is dangerous. But nowadays schools do all they can to avoid adventure and risk.

Interviewer Why do you think schools have become so obsessed with eliminating risk?

Sue I think it's because schools and teachers are so worried nowadays that if a child has an accident of any kind, however small, that the child's parents will sue the school for huge amounts of money and maybe even put them out of business.

Interviewer Have you ever had any problem with parents?

Sue Oh, on the contrary. They are extremely positive about the school and our teaching methods and philosophy. I've heard parents say that children who come to our school are healthier and stronger than other children – and that's in spite of being out in the rain – or maybe it's because of it. I think, and the parents agree with me, that the way we are teaching is the way that childhood should be.

Interviewer Well, thank you very much, Sue.

3.13 **Interviewer** EZ is a free runner who started the organization Urban Freeflow. Free runners use obstacles in a town or city to create movement, by running, jumping, and climbing. Can you do free running anywhere, I mean, for example, if you're on your way somewhere?

EZ Yeah, I mean if you wanted to, you could kind of do it anywhere, you know, and if you're on your way to work, you could do it. But generally the people who practice would go to a particular spot and practice there and then move on elsewhere.

Interviewer Where do you most enjoy doing free running?

EZ The most rewarding for me would be running in London, here, I mean, around the South Bank. And we'd do it in a team of maybe ten of us, and just, you know, like someone leading the way and the rest following, and just using basic obstacles, like lampposts and walls and just moving.

Interviewer How did you first get into free running?

EZ Well, my background is in boxing, which I did for about 20 years, and I boxed at international level. And I got married and had a kid and I had to just change my life around and become sensible all of a sudden. So I gave up the boxing and there was a huge void in my life, so I drifted into martial arts, which didn't really do it for me. And I was looking for the next thing to do and I saw this on TV one day, and I remember sitting in bed watching it and I said, "That's what I'm looking for."

Interviewer Tell us about the organization Urban Freeflow.

EZ Well, Urban Freeflow started out as a website, but then we devised a performance team. We have 20 athletes in the team now, eight who are very, very high-profile; we're sponsored by Adidas now. We take care of all sorts of commercials and movies in that sense. We teach as well, we teach in schools, we've taught the army, the police.

Interviewer How do you help the police?

EZ The police run these schemes for youth offenders, and they're trying to get them out of, you know, doing bad things. So it's seen as a positive thing to do, it's seen as a very cool thing to do, and for the youths it's very engaging, so that's what we do for them.

Interviewer And how does it help schools?

EZ In terms of schools, same again. There's a big problem in the UK with obesity, and kids just aren't practicing anything. They're not doing any PE, they're not doing any kind of sports, whereas what we do is perceived as being very cool, and unwittingly they're taking part and exercising, so that seems to be a very positive thing.

3.14 **Interviewer** How dangerous is free running?

EZ On the face of it, what we do seems to be quite dangerous, but it doesn't touch on what we do, we're very, very safety conscious, we work in movies and commercials where safety is paramount, I mean, everything we do is calculated, there's no risk-taking. If you see a big jump being done, we'd have practiced that at ground level thousands of times, over and over and over. I think if anything, the key word for what we do is repetition.

Interviewer What attracted you to free running? Was it the risk element?

EZ To a degree, the risk element played a part, but it was more about the sense of freedom, the way to be able to move within your environment with no limitations, you know. You don't need any equipment to take part, no skateboard, or no BMX, you can just… a pair of trainers and I'm ready to go. That was the real draw for me, just the freedom aspect.

Interviewer Have you had many accidents since you started doing free running?

EZ Well, if you're practicing this sport, you will pick up the odd scrapes here and there, you know, you'll get blisters on your hands, and calluses, which is normal. You might get the odd sprained ankle. Personally, I fell out of a tree once, and fell on my head, which wasn't very nice and I had to go to hospital here.

Interviewer Is free running really something that anyone can do?

EZ It helps if you have a background in some kind of sport, but it isn't essential, you can start from being a complete beginner. Gymnastics would help, but you could be, you know, just someone who plays football, or does a bit of running and pick it up straight away. As long as you start out very small scale, take your time, there's no problem.

3.16 **Interviewer** Have you ever done any high-risk sports or activities?

Tim Uh, yeah, I raced cars for 20 years before I got married and had children and that quickly ended.

Interviewer What was it like?

Tim Uh, it's what I did since I was 10 years old. It was probably where I felt most comfortable – behind the wheel of a race car. Uh… it was a rush, it was a lifestyle that I enjoyed, it took me around the world… So it was what I wanted to do for a long time.

Interviewer Is there anything else you'd like to try?

Tim Uh… I would probably have a few. My wife, I'm not sure she would be excited about. Parachuting probably, jumping out of an airplane. My parents both did it, and I was supposed to get it for my 18th birthday and I never followed up on it with them. So, we'll see… someday… someday…

Interviewer Have you ever done any high-risk sports or activities?

Duey High risk?… Um, depends on how you define it. I've done bungee jumping, I've done skydiving, I've done scuba diving. Uh… Next month, I'm going to try out rock climbing. So I guess those are pretty extreme sports.

Interviewer What was skydiving like?

Duey Skydiving was probably one of my favorite things to do. It's just the adrenaline rush, where it only lasts seconds but, you know, I did that several years back and I still remember, recall how that feels, such a jump out of a plane.

Interviewer Is there anything else you'd like to try?

Duey Um… I think I would want to give sky… uh…scuba diving a chance again. I ruptured my ear diving in the Great Barrier reefs, so it hasn't been the same ever since, I've been a little bit scared to go back and try that out again. But it would be great to, uh, give it another chance.

Interviewer Have you ever done any high-risk sports or activities?

Josh The only high-risk sport I've ever done would be jet skiing.

Interviewer What was it like?

Josh Just a total new experience for me, and jumping up in the air after huge waves was just awesome and kind of nerve-wracking at the same time.

Interviewer Is there anything else that you'd like to try?

Josh I cannot see myself doing any high-risk sports. I get too nervous, and jumping out of a plane isn't for me.

Interviewer Have you ever done any high-risk sports or activities?

Christina After I turned 18, I did participate in a high-risk activity. I went skydiving. My mom, especially at the beginning, was very hesitant to let me go. But I eventually convinced her, and it was one of the best things I have ever done in my entire life.

Interviewer What was it like?

Christina It was really like an out-of-body experience, I guess. It wasn't anything like, um, like I've ever experienced before, and I definitely recommend it to everyone.

Interviewer Is there anything else that you'd like to try?

Christina My dad goes white-water rafting and I've always wanted to try that with him, so I would definitely love to get into white-water rafting.

4.3 Yossi and Kevin soon realized that going by river was a big mistake. The river got faster and faster, and soon they were in rapids.

The raft was swept down the river at an incredible speed until it hit a rock. Kevin managed to swim to shore, but Yossi was swept away by the rapids.

But Yossi didn't drown. He came up to the surface several kilometers downriver. By an incredible stroke of luck, he found their backpack floating in the river. The backpack contained a little food, insect repellent, a lighter, and most important of all… the map. The two friends were now separated by a canyon and six or seven kilometers of jungle.

4.4 Kevin was feeling desperate. He didn't know if Yossi was alive or dead, but he started walking downriver to look for him. He felt responsible for what had happened to his friend. Yossi, however, was feeling very optimistic. He was sure that Kevin would look for him, so he started walking upriver, calling his friend's name. But nobody answered.

At night Yossi tried to sleep, but he felt terrified. The jungle was full of noises. Suddenly, he woke up because he heard a branch breaking. He turned on his flashlight. There was a jaguar staring at him…

Yossi was trembling with fear. But then he remembered something that he once saw in a movie. He used the cigarette lighter to set fire to the insect repellent spray, and he managed to scare the jaguar away.

4.5 After five days alone, Yossi was exhausted and starving. Suddenly, as he was walking, he saw a footprint on the trail – it was a hiking boot. It had to be Kevin's footprint! He followed the trail until he discovered another footprint. But then he realized, to his horror, that it was the same footprint, and that it wasn't Kevin's… It was his own. He had been walking around in circles. Suddenly, Yossi realized that he would never find Kevin. He felt sure that Kevin must be dead. Yossi felt depressed and was at the point of giving up.

4.6 But Kevin wasn't dead. He was still looking for Yossi. But after nearly a week, he was weak and exhausted from lack of food and lack of sleep. He decided that it was time to forget Yossi and try to save himself. He had just enough strength left to hold onto a log and let himself float down the river.

Kevin was incredibly lucky – he was rescued by two Bolivian hunters in a canoe. The men only hunted in that part of the rainforest once a year, so if they had been there a short time earlier or later, they would never have seen Kevin. They took him back to the town of San José, and he spent two days recovering.

4.7 As soon as Kevin felt well enough, he went to a Bolivian Army base and asked them to look for Yossi. The army soldiers were sure that Yossi must be dead, but Kevin finally persuaded them to take him up in a plane and fly over the part of the rainforest where Yossi could be. It was a hopeless search. The plane had to fly too high and the forest was too dense. They couldn't see anything at all. Kevin felt terribly guilty. He was convinced that it was all his fault that Yossi was going to die in the jungle. Kevin's last hope was to pay a local man with a boat to take him up the river to look for his friend.

4.8 By now, Yossi had been alone in the jungle for nearly three weeks. He hadn't eaten for days. He was starving, exhausted, and slowly losing his mind. It was evening. He lay down by the side of the river ready for another night alone in the jungle. Suddenly, he heard the sound of a bee buzzing in his ear. He thought a bee had gotten inside his mosquito net. When he opened his eyes, he saw that the buzzing noise wasn't a bee… It was a boat.

Yossi was too weak to shout, but Kevin had already seen him. It was a one-in-a-million chance, but Yossi was saved.

When Yossi had recovered, he and Kevin flew to the city of La Paz and went directly to the hotel where they had agreed to meet Marcus and Karl. But Marcus and Karl were not there. The two men had never arrived back in the town of Apolo. The Bolivian army conducted a search of the rainforest, but Marcus and Karl were never seen again.

4.14 In life we sometimes have disagreements with other people. It could be with your spouse, with your boss, with your parents, or with a friend. When this happens, the important thing is to try not to let a calm discussion turn into a heated argument. But of course this is easier said than done.

The first thing I would say is that the way you begin the conversation is very important. Imagine you are a student and you share an apartment with another student who you think isn't doing their share of the housework. If you say, "Look, you never do your share of the housework. What are we going to do about it?," the discussion will very soon turn into an argument. It's much more constructive to say something like, "I think we'd better take another look at how we divide up the housework. Maybe there's a better way of doing it."

My second piece of advice is simple. If you're the person who is in the wrong, just admit it! This is the easiest and best way to avoid an argument. Just apologize to your roommate, your parents, or your spouse, and move on. The other person will have much more respect for you in the future if you do that.

The next tip is, don't exaggerate. Try not to say things like "You always come home late when my mother comes to dinner" when that might have only happened twice, or "You never remember to buy toothpaste." This will just make the other person think you're being unreasonable and will probably make him or her stop listening to what you are saying.

Sometimes we just can't avoid a discussion turning into an argument. But if you do start arguing with someone, it is important to keep things under control, and there are ways to do this.

The most important thing is not to raise your voice. Raising your voice will just make the other person lose their temper, too. If you find yourself raising your voice, stop for a moment and take a deep breath. Say "I'm sorry I shouted, but this is very important to me," and continue calmly. If you can talk calmly and quietly, you'll find the other person will be more willing to think about what you are saying.

It is also very important to stick to the point. Try to keep to the topic you are talking about. Don't bring up old arguments or try to bring in other issues. Just concentrate on solving the one problem you are having, and leave the other things for another time. So, for example, if you're arguing about the housework, don't start talking about cell phone bills, too.

And my final tip is that, if necessary, call "Time out," like in sports. If you think that an argument is getting out of control, then you can say to the other person, "Listen, I'd rather talk about this tomorrow after we've both calmed down." You can continue the discussion the next day when perhaps both of you are feeling less tense and angry. That way there is much more chance that you will be able to reach an agreement. You'll also probably find that the problem is much easier to solve after you've both had a good night's sleep.

Well, those are my tips. But I want to say one last important thing. Some people think that arguing is always bad. This is not true. Conflict is a normal part of life, and dealing with conflict is an important part of any relationship, whether it's three people sharing an apartment, a married couple, or just two good friends. If you don't learn to argue appropriately, then when a real problem comes along, you won't be ready to face it together. Think of the smaller arguments as training sessions. Learn how to argue cleanly and fairly. It will help your relationship become stronger and last longer.

4.17 **Presenter** And welcome to tonight's edition of *Use Your Senses*. First, let's meet Joanna and Steve from Chicago.

Joanna and Steve Hi. / Hello.

Presenter Now, the blindfold is on – you can't see anything, can you?

Steve and Joanna No, nothing. / No, nothing, no.

Presenter OK, so first the mystery drink. Remember, you can smell it, but you can't taste it… Starting… now!

Joanna It doesn't really smell like anything.

Steve It smells fruity to me, not very strong, but definitely fruity.

Joanna Yeah, it smells a little like orange juice but sweeter.

Steve It could be [*beep*].

Presenter OK, so now the food. This you can taste, but you can't see, of course… Ready? Now!

Joanna Well, it's meat, right? It tastes a little bit like chicken, but I don't think it *is* chicken.

Steve I don't think I've had it before – the texture isn't exactly like chicken – it tastes fairly light; I don't think it's duck…

Presenter You've got ten more seconds…

Joanna It must be [*beep*].

Steve OK.

Presenter Now the object.

Steve It feels like a coin.

Joanna Can I feel it? Yes, it definitely feels metallic, but it's completely smooth – it doesn't seem to have any markings – oh, it has two tiny little holes in the middle. I know, it's a [*beep*].

Steve Yeah, yeah. That's it.

Presenter So now we're going to take off the blindfolds – there we are.

Joanna and Steve Thanks. / That's a lot better.

Presenter And now to the sound effect. I'm going to play you a sound, and you have to decide what it is you're hearing. Remember, you can hear it only twice. Ready? Now…

Steve It sounds like thunder to me.

Joanna Well, maybe, but it sounds very distant. Could it be a train?

Steve No, I think it's something natural, you know, not a machine. Can we hear it again, please?

Presenter Of course.

Steve Yes, I think it's [*beep*]. What do you think?

Joanna Could be. I'll go with that.

Presenter OK. Time's up. So now, the moment of truth. Did Steve and Joanna get it right? Remember, you need all the answers right to win today's prize. Our assistant Vanessa will give us the answers; a round of applause for Vanessa.

4.23 **Interviewer** Trevor White is a Canadian actor. Can you tell us a little bit about the kind of acting you do?

Trevor Uh… There isn't much I don't do, I guess, as far as acting goes. There's theater, obviously, film work, television work, sometimes commercials and even voice-over work, which is for radio or for television or even sometimes animated shows where you lend your voice to those as well. So, I've rarely said "no" to an acting job.

Interviewer Did you always want to be an actor?

Trevor Well, it's something that I always loved to do, act, as a kid in high school, in school plays, and in my spare time, just playing around with friends. You know, acting and improvising and that kind of thing. But I don't think I ever believed that I could… or ever took it seriously to act as a profession or for the rest of my life. So I went in to university and took economics as a more practical thing to do, but I didn't really enjoy it, I guess, and ultimately, after university, I started taking some acting classes and really enjoyed that. And then started doing student films and fringe theater and unpaid work just to get experience in acting and loved it and then started doing it more seriously and got an agent and started getting proper acting jobs, and that was about 13 years ago.

Interviewer What's the most difficult thing about preparing for a new role?

Trevor It really depends. When you do a play, for example, you have three, four, sometimes even six weeks to rehearse with the other people and the director and the props and everything, so you have a long time to learn your lines, to, as it were, find the character. The memorization is the most like real work, that can be difficult, you know, just memorizing lots of lines. But, uh… in film and television you don't have the benefit of rehearsal. You just show up and you're expected to know all your lines and then you do it a few times and that's it. So you have to be very disciplined and get all that ready in advance.

Interviewer How do you learn your lines?

Trevor I have a Dictaphone actually, which I just record the other people's lines, obviously in my voice, I don't do strange character voices because that would be weird… And, you know, I just say their line, I stop it, I say my line, I play the next line, so you just basically record all the other lines in any given scene and play it back and just work through it slowly. It's amazing the difference it makes when the writing is good and it makes sense. It's much easier to memorize. But if sometimes you audition for a bad science fiction TV show or a horror movie or something, you often have a much harder time memorizing poorly written lines, because they are just bad. But of course it's your job, so you do it.

4.24 **Interviewer** Is there any role you've particularly enjoyed?

Trevor There's a few roles that I've played or oftentimes when you do something it's the whole experience of a job, not necessarily just the part you have in it. Earlier this year, I got to work for the Royal Shakespeare Company for the first time, and we did *Coriolanus*, one of Shakespeare's lesser performed plays, in Stratford, in Washington in America, also in Newcastle here in the United Kingdom, and in Madrid in Spain for five months, which was amazing.

Interviewer What's the most difficult role that you've ever had to play?

Trevor Well, I suppose, this last role that I played is one of the most difficult parts, Tullus Aufidius in *Coriolanus*, because there were lots of things that were very demanding about the part. We had to do a huge sword and ax fight in the middle of the play. Which… I'd done stage combat before, but never anything like this, we were using actual… I mean, they were blunt swords and axes, but they were still very large pieces of metal. And we had a couple of small accidents, but no major ones, luckily. I gave the other guy three stitches on his fingers at one point when he parried in the wrong place – that's my opinion anyway.

Interviewer Do you prefer working in the theater or in movies and TV?

Trevor I think theater is the most satisfying work in acting oftentimes, because you get to do it over and over again in front of a live audience, but it doesn't tend to pay as well as film and television, which is also fun, but not as glamorous as people might think it is, I guess.
Interviewer So being an actor isn't really glamorous?
Trevor No, I don't think acting is a glamorous life, particularly in… well, I guess in any way. In theater it's, you know, you don't really earn that much money and you, you know, work hard. Yeah, and film and television work is, you know, can be a lot of fun, you can get to work with some famous people sometimes or some very talented people that you admire, and that's a thrilling thing, and you get to shoot guns or, you know, go on car chases, and all those things are really fun, but most of the time, the 90% of the day, even when you're doing exciting things, you're just sitting and waiting around, you're always waiting around, they're always fixing lights, setting up new camera positions, trying to figure out who's going where, when, and, it's, uh, you know… it takes them…To film a proper feature film takes months and maybe in all that time only two or three of those days all told is actually you doing anything. So, yeah, I think a lot of people get into extra work and stuff because they think, "Oh, this will be really glamorous," but you end up sort of reading a book about nine hours a day. Uh, so, yeah. And I've never been on a red carpet, so I suppose I can't judge. That looks glamorous.

4.26 **Interviewer** Have you ever acted?
Rachel When I was in high school, I had to act in some plays for a drama class that I was in. So we did performances for the student body.
Interviewer How did it make you feel?
Rachel It made me feel that I really wasn't meant to be an actor specifically. But it was a good experience and it was a start in public speaking – so that was valuable.
Interviewer Have you ever acted?
Josh I've done a little bit of acting. I started a few years ago doing more serious work for more commercial print, uh, and commercials as well as independent films and a little bit of extra work on major motion pictures.
Interviewer How does it make you feel?
Josh I love doing acting. I think it's so much fun portraying a different person. And it's just a ton of fun doing different projects.
Interviewer Have you ever acted?
Kerrie Uh… yes, I used to act in college musicals when I was at college – which is a long time ago now.
Interviewer How did it make you feel?
Kerrie Lots of fun. I love dancing, so I used to do lots of dancing when I was growing up. So it just was a continuation of that experience.
Interviewer Have you ever acted?
Shelly Well, I did some acting in high school. I did a couple of musicals in my junior and senior years – one of them was *Fiddler on the Roof*.
Interviewer How did it make you feel?
Shelly It was a lot of hard work, but I felt really great doing it. I was nervous, at first, when I got on stage, but it was pretty clear that the audience was enjoying themselves and by the end, when they're applauding, you feel fabulous.
Interviewer Have you ever acted?
Juan I acted once. I was in one of my theater classes in high school. I was a sophomore, and we just made up our own play and, uh, that was… that was one of the premier highlights of my acting career and one of the last highlights.
Interviewer How did it make you feel?
Juan It was very nerve-wracking because you had to remember all your lines and you had an audience, which is something that I was always terrified of.

5.2 I think it's very interesting that human beings are the only animals which listen to music for pleasure. A lot of research has been done to find out *why* we listen to music, and there seem to be three main reasons. Firstly, we listen to music to make us remember important moments in the past, for example, when we met someone for the first time. Think of Humphrey Bogart in the film *Casablanca* saying, "Darling, they're playing our song." When we hear a certain piece of music, we remember hearing it for the first time in some very special circumstances. Obviously, this music varies from person to person.

Secondly, we listen to music to help us to change activities. If we want to go from one activity to another, we often use music to help us to make the change. For example, we might play a certain kind of music to prepare us to go out in the evening, or we might play another kind of music to relax us when we get home from work. That's mainly why people listen to music in cars, and they often listen to one kind of music when they're going to work and another kind when they're coming home. The same is true of people on buses and trains with their iPods.

The third reason why we listen to music is to intensify the emotion that we're feeling. For example, if we're feeling sad, sometimes we want to get even sadder, so we play sad music. Or we're feeling angry and we want to intensify the anger… then we play angry music. Or when we're planning a romantic dinner, we lay the table, we light candles, and then we think, "What music would make this even more romantic?"

5.3 Let's take three important human emotions: happiness, sadness, and anger. When people are happy, they speak faster, and their voice is higher. When they're sad, they speak more slowly and their voice is lower, and when people are angry, they raise their voices or shout. Babies can tell whether their mother is happy or not simply by the sound of her voice, not by her words. What music does is it copies this, and it produces the same emotions. So faster, higher-pitched music will sound happy. Slow music with lots of falling pitches will sound, feel sad. Loud music with irregular rhythms will sound angry. It doesn't matter how good or bad the music is, if it has these characteristics, it will make you experience this emotion.

Let me give you some examples. For happy, for example, the first movement of Beethoven's *Seventh Symphony*. For angry, say *Mars*, from *The Planets* by Holst. And for sad, something like Albinoni's *Adagio for strings*.

Of course the people who exploit this most are the people who write film soundtracks. They can take a scene which visually has no emotion, and they can make the scene either scary or calm or happy just by the music they write to go with it. Think of the music in the shower scene in Hitchcock's film *Psycho*. All you can see is a woman having a shower, but the music makes it absolutely terrifying.

5.11 **Presenter** Now I imagine some of you are finding this story a little difficult to believe, so I've invited into the studio Professor Miller, who is an expert in sleepwalking. Professor Miller, does this story surprise you?
Professor Not at all. I have treated people who have driven cars, ridden horses… and I had one man who even tried to fly a helicopter while he was asleep.
Presenter But how did this girl manage to climb a 130-foot crane?
Professor It would have been no problem for her. She would climb the crane just as easily as if she were awake.
Presenter And would her eyes have been open?
Professor Yes, sleepwalkers usually have their eyes open. That's why sometimes it's difficult to know if someone is sleepwalking or not.
Presenter Is sleepwalking very common?
Professor Yes. Research shows that about 18 percent of the population has a tendency to sleepwalk. In fact, it's much more common in children than in teenagers or adults. And curiously it's more common among boys than girls. Adults who sleepwalk are usually people who used to sleepwalk when they were children. Also, adult sleepwalking often happens after a stressful event, for example, after a car accident.
Presenter People always say that you should never wake a sleepwalker up when they're walking. Is that true?
Professor No, it isn't. People used to think that it was dangerous to wake up a sleepwalker. But, in fact, this isn't the case. You *can* wake up a sleepwalker without any problem, although if you do, it is quite common for the sleepwalker to be confused, so he or she probably won't know where they are for a few moments.
Presenter So if we see someone sleepwalking, should we wake them up?
Professor Yes, you should remember that another of the myths about sleepwalkers is that they cannot injure themselves while they're sleepwalking. But this isn't true. If a sleepwalker is walking around the house, they can trip or fall over a chair or even fall down stairs. The other day there was a case of a nine-year-old girl who opened her bedroom window while sleepwalking and fell 30 feet to the ground. Luckily, she wasn't seriously injured. So, you see, it is definitely safer to wake a sleepwalker up.
Presenter Hmm… How long does sleepwalking last?
Professor It can be very brief, for example, a few minutes. The most typical cases are of people getting up and getting dressed, or going to the bathroom. But it can occasionally last much longer, maybe half an hour or even more.
Presenter And what happens when sleepwalkers wake up? Do they remember the things they did while they were sleepwalking?
Professor No, a sleepwalker usually doesn't remember anything afterward. So, for example, the girl who climbed up the crane will probably have no memory of the incident.
Presenter So, is a sleepwalker responsible for his or her actions?
Professor A very good question, actually. A few years ago a man from Canada got up in the middle of the night and drove 12 miles from his home to the house where his parents-in-law lived and, for no apparent reason, he killed his mother-in-law. The man was charged with murder, but he was found not guilty because he had been asleep at the time he committed the crime.

5.15 The best thing about my job is that I get to go to the best restaurants in the country, and sometimes abroad, and I don't have to pay the check at the end of the evening. I get the chance to eat the most wonderful, exquisite food in restaurants that I wouldn't normally be able to afford, and I can order the most expensive dishes and drinks without worrying about what it's going to cost.

The other great side of the job is that I can take a friend with me, so it's a good way of catching up with old friends who I may not have seen for a while. And everyone loves a free meal in a fancy restaurant, so I rarely have to eat by myself.

The downside? Well, there are several. I frequently have to eat a lot when I'm not really hungry. To do my job well, I have to try all the courses – you know, appetizer, main course, dessert, and sometimes I don't feel like eating so much, but I have to do it. I also have a problem with my weight now – it's very easy to put on weight when you eat out several times a week. In fact, most restaurant critics have a weight problem. Another problem is that if I write a bad review of a meal I have, it's difficult for me to ever go to that restaurant again, because the owner of the restaurant will probably recognize me. Another disadvantage of the job is that because I do it so often, eating out has lost a lot of its attraction for me. When the weekend comes, I prefer to eat at home rather than go out for a meal.

5.16 Nearly all the foreign correspondents and war reporters that I've met are people who were looking for adventure. They're not the kind of people who would be happy with a nine-to-five job. They are people who got into the job precisely because it has very odd hours and involves going to difficult places. I mean, to some extent the things that are difficult and potentially dangerous about the job are also the things that made you want to do the job in the first place and the reason why the job is so exciting.

Something else I really like about the job is that I work as part of a team – you sit down and have dinner together at the end of the day and talk things through with other journalists and photographers, and you're talking to people who have experienced the same things as you and seen the same things as you. And that's very important in this kind of work.

One of the problems of the job is seeing a lot of horrific things and then going back home to normality. I remember a few years ago coming back from a war zone where I'd been for a long time, and I'd seen a lot of death and destruction, and then I went to a friend's wedding in my hometown. It was a beautiful day, everyone was having fun and talking about unimportant things, and I wanted to say, "Hang on, can't you see that there is something awful happening in the world?"

Another major worry about my job these days is the risk of being killed. Journalists used to get killed only by accident, but now there are more and more cases of journalists being killed simply because they are journalists, and they are also becoming the target of kidnappers. Two of my colleagues have been kidnapped recently and a very good friend of mine was killed last year.

5.17 **Interviewer** Sir Nicholas Kenyon was the director of a music festival in London called the Proms for 12 years. How did the Proms start?

Nicholas The Promenade Concerts started way back in 1895 when a brilliant impresario wanted to use a newly-built concert hall in London, the Queen's Hall, for a series of popular concerts that really brought classical music to the widest possible audience. There were important classical concerts during the year, but in the summer people tended to go away, society life finished, and so he had the brilliant idea of taking away all the seats on the floor of the hall, where the expensive people usually sat, and letting people come in and stand there and walk around and have a very informal experience of concert-going. The name "Proms" is an abbreviation of "Promenade Concerts" and it basically means that people are able to walk around and stand during the music.

Interviewer How long do the Proms last?

Nicholas The Proms lasts for two months in the summer, from the middle of July to the middle of September, and during that period there's one concert every day, two concerts on many days, three concerts on some days. So it's a very, very intense period of music-making, and people buy season tickets in order to be able to attend all the concerts, whether they do or not – very few people attend actually all of them, except me – and they come and they queue during the day in order to get the best places in the floor of the hall, where they stand.

Interviewer World-class musicians perform at the Proms for much lower fees than they usually receive. Why do you think that is?

Nicholas I think the Proms has an absolutely unique atmosphere... that's what orchestras and conductors who come here say. And so people do want to come and perform. What you get at the Proms is a wonderful mixture of total informality and total concentration. So that although people don't dress up to come to the Proms, they behave how they want, they actually absolutely listen to the music and that is a feature that so many conductors and orchestras really comment on – the level of concentration is absolutely amazing.

5.18 **Interviewer** There must have been many truly memorable concerts during your time as director of the Proms. Could you tell us about one of them?

Nicholas The death of Princess Diana was particularly difficult because, of course, she lived just across the road in Kensington Palace from where the Proms happen, in the Royal Albert Hall. We changed some programs to make them more appropriate. On the day of her funeral, we put in Fauré's requiem to the program. Very oddly we had programmed two or three requiems in that last two weeks of the season and they fitted very, very well. We then lost another major figure of the musical world, the conductor Sir Georg Solti, who was to have conducted the Verdi requiem on the last Friday of the season, and he was... he had been a very good friend of Princess Diana and indeed had rung me up just after Diana's death to say that he wanted to dedicate this Verdi requiem to her memory. As it turned out, he died just a week later and so another conductor, Colin Davies, took over that Verdi requiem and dedicated it to both of them, and it was a fantastically charged atmosphere in the hall. I can't remember such an electric occasion as that.

Interviewer There was also another strange coincidence in the program at the time of Princess Diana's death in 1997. Could you tell us about it?

Nicholas A wonderful American composer called John Adams had written an absolutely wonderful piece, which we were going to do on the last night of the Proms in 1997. Unfortunately... I mean, it could have been called absolutely anything this piece, it's a whirling abstract piece of fanfare music. Unfortunately, he had called it *Short Ride in a Fast Machine*. And so it was perfectly obvious from the first moment that we had to take that piece out and change the program.

Interviewer Are there any embarrassing or amusing experiences you remember?

Nicholas One of the things that was a real challenge to the Proms was the arrival of the mobile phone, because in the beginning, people didn't know how to use them, when to switch them off, and the Albert Hall is a very, very big space and mobile phones would go off in concerts and it could be very embarrassing. Usually, because they were in the middle of the music, conductors just ignored them and people got embarrassed and switched them off. But there was one particular incident that was just so awful because Stravinsky's *The Rite of Spring* starts with a very, very exposed quiet bassoon solo, and Simon Rattle and the Berlin Philharmonic, making one of their first appearances together at the Proms, had just begun that piece when a mobile phone went off very loudly in the stalls and Simon Rattle stopped the bassoonist and turned round and glared at this person in the stalls, and there was a round of applause and everything. So anyway, it restarted and the performance was a spectacular success and it was wonderful. But this was such an incident, that he had actually stopped it, that it became the subject of a lot of media attention and there were paragraphs in the papers, and I had to go and be interviewed the next day at home for a Radio 4 program about mobile phones going off in concerts, and in the middle of this interview, my own phone went off and it's a wonderfully classic little bit of tape, my embarrassment at the same thing happening to me.

5.20 **Interviewer** Have you ever been to a music festival?

Savanna Yes, I'm from Austin, Texas, and so I've been to the Kerrville Folk Festival and the Austin City Limits Music Festival.

Interviewer What are they like?

Savanna The Kerrville Folk Festival is a little bit more laid-back. And it's beautiful country, it's out in the country, so it's kind of a camping experience, a lot of fun, great food. And Austin City Limits, which is also called ACL, is usually very hot because it's in September and it's urban and a lot of great music acts. I just remember it always being very hot.

Interviewer Have you ever been to a music festival?

Tim Yes. The Lollapaloozas, way back – not to date myself, but it was a while ago.

Interviewer What was it like?

Tim Uh... It was a lot of fun. I mean, I was... I've been to probably a hundred shows and it was a fantastic one. And it had... the first couple had, you know, my favorite bands – Jane's Addiction, uh, Soundgarden early on – so all those were sort of what I was listening to at the time, so it was perfect. It was great.

Interviewer Have you ever been to a music festival?

Christina Oh, I've been to one huge music festival, uh, which is called EarthFest. And it's one day of bands coming right along the water and they play and there's food concession stands and lots of people, so it's a lot of fun.

Interviewer Tell us more. What was it like?

Christina When we got there first we picnicked a little bit during the morning and then in the afternoon we would walk around. And there's a lot of... companies that come and bring samples, so we would walk around and sample the food and then we would walk to the music, listen to some of the bands play, and then just hang out there for the rest of the day.

Interviewer Have you ever been to a music festival?

Curt Uh, yeah, I have been to the Sounds of the Underground festival, which is a big national heavy metal tour. I took my 14 year old cousin – I think I was the oldest guy there. It was... It was pretty fun.

Interviewer What was it like?

Curt Uh, well, you know, I was... I was big into metal when I was young and his age, and used to go to a ton of shows, so it was like being in that environment, but now being just a little bit too old, and it made me really uncomfortable. But the new bands are great! And it was fun to watch the ones that have been around since I was into it, still up there rocking out.

6.5

1 I was giving a talk to about two hundred people in a large hotel room in Poland. About halfway through the talk, I realized that something was flying around the room. At first, I just ignored it, since I thought it was probably a bird that had come in through the window, but after a while I noticed that the women in the audience were following its movements with their eyes and were not looking very happy. It was then that I realized that it was a large bat. The next moment, I could see from the audience's eyes that it was directly above my head. I'm really frightened of bats, and I just panicked. I tried to continue, but I couldn't concentrate, and I kept forgetting what I was going to say. So I hurried through the last part of the talk, and then as soon as I finished, I rushed out of the room. It was awful; I'll never forget it!
2 I get invited to talk to teachers all around the world, and this time I was in Mexico giving a talk to some English teachers. I think I'm a good speaker, if I do say so myself, and usually the audiences enjoy my talks and are interested in what I'm saying. But after about ten minutes, I realized that something was wrong. The audience wasn't laughing at my jokes, and some people were looking very unhappy. Then I saw several people get up and walk out of the hall. I just couldn't figure out what was going on. I'd given a presentation there the year before, and the audience had been really enthusiastic. Finally, I just stopped and asked them, "Is anything the matter? You don't seem to be enjoying this." And one teacher said "Actually, the problem is that you gave exactly the same talk last year, so we've heard it all before." I didn't really know what to do at this point. I just apologized profusely and invited the people who had already heard the talk to leave, which, unfortunately, was almost everybody.
3 I was giving a presentation to a rather serious group of business people in Germany. They listened politely for 45 minutes, and at the end I asked for any questions. Nobody said anything. Then a young

man stood up and said to me, "Sir, your fly is open." I looked down at my zipper and realized that it was.

4 I had to give a talk to some students at a university in Washington, D.C. It was in the science and technology department of the university, so I didn't think there would be any problems with the equipment. I'd seen the auditorium before, and it was a nice room, good sound and screen, and so forth. But as soon as I began my talk, people started complaining that they couldn't see the slides – there was something wrong with the projector and the screen was too dark. So I started touching keys on my laptop, and I don't know what I did, but I managed to delete the whole presentation. So there I was with no presentation notes at all, nothing, and I had to improvise from what I could remember. It was all very embarrassing.

5 I had to give a business presentation to a company in Montreal one time. I flew in from Chicago that morning, and after I'd gotten to my hotel and checked in, I thought I'd go for a walk since it was such a beautiful day and I had plenty of time. My talk wasn't until one o'clock, and I was well prepared. I was strolling along by the river, enjoying the sunshine, when I noticed that several people at the cafes were already having lunch. I thought it was a little early for lunch and checked my watch – it was only a quarter to twelve. And then I suddenly realized that I'd forgotten to change my watch. Chicago is one hour behind Montreal, so that meant it was actually a quarter to *one*. My presentation was supposed to start in 15 minutes. I desperately looked for a taxi to take me first back to my hotel and then to the company's offices where I was going to give the presentation. I finally arrived 20 minutes late and very stressed – and the worst thing of all was that the title of the talk I was giving was "How to manage your time better"!

6.9 **Interviewer** What advice would you give to someone visiting Chicago for the first time?

Travel writer Take an architectural boat tour along the Chicago River. Chicago is the birthplace of the modern skyscraper and has some of the most spectacular architecture in the United States. You can get a great view of the famous buildings and bridges while you're enjoying a cruise down the river.

Interviewer What's the one thing that someone visiting Chicago should do or see?

Travel writer Outdoors: take a stroll in Millennium Park, with its beautiful gardens and amazing fountains. The Crown Fountain, for example, has faces of different Chicagoans projected on a huge tower, with water cascading down from the top. It's fabulous! Indoors: the Chicago Museum of Science and Industry. It's a "hands-on" type of museum, where you can see a coal mine or look inside the Apollo 8 space capsule!

Interviewer And what's the best place to have your photo taken?

Travel writer In front of an outdoor sculpture called "Cloud Gate" by Anish Kapoor. Its surface is like a mirror that reflects the city skyline, and it's breathtaking on a clear day, a perfect background for a photo.

Interviewer What's your favorite landmark?

Travel writer Tough question… There are so many. I'd have to say the John Hancock Building. It's not the tallest skyscraper, but for some of us, it's the most graceful, with its bold design and cross-braced steel on the outside.

Interviewer What's the best place to watch the sunset?

Travel writer I imagine the Ferris Wheel at Navy Pier would be a good spot, but I am ashamed to say I have never been on it. Of course, the views from the skyscrapers, like the Sears Tower, are always stunning.

Interviewer What would be a good place to go on a scorching hot day?

Travel writer That would be Lake Michigan. Chicago is unique in that it's the only big city in the US with a beach right in the heart of the city. In the summer, the lake is full of swimmers and sailboats, and there's an 18-mile bicycle path along the lakefront.

Interviewer Sounds good. What's your favorite sports venue?

Travel writer For me, it's Wrigley Field, where the Chicago Cubs play baseball. It was built in 1914 and still has ivy-covered walls and a hand-operated scoreboard. Cubs fans are incredibly loyal, so most games are sold out. Fans even stand out on the street, hoping to catch a baseball if a home run is hit outside the stadium.

Interviewer What's a good thing to do that's absolutely free?

Travel writer Spend a day at the Lincoln Park Zoo, where admission is free every day of the year. The zoo is famous for its collection of apes, monkeys, and other primates.

Interviewer What do you think is the most romantic thing to do in Chicago?

Travel writer A horse-drawn carriage ride down Michigan Avenue is very romantic. The ride goes through a historic district, making it seem all the more magical. In fact, my husband proposed to me on one of those carriage rides!

6.11 **Presenter** And tonight on the program we're reviewing a book called *Did You Spot the Gorilla?* by Dr. Richard Wiseman, who's an expert on creative thinking. With us tonight to talk about this book is Steven Hutchinson, a freelance journalist. So, Steven, what exactly is Dr. Wiseman's main message?

Steven Well, Dr. Wiseman's theory is that most people don't think creatively because they concentrate so hard on the small, specific job that they are working on that they don't see the bigger picture. That's what the gorilla experiment proves.

Presenter What was the gorilla experiment?

Steven Well, a study was carried out by two researchers, Daniel Simons and Christopher Chabris, at Harvard University in 1999. They got volunteers to watch a 75-second film of people playing basketball. There were two teams. One team was wearing black T-shirts and the other team was wearing white ones. They gave the volunteers a simple task: they just had to count the number of passes made by one team. Afterward, they were asked how many passes they had counted, and most people got the answer right. Then they were asked if they had seen anything unusual, and at least half of them said no. And that's really amazing because, during the film, while the two teams were playing basketball, a woman dressed as a gorilla walked onto the court and beat her chest at the camera, and then slowly walked off the court. And half of the volunteers just didn't see it!

Presenter That's incredible. Why not?

Steven Because they were so busy trying to count the passes that they didn't notice the gorilla! Dr. Wiseman repeated this experiment many times, and the result was always the same. In fact, he actually tried it on a group of top scientists, and not one of them saw the gorilla.

Presenter That's amazing!

6.12 **Steven** The gorilla experiment is a perfect demonstration of how we usually focus only on what we're looking for and don't see outside it. So, we sometimes miss really important discoveries that are right in front of us because we just don't see them. That's why when something is invented, people often say, "Why didn't anybody think of that before?" Well, they didn't because they didn't think creatively.

Presenter Dr. Wiseman gives some examples of people who he says *are* creative thinkers, doesn't he?

Steven Yes, people like the man who invented Post-it notes. He was actually trying to develop a really strong kind of glue, but he could only manage to make a very weak one. But instead of just thinking, "Oh that's no good," he actually thought of a way to use the weak glue to make Post-it notes, notes that would stick to something, but not too much.

Or the man who set up IKEA, the furniture company. I mean, for years people had been wanting cheap furniture that was well designed, but nobody made it. Or the idea of cheap air travel. People just accepted the idea that it was impossible. But then somebody said, "It *is* possible, and I'm going to do it." And that's how we got discount airlines like JetBlue.

Presenter Can we make ourselves into creative thinkers?

Steven Yes, Dr. Wiseman has lots of tips on how we can become more creative. One of the things he recommends is to try to do the *opposite* of what you usually do. For example, he told a group of journalists to try to think of articles that *nobody* would find interesting – he said that from that, possibly a brilliant idea for something interesting would come up. His book is full of tips – it's really worth reading.

Presenter And has he had any "eureka moments" himself?

Steven Yes, as a matter of fact, he thought up a great idea for book lovers. His idea is to print a book that contains the first chapters of 15 different books. This book has a book token in the back, a voucher that you can use to buy another book. The idea is that you read the beginnings and then choose which book you want to read more of and buy it with the book token.

Presenter What a great idea! Now that's creative thinking for you.

6.16 **Interviewer** Graham Bull is a "conDUCKtor," or a tour guide, of Boston Duck Tours. The company uses vehicles, called "Ducks," that can travel on land or water. How did the Boston Duck Tours start?

Graham The company was founded by a fellow by the name of Andy Wilson, I believe 14 years ago. Uh… He was a fellow who was traveling about and he saw a Duck being used, uh, I believe on a tour, and he thought, "Oh, that would be great in Boston – we've got the Charles River, we've got all the historical sights."

Interviewer In your opinion, what makes a Duck tour special?

Graham Boston Duck Tours is special for two reasons, actually. One is that we actually… it is an amphibious tour – we go on the river, there is a wonderful view of Boston. But that and the fact there is levity in the tour, there is a good deal of sense of humor involved, and it works out very well. It's a special, special occasion.

Interviewer What are the most popular sights on the tour?

Graham The most popular sights are difficult to determine because different people have different interests. I think there is a high degree of interest in the… uh… in Beacon Hill because people have heard of Beacon Hill, the home of the double-rich, our Boston Brahmans. Uh… I think they are interested also in Faneuil Hall, which is where Sam Adams did his work in the pre-revolutionary days…

Interviewer What would you say is the best thing about Boston for a tourist?

Graham For a tourist in Boston, I think the best thing is really the friendliness of the city. It's a very friendly city. And it is also a safe city… to walk around downtown, you are safe at anytime of the night or day – it's really not a dangerous spot. So those, I think, are the two best things about the city in general.

Interviewer And what is the worst thing?

Graham The worst thing about being a tourist in Boston is, without question, the matter of driving a car. Do not drive a car in Boston unless you live here and know your way around. It is an impossibility. The streets are almost all of them one way; sometimes you can run onto five, six, seven streets in a row – they are all one way the wrong way. And people who don't know their way around can get badly, badly lost.

6.17 **Interviewer** Have you had any interesting or amusing incidents during the tour that you can tell us about?

Graham There's one particularly funny, uh…, funny instance that occurred. On rare occasions we will get a passenger on board who is not aware that the tour is amphibious, that the Ducks are intended to go into the river. And, uh… I think it was two or three years ago. I had a family that had arranged a surprise birthday for their mother. Now, she was not a youngster. I mean, I would've… I would guess she was probably in her seventies. And we did the tour and she was enjoying it and she was, you know, obviously enjoying this birthday present from her children. We got to the river and we have a ramp that goes down at a rather steep angle into the river. And when you're on the ramp there is that kind of roller-coaster sensation of "oh-we're-going-down". And at that point I turned around and I could see on her face this look of what appeared to me to be excited glee. And it's not uncommon for people to shriek with glee, especially the children. Well, she was shrieking her brains out! And when we got onto the water, it became clear that she didn't know this tour was an amphibious tour and she was really freaking out.

Interviewer Do you tell any funny stories about the city, too?

Graham There is… There's a funny story about Boston Garden – our magnificent premier downtown sports arena where the Celtics reign supreme. The Garden that we have now is the new Garden, but it was preceded by the old original Boston Garden right in the very same location. And, uh, they had a ghost. True story, they had a ghost in the old Boston Garden. The janitors came into work one morning and they found rubbish strewn all over the floor, where they cleaned up the night before after an athletic event. And they assumed that they had a vandal in the building, so they dismissed it, they weren't at all concerned. But the following morning this rubbish shows up again and the following morning, the following morning. Well, to make a long story short: days turn into weeks, weeks turn into months and this rubbish keeps showing up, and these… these janitors are flummoxed by this. Months turn into years and this keeps going on and by this time they've cemented into their minds that they have a ghost in the old Boston Garden. And when they tore down the old building to replace it with the new Garden, what did they find? This is a true story. They found the remains of a monkey! He'd escaped from the Ringling Brothers Barnum and Bailey Circus years ago and had been living in the rafters of the Boston Garden for years undetected. And, I mean, if you've ever been to one of these sports arenas, you know, there are tens of thousands of sports spectators, television sweeping every inch of the arena and never once was that monkey ever detected! Can you imagine that?!

6.19 **Interviewer** What's your favorite city in the world?

Christina My favorite city in the world would have to be Dublin in Ireland. I was there two years ago with my friends and I've had… I had the most wonderful time. The people were awesome, the city was absolutely gorgeous, the weather could have been better because it rains all the time, but it was a lot of fun.

Interviewer What city would you most like to visit?

Christina I would love to go to Prague just because I've never been there and I've heard great things about it. So it's definitely one city I would love to visit before I'm done.

Interviewer What is your favorite city in the world?

Juan My favorite city in the world would have to be Miami. Uh… The reason being the weather's beautiful, you can't complain. Uh… My family… I have a lot of family that lives down there. The diversity down there, it's a high… it's a fast-paced lifestyle… and… it's just gorgeous.

Interviewer What city would you most like to visit?

Juan City anywhere in the world… that would probably have to be Rome. And the reason being for that is… it's just gorgeous out there, it's different. I mean, it's Europe. Everybody wants to go out there, it's beautiful.

Interviewer What's your favorite city in the world?

Sophie My favorite city in the world would have to be Cambridge, Massachusetts, because I think it's really cute, and everyone's really nice, and it's like a perfectly sized city.

Interviewer What city would you most like to visit?

Sophie I think I would like to visit Athens, Greece. I think it has a lot of historical, I don't know, value and I think it would be very cool to see.

Interviewer What's your favorite city in the world?

Tim Oh, favorite city in the world… Uh… Well, to be a little cliché… Paris. I went to when I was 17 or 18 and I always wanted to take someone special back there. And I was fortunate to be able to do that with my then girlfriend, now wife – back then fiancée, now wife – she and I got to go back there and spent about ten days and… So that was… that was pretty neat, I really enjoyed that.

Interviewer What city would you most like to visit?

Tim Uh… probably… probably Tokyo. I was there for a day, but didn't get a chance… I kind of felt like I had an opportunity to see it and wasn't able to. So back there to see… to see it again or to see more of it would be great.

Interviewer What's your favorite city in the world?

Rachel My favorite city in the world is New York City, where I went to college, because it was where I did a lot of my growing up.

Interviewer What city would you most like to visit?

Rachel I would really actually like to visit Rio, because now that I have friends there, it would be a… it would be a different experience of getting a sense of other cultures. I haven't been to South America at all.

7.3

1 When I was a young man, about 17, I was working in Spain as an electrician for the German car company Mercedes. A man from the engineering company Bosch visited Mercedes, and he liked the way that I worked, and he offered me a job in Germany. I suppose it is what you would call "an apprenticeship." I would have learned to become an engineer. I really wanted to do it, but my parents didn't want me to leave home and go and work in a foreign country. In those days not many people did that. So, in the end I didn't go. But I really wish that I'd taken that job because I think it would have opened doors for me, and my professional life would have been more fulfilling.

2 Three years ago I was going to take part in a dance contest. I was a little bit pale, so I decided to go to a tanning salon the day before the contest. I didn't have much time, and I wanted to get a nice tan really quickly, so I stayed under the lamp about 20 minutes. Unfortunately, that was too long and I got burned. The top and the skirt I wore the next day for the contest were really skimpy, and so everyone in the audience could see how red my skin was. I felt really stupid and really wished I hadn't done it.

3 I really wish I'd been able to know my grandmother better. She died when I was 12, and since then I've discovered that she must have been a fascinating person, and there are so many things I would love to have been able to talk to her about. She was Polish, but she was in Russia, in St. Petersburg, during the Russian Revolution, and she knew all kinds of interesting people at the time: painters, writers, people like that. I was only a child, so I never asked her much about her own life. Now I'm discovering all about her through reading her old letters and papers, but I wish she had lived longer so that I could have talked to her about those times face-to-face.

4 The only thing I really regret is not having had the courage to talk to a guy who I saw at a party last summer. I really liked him – he was very good-looking – but I just wasn't brave enough to start a conversation. I wish I'd tried. I'm absolutely positive we would have gotten along well. And now it's too late – he's engaged to another woman!

5 My biggest regret is how I spent my time in college. I studied English literature, which was something I was interested in, but it certainly wasn't the most important thing in my life. I played a lot of sports, I played in a band, and I listened to a lot of music, but I also spent most of my time either socializing or sleeping. And in terms of studying, I just did the bare minimum – I read what I had to, but never anything more. I only went to the compulsory lectures, never the optional ones, and I left all my essays until the last minute and kept them as short as I could. OK, I passed my exams and I got my degree in the end, but I've always regretted not taking more advantage of those four years. I wish I'd realized at the time that this was a unique opportunity to read lots of novels, to learn about great writers, and to listen to people who really knew what they were talking about. Now I'm working and have small children, so I don't have time to read anything.

7.5 When Paul Feldman started his business, he projected that at least 95 percent of the people would pay for their bagels. He made this forecast presumably because that was the payment rate that he got in his own office. But in fact, that rate wasn't representative at all. In his office, most people paid probably just because Feldman worked there himself, and they knew him personally and probably liked him.

So when Feldman began his project of selling bagels in other offices, he had to accept less. After a while, he considered that a company was "honest" if over 90 percent of the people paid. Between 80 and 90 percent was what he considered to be normal, or the average rate. He didn't like it, but he had to accept it. It was only if a company habitually paid less than 80 percent – which luckily not many did – that he would feel he had to do something. First, he would leave a note, sort of giving them a warning, and then, if things didn't improve, he would simply stop selling there. Interestingly, since he started the business, the baskets he leaves to collect the cash have hardly ever been stolen. Obviously, in the mind of an office worker, stealing a bagel isn't a crime – but stealing the money basket is.

So, what do the bagel data tell us about the kind of offices that were not honest, the ones that *didn't* pay? Well, first of all, it shows that smaller offices are more honest than big ones. An office with 20 to 30 employees generally pays 3-5 percent more than an office with two to three hundred employees. This seems to be because in a smaller community, people are more worried about being dishonest – probably because they would feel worse if they were caught.

The bagel data also suggest that your mood, how you feel, affects how honest you are. For example, the weather is a really important factor. When the weather is unusually good, more people pay, but if it's unusually cold or rainy, fewer people pay. And people are also affected by public holidays, but in different ways – it depends on *which* public holiday. Before Christmas and Thanksgiving, people are less honest, but just before the 4th of July and Labor Day, they are *more* honest. This seems to be because holidays like the 4th of July, are just a day off work, and people always look forward to them. But Christmas and Thanksgiving are holidays when people often feel very stressed or miserable. So their bad mood makes them less honest.

The other thing Feldman believes affects how honestly people behave is the morale in an office. When employees like their boss and like their job, then the office is more honest. He also thinks that the higher the position people are promoted to, the less honest they are. He reached this conclusion because over several years he'd been delivering three baskets of bagels to a company that was on three floors: the top floor was the executive floor, and the two lower floors were for people who worked in sales and service, and administration. Well, it turned out that the least honest floor was the executive floor! It makes you wonder whether maybe these guys got to be executives because they were good at cheating!

But, in general, the story of Feldman's bagel business is a really positive one. It's true that some people *do* steal from him, but the vast majority of customers are honest, even though no one is watching them.

7.7 **Presenter** Now it's time for our regular Wednesday afternoon program about words and their origins. And I have with me, as usual, our English language expert, Sally Davies. So what are the three words you are going to tell us about today, Sally?

Sally Hello, John. My three words today are *ketchup*, *orange* – that's the fruit, the color came later – and *tennis*.

Presenter OK, well, let's start with *ketchup*.

Sally Well, the Chinese invented a sauce called "ke-tsiap," spelled K-E-hyphen-T-S-I-A-P, in the 1690s. It was made from fish and spices, but no tomatoes. By the early 18th century, its popularity had spread to Malaysia, and that is where British explorers first found it, and obviously, really liked it. By 1740 the sauce was part of the English diet – people were eating a lot of it, and it was also becoming popular in the American colonies. And they renamed the sauce "ketchup," because it was a little bit easier for the English to pronounce. Then about 50 years later, in 1790, some Americans in New England mixed tomatoes into the sauce and it became known as "tomato ketchup."

Presenter Well, so it is American after all?

Sally Well, tomato ketchup is.

Presenter So, tell us about *orange*.

Sally Well, it's very interesting that neither *orange* in English nor *naranja* in Spanish or *arancia* in Italian come from the Latin word for *orange*, which was *citrus aurentium*. Instead, they all come from the ancient Sanskrit word *narangah*. There is also an interesting story about where this word, *narangah*, comes from. It's said that it comes from *naga ranga*, which literally means "poison for elephants."

Presenter Poison for elephants?

Sally Yes, apparently, one day, an elephant was passing through the forest when he found a tree that he had never seen before. This tree was full of beautiful, tempting oranges. As a result, the elephant ate so many that he died. Many years later, a man came to the same spot and noticed the remains of the elephant with some orange trees growing from what had been its stomach. The man then exclaimed, "These fruits are naga ranga," that is, "poison for elephants."

Presenter So is this true?

Sally Well, I don't know, but it's a nice story!

Presenter Yes, it is. And finally our last word is *tennis*.

Sally This is my favorite one, and it shows that English speakers have always had their own special way of pronouncing foreign languages.

Presenter What do you mean?

Sally Well, tennis is a sport that first developed in France. The name was originally *tenez*, which is from the French verb *tenir*, which means, in this case, something like "Here you are." Players used to say "Tenez" when they hit the ball, meaning something like "There, try to get this one." But the sport lost popularity in France and gained popularity in England at the same time. So, English people were still using the word tenez each time they hit the ball, but they were saying it with the English accent, which sounded more like "tennis," and eventually it took on this new spelling. Then the sport gained popularity worldwide and was taken up by many nationalities, including the French – but they now had to call it "le tennis!"

Presenter That's fascinating! Well, thank you very much for those three words, Sally, and we'll look forward to next week's program.

7.9 **Interviewer** Jesse Sheidlower is one of the main editors of the *Oxford English Dictionary*, also known as OED. Could you give us an estimate of how many new words come into the English language every year?

Jesse It's very hard to give an exact number for the number of new words that enter the language in a given year. There is just no way to figure out which are really new words, which are going to stay around. Um… There are going to be words that come in very briefly, but no one really pays attention to, or people pay attention to only because they are new, but they are not going to be a part of the language. The OED puts in around a thousand new words every year. And that's a number with some meaning, but it doesn't tell you anything about how large the language is or anything like that, but it's one useful figure you can look at.

Interviewer And how long does it usually take for a new word to get into the dictionary?

Jesse There's no easy way to say exactly how long it will take for a new word to make it into the dictionary. In some cases it can be very fast. If you have a term for something that is very important and you know it's important and that's *a* term that describes that, uh, it can go in very quickly.

Interviewer Can you give us an example of a word that entered the dictionary very quickly?

Jesse Typically, when you have a word that enters the dictionary very quickly, it's a technical term or something where you have a new invention and that becomes very popular very quickly, and you know then that as soon as there is a word coined for that, it's got to go in pretty quickly if the term is important enough. And I think the best recent example is *podcasting*, where I think the first example we have from that is 2003, but it became so ubiquitous, so quickly, and this was *the* term for it, there was no other term, there were no competing terms, there were no other descriptions, uh, this was it. And we waited a very short amount of time before saying, "Well, you know, even though this is very, very recent, um, this is clearly such a big thing that it has to go in right away."

Another good example of a new word that came into the language very quickly is *google* as a verb – uh, meaning to use the Google search engine to look for information on the Internet – uh, which happened to have been coined very soon after Google started in the late 1990s. But because of how prominent Google is and how many people use it, um, it's – all people use it now – it's *the* word for searching for things on the Internet. You know, if you want to find out what something is, you *google* it.

7.10 **Interviewer** How are new words formed?

Jesse There are a number of different ways that words can be formed in English. One of the most common ways is "compounding," where you take two separate words and use them together in a particular way. For example, one of the recent entries in the OED is the word *hang time*, which refers to the amount of time that a ball kicked or thrown stays in the air or that a person jumping stays in the air – a relatively recent term in sports, which is formed from taking two words and using them together.

Another example is *time-shift*, which is typically used to refer to, uh, video recording or digitally recording, television shows that you can watch at a later time. So you're just shifting the time you're watching it.

Interviewer Are there also new words that come from other languages?

Jesse There are a number of words that enter the OED from foreign languages all the time. *Hawala*, a term from Arabic, which refers to an informal system of uh… a sort of informal banking system where people pay debts on behalf of other people in different places. *Ki*, K-I, which is a Japanese term, uh, for a sort of, you know, a life force or a strong force of nature. It's the equivalent of *chi* in Chinese.

Interviewer Are there any interesting stories about new words entering the dictionary?

Jesse One of the famous stories in the history of the OED is that when the OED was first being… at the very earliest stages, when they were working the letter A, it was decided to keep the word *appendectomy* and *appendicitis* out of the dictionary because these were thought to be too technical. And the editor of the OED at the time actually wrote to a consultant, who was the professor of medicine at Oxford, asking about these words, and he said, "Oh, no, no, no one will ever use these. These are too technical. You can keep them out." And then a few years later, when the coronation of King Edward had to be delayed because he had appendicitis and had to have an appendectomy, people looked at the OED and said, "Well, you don't have these words in. What's wrong with you?" So it's very hard to predict what's going to become prominent and why. All you can do is use your best judgment for what's common enough to be put in.

7.12 **Interviewer** Are there any English words that are used in your language?

Mateusz Yes, for example, *hamburger*. It is used, I think, worldwide, but in Poland we say "hamburger." Yes, maybe *computer*, in Poland "komputer," there are plenty of words like that, plenty of words that are about cuisine, *hot dog*, "hot dog" in Polish. Really, plenty of words like that.

Interviewer Do you think it would be better to use your own words?

Mateusz No, I don't think so, because they are used everywhere in this world and why not in Poland?

Interviewer Are there any English words that are used in your language?

Victoria Uh… yes. Well, no, there are not… I don't think there are a lot of English words, but there are a lot of French words that sound English, like *parking*, which actually doesn't make sense in English. It's a car park and we call it "parking" and it's not French at all. But we have a lot of things like that because English is cool, so we try to make our words sound English.

Interviewer Do you think it would be better to use your own words?

Victoria No, we should… I like the idea that there are words that you can understand in every country, it makes us… brings nations, people closer, you know.

Interviewer Are there any English words that are used in your language?

Matandra An English word that is used in the Italian language, well, everything to do with technology, everything to do with the Internet, and *Internet* itself. Well, someone could argue that *Internet* is actually Latin but… Say, *download*, we've given up saying the Italian version of *downloading*, which is "scaricare," so most people just go with "downloadare," which sounds very odd to the Italian ear, but we… we're going with it.

Interviewer Do you think it would be better to use your own words?

Matandra I don't think it's necessary to… to set off on a crusade to defend language in so much as, you know, there are specific areas which are just the domain of another language. Italian is the main domain in, say, music. No one complains around the world because you say *pianissimo* when you have to play softly.

Interviewer Are there any English words that are used in your language?

Volke Too many, too many, I must say. We forget a lot of German words and replace them by English words and they are pronounced in the same way. I miss that, because I like Spanish as well and they have so many, they have, like, words for *computer* or *skateboard* and things like that, which we don't have, and we take all the English words. And if there are new inventions and stuff like that, we don't invent new words – we just take them – and I think it's a pity not to do the opposite.

Interviewer Do you think it would be better to use your own words?

Volke It's part of culture. And I think we should maintain that. You can be open to other languages and cultures, but at the same time you should keep your own one, I think.

1

1A question formation

1 **Can you** drive? Why **are you** crying?
2 Where **do you** live? **Did you** go out last night?
3 Why **didn't you** like the play? **Isn't this** a beautiful place?
4 **What** are they talking **about**? **Where** is she **from**?
5 **Who lives** in this house? **How many people came** to the party?
6 Could you tell me **where this bus goes**?
Do you know **if he's coming**?

1 To make questions with modal verbs and with tenses where there is an auxiliary verb (*be*, *have*, etc.), invert the subject and the modal / auxiliary verb.
2 With the simple present and simple past, add *do* / *does* or *did* before the subject.
3 We often use negative questions to show surprise or when we expect somebody to agree with us.
4 If a verb is followed by a preposition, the preposition often comes at the end of the question, e.g.,
What are you talking about? NOT ~~*About what are you talking?*~~
- We often use just the question word and the preposition, e.g.,
A *I'm thinking.* **B** *About what?* OR *What about?*

5 When *who* / *what* / *which*, etc. is the **subject** of the question, don't use *do* / *did*, e.g., *Who wrote this?* NOT ~~*Who did write this?*~~
6 Use indirect questions when you want to ask a question in a more polite way.
Where does she live? (direct) *Could you tell me where she lives?* (indirect)
- In indirect questions the order is subject + verb.
Can you tell me where **it is**? NOT ~~*Can you tell me where is it?*~~
- Don't use *do* / *did* in the second part of the question, e.g.,
Do you know where he lives? NOT ~~*Do you know where he does live?*~~
- You can use *if* or *whether* after *Can you tell me, Do you know*, etc., e.g.,
Can you tell me if / *whether he's at home?*

1B auxiliary verbs

1 **A** **Do** you speak Chinese? **B** Yes, **I do**. Fairly well.
2 I like dogs, but my husband **doesn't**. Jim's coming, but Anna **isn't**.
3 **A** I loved the movie. **B** **So did I.**
A I haven't finished yet. **B** **Neither have I.**
He's a doctor and **so is his wife.**
4 **A** I went to a psychic yesterday. **B** **You did?**
A I'll make the dinner. **B** **You will?** That's great!
5 **A** You didn't lock the door! **B** I **did** lock it, I promise.
A Silvia isn't coming. **B** She **is** coming. I just spoke to her.
6 You won't forget, **will you**? Your wife can speak Portuguese, **can't she**?

Use auxiliary verbs (*do, have*, etc.) or modal verbs (*can, must*, etc.):
1 in short answers, instead of answering just *Yes* / *No*.
2 to avoid repeating the main verb / verb phrase, e.g.,
I like dogs, but my husband doesn't (~~like dogs~~).
3 with *so* and *neither* to say that something is the same.
Use *so* + auxiliary + subject to agree with an affirmative statement.
Use *neither* (or *nor*) + auxiliary + subject to agree with a negative statement.
4 to make "echo questions," to show interest.
5 to show emphasis in an affirmative sentence.
With the simple present and simple past, add *do* / *does* / *did* before the main verb. With other tenses, stress the auxiliary verb.
6 to make tag questions. Use an affirmative tag question after a negative statement and a negative tag question after an affirmative statement.
- Tag questions are often used simply to ask another person to agree with you, e.g.,
It's a nice day, isn't it?
In this case the tag question is said with falling intonation, i.e., the voice goes down.
- Tag questions can also be used to check something you think is true, e.g.,
She's a painter, isn't she?
In this case the tag question is said with rising intonation, as in a regular Yes / No question.

1C present perfect (simple and continuous)

present perfect simple: *have* / *has* + past participle

1 **I've been** to Brazil.
Have you ever broken your leg?
2 **We haven't called** the doctor **yet**.
I've already finished my lunch.
3 It's the best book **I've** ever **read**.
It's the first time **we've done** this.
4 All the guests **have arrived**.
5 **I've known** her **since** I was a child.
She's had the job **for** six months.
6 **How many** of his books **have you read**?
She's been out twice this week.

Use the present perfect simple:
1 to talk about past experiences when you don't say when something happened.
2 with *already* and *yet*.
3 with superlatives and *the first, second, last time*, etc.
4 for finished actions (no time is specified) that are connected in some way with the present.
5 with *How long?* and *for* / *since* with **non-action** verbs (= verbs not usually used in the continuous form, e.g., *be, have, know, like*, etc.) to say that something started in the past and is still true now.
6 when we say / ask *how much* / *many* we have done or *how often* we have done something up to now.

present perfect continuous: *have* / *has* + *been* + verb + *-ing*

1 **How long have you been feeling** like this?
I've been working here **for** two months.
2 **I haven't been sleeping** well recently.
It's been raining on and off all day.
3 **I've been shopping** all morning. I'm exhausted.
A Take your shoes off. They're filthy.
B Yes, I know. **I've been working** in the garden.

Use the present perfect continuous:
1 with *How long?* and *for* / *since* with **action** verbs to say that an action started in the past and is still happening now.
2 for repeated actions, especially with a time expression, e.g., *all day, recently*.
3 for continuous actions that have just finished (but that have present results).

present perfect simple or continuous?

1 **We've lived** / **We've been living** in this town since 1980.
We've been living in an apartment for the last two months.
2 **I've read** that book. **I've been reading** that book.

1 With *How long...?* and *for* / *since* you can often use the present perfect simple or continuous. However, we often prefer the present perfect continuous for shorter, more temporary actions.
2 The present perfect simple emphasizes the completion of an action (= I've finished reading the book). The present perfect continuous emphasizes the continuation of an action (= I haven't finished reading the book).

1A

a Order the words to make questions.

friend known long best have How you your

How long have you known your best friend?

1 you messages send ever text Do
2 party was a time you to the When last went
3 if Could bank here a you me near tell is there
4 dinner usually Who the cooks
5 shopping do going Who like you with
6 on don't weekends you What doing like
7 car to would What you kind like buy of
8 you time concert know ends Do what the

b Complete the questions.

Where *did you go* on vacation last year? (you / go)

1 How often ________ exercise? (you / do)
2 Who ________ *Crime and Punishment*? (write)
3 Could you tell me how much ________? (this book / cost)
4 What ________ at the end of the movie? (happen)
5 ________ your trip to Peru last summer? (you / enjoy)
6 What kind of music ________? (Tim / usually listen to)
7 Who ________ Mia's backpack? (steal)
8 Do you know when ________? (the swimming pool / open)
9 Where ________ your boyfriend tonight? (you / meet)
10 Can you remember where ________? (she / live)

1B

a Complete the dialogues with an auxiliary.

A You didn't remember to buy coffee. **B** I *did*. It's on the shelf.

1 **A** It's cold today, ________ it? **B** Yes, it's freezing.
2 **A** So you didn't go to the meeting?
B I ________ go to the meeting, but I left early.
3 **A** What did you think of the movie?
B Hiro liked it, but I ________. I thought it was awful.
4 **A** I wouldn't like to be famous. **B** Neither ________ I.
5 **A** Claudia doesn't like me.
B She ________ like you. She thinks you're very nice.
6 **A** Sarah had a baby.
B She ________? I didn't know she was pregnant!
7 **A** Will your boyfriend be at the party?
B No, he ________. He's away this week.
8 **A** I can't come tonight.
B You ________? Why not?

b Complete the conversation with auxiliary verbs.

A You're Marco's sister, *aren't* you?
B Yes, I [1] ________.
A It's a great club, [2] ________ it?
B Yes, it [3] ________. But I don't like the music much.
A You [4] ________? I love it!
B Really? [5] ________ you been here before?
A No, I [6] ________.
B Neither [7] ________ I.
A So you [8] ________ go out much, then?
B Well, I [9] ________ go out, but I [10] ________ go to clubs very often.
A Oh, I [11] ________. I love clubbing.
B I'd like something to drink.
A So [12] ________ I. Let's go to the bar.

1C

a Circle the correct form of the verb. Put a check (✔) next to the sentence if both forms are correct.

Have you ever *(tried)* / *been trying* caviar?

1 *She's lived* / *She's been living* here for years.
2 Your boss *has called* / *has been calling* three times this morning!
3 The kids are exhausted because *they've played* / *they've been playing* outside all day.
4 *He hasn't seen* / *He hasn't been seeing* the new James Bond movie yet.
5 *I've never met* / *I've never been meeting* his wife. Have you?
6 *We've studied* / *We've been studying* English all our lives.
7 *I've cleaned up* / *I've been cleaning up* the garage all afternoon. I'm nearly finished.
8 *We've already had* / *We've already been having* breakfast.
9 How long *have you had* / *have you been having* your car?
10 The train *has left* / *has been leaving* the station. The next one leaves in an hour.

b Complete the sentences with the present perfect simple or continuous.

I've bought a new car. Do you like it? (buy)

1 We ________ Jack and Ann for years. (know)
2 You look hot. ________? (you / run)
3 Rose ________ her homework, so she can't go out. (not do)
4 Did you know that ________? They live in Boston now. (they / move)
5 How long ________ together? Five months? (Laura and Adam / go out)
6 I ________ time to cook dinner. Why don't we get a pizza? (not have)
7 We ________ for hours. I think we're lost. (drive)
8 ________ my cookies? There are only a few left! (you / eat)

2

2A adjectives as nouns, adjective order

nationalities

1 **The English** are famous for drinking tea. **The Dutch** make wonderful cheeses. **The Chinese** invented paper.
2 **The Argentinians** invented the tango. **The Greeks** are very outgoing.
3 **The Turks** drink a lot of coffee. **The Poles** play a lot of basketball.

1 You can use *the* with the nationality adjectives that end in *-sh*, *-ch*, *-ss*, or *-ese*. Don't add *s* to these words or use them without *the*.
2 Nationality words that end in *-an* and a few others, e.g., *Greek* and *Thai*, are both adjectives and nouns. To talk about the people from that country use a plural noun ending in *-s*.
3 Some nationalities have a special noun for the people. The noun is different from the adjective, e.g., *Polish* = adjective, *Pole* = noun. To talk about the people you can either use *the* + adjective or *the* + plural noun, e.g., *the Polish* or *the Poles*.

⚠ With any nationality, you can also use the adjective + *people*, e.g., *Korean people.*

⚠ To talk about one person from a country, you can't use *a* / *an* + adjective alone:
1 *a Japanese man / woman / person, an Englishman / Englishwoman / English person*, NOT ~~*a Japanese*~~, ~~*an English*~~, etc.
2 but: *an Italian, a Greek, a Peruvian*, etc. (These are nouns.)
3 *a Turk, a Pole*, etc. (These are nouns.)

specific groups of people

The poor are getting poorer and **the rich** are getting richer.
The government should create more jobs for **the unemployed**.

- You can use *the* + some adjectives to talk about specific groups in society, e.g., *the young, the blind, the homeless, the old, the elderly, the sick.* These expressions are always plural.

one, ones

A **Which one** would you like? **B** **The red one**, please.
Two ice creams, please. **Big ones**.

- When we don't want to repeat a noun after an adjective because it is already clear what we are talking about, we use the adjective + *one* (singular) or + *ones* (plural).

adjective order

They live in **a charming old house** near the lake.
She has **long black** hair.
I bought a **beautiful Italian leather** belt.

- You can put more than one adjective before a noun (often two and occasionally three). These adjectives go in a particular order, e.g., NOT ~~*an old charming house*~~.
- Opinion adjectives, e.g., *beautiful, nice, charming*, usually go before fact adjectives, e.g., *blue, old, round.*
- If there is more than one fact adjective, they go in this order:

size	age	shape / style	color / pattern	nationality	material	noun
big	*new*	*long*	*pink, striped*	*Italian*	*silk*	*scarf*

2B narrative tenses: simple past, past continuous, past perfect, past perfect continuous

narrative tenses

1 We **arrived** at the airport and **checked in**.
2 We **were having dinner** when the plane hit some turbulence.
3 When we arrived at the airport, we suddenly realized that **we had left** one of the suitcases in the taxi.
4 **We'd been flying** for about two hours when the captain told us to fasten our seat belts because we were flying into some very bad weather.

1 Use the **simple past** to talk about consecutive actions in the past, i.e., for the main events in a story.
2 Use the **past continuous** (*was* / *were* + verb + *-ing*) to describe a longer continuous past action that was in progress when another action happened.
3 Use the **past perfect** (*had* + past participle) to talk about the "earlier past," i.e., things that happened before the main event(s).
4 Use the **past perfect continuous** (*had been* + verb + *-ing*) to talk about a longer continuous action that was going on before the main events happened. Non-action verbs (e.g., *know, like, have*) are not generally used in the past continuous.

past perfect simple or continuous?

She was crying because **she'd been reading** a very sad book.
She didn't want to see the movie because **she'd read** the book.

The past perfect continuous emphasizes the continuation of an activity. The past perfect simple emphasizes the completion of an activity.

2C adverbs and adverbial phrases

1 I don't understand you when you speak **quickly**. The driver was **seriously** injured.
2 I **never** have breakfast. He's **always** late.
3 They'll be here **soon**. It rained **all day yesterday**.
4 I'm **nearly** finished. We're **incredibly** tired. He works **a lot**.
5 **Unfortunately**, we arrived half an hour late. **Ideally**, we should leave at 10:00.

- Adverbs can describe an action (*He walked slowly*) or modify adjectives or other adverbs (*It's incredibly expensive; He works very hard*). They can either be one word (*often*) or a phrase (*once a week*).

1 **Adverbs of manner** (how somebody does something) usually go after the verb or phrase. However, with passive verbs they usually go in mid-position (before the main verb but after an auxiliary verb).
2 **Adverbs of frequency** generally go before the main verb but after the verb *to be.*

⚠ *sometimes / usually / occasionally* can go at the beginning of a sentence, too.

3 **Adverbs of time** usually go at the end of a sentence or clause.
4 **Adverbs of degree** (which describe how much something is done or modify an adjective).

- *extremely, incredibly, very*, etc. are used with adjectives and adverbs and go before them.
- *much* and *a lot* are often used with verbs and go after the verb or verb phrase.
- *a little / a little bit* can be used with adjectives or verbs, e.g., *I'm a little tired. She sleeps a little bit in the afternoon.*

5 **Comment adverbs** (which give the speaker's opinion) usually go at the beginning of a sentence or clause. Other usual comment adjectives are *luckily, clearly, obviously, apparently*, etc.

⚠ Most other adverbs go in mid-position, e.g., *She didn't* ***even*** *say good-bye. You* ***just*** *have to talk to me.*

2A

a Rewrite the underlined phrase using *the* + an adjective.

The people who live in Vietnam like to eat spicy food. *the Vietnamese*

1 The people from the Netherlands are very good at languages.
2 The people who had injuries were taken to the hospital.
3 The system of reading for people who can't see is called Braille.
4 The people from China have a fascinating history.
5 A nurse's job is to take care of the people who aren't well.
6 I think the people from Switzerland are very punctual.
7 The worst season for people without a home is winter.
8 There is a discount for students and people without a job.

b Write the adjectives in parentheses in the right place.

a big parking lot (empty) *a big empty parking lot*

1 an attractive man (young)
2 dirty shoes (old)
3 a leather jacket (purple / stylish)
4 a tall woman (thin)
5 a sandy beach (long)
6 a new floor (beautiful / wooden)
7 a stylish suit (Italian)
8 a romantic cafe (French / little)
9 an old dog (black / friendly)

2B

a Put the verb in parentheses in the past perfect simple (*had done*) or past perfect continuous (*had been doing*). If you think both are possible, use the continuous form.

His English was very good. He*'d been studying* it for five years. (study)

1 My feet were aching. We ______ in line for hours. (stand)
2 She went to the police because someone ______ her bag. (steal)
3 The streets were wet. It ______ all morning. (rain)
4 She got to work late because she ______ an accident on the way. (have)
5 I almost didn't recognize him. He ______ a lot since I last saw him. (change)
6 They were very red. They ______ all morning, but they ______ any sunscreen. (sunbathe, not put on)
7 I could see from their faces that they ______. (argue)
8 Jess had a bandage on her arm. She ______ off her bike the day before. (fall)

b Circle the correct verb form.

My British friends, Meg and Jack McGowan (*got*) / *were getting* a nasty surprise when they [1]*had checked in / were checking in* at Heathrow Airport yesterday with their baby Sam. They [2]*had won / were winning* three free plane tickets to Rome in a contest, and they [3]*looked forward to / had been looking forward to* their trip for months. But, unfortunately, they [4]*had been forgetting / had forgotten* to get a passport for their son, and so Sam couldn't fly. Luckily, they [5]*had arrived / were arriving* very early for their flight so they still had time to do something about it. They [6]*had run / ran* to the police station in the airport to apply for an emergency passport. Meg [7]*was going / went* with Sam to the photo booth while Jack [8]*had filled out / was filling out* the forms. The passport was ready in an hour, so they [9]*hurried / were hurrying* back to check-in and finally [10]*caught / had caught* their flight.

2C

a Underline the adverb(s) or adverbial phrase(s) and correct the sentences that are wrong.

We're going to be unfortunately late. ✘ *Unfortunately, we're going to be late.*

We rarely go to bed before 11:30. ✔

1 She likes very much the theater.
2 Dave was late for work yesterday.
3 Immediately the ambulance arrived.
4 They go usually jogging after work.
5 I was extremely tired last night.
6 They won easily the game because they played so well.
7 I forgot your birthday almost.
8 We luckily had taken an umbrella.
9 She always eats healthily.
10 He's been apparently fired from his job.

b Put the adverbs in parentheses in the usual position in these sentences.

Sadly I don't speak *very* good English. (sadly, very)

1 The building was damaged in the fire. (badly, last week)
2 We need to do something. (obviously, quickly)
3 Ben is at his friend's house. (often, in the evening)
4 She walked out and didn't say good-bye. (just, even)
5 He drives fast. (always, extremely)
6 She danced at the ballet. (beautifully, last night)
7 She wasn't injured when she fell. (luckily, seriously)
8 He broke his leg when he was skiing. (apparently, nearly)
9 My father sleeps in the afternoon. (usually, a little)

3A passive (all forms), *it is said that ..., he is thought to ...*, etc.

the passive (all forms)

simple present	Murderers **are** usually **sentenced** to life imprisonment.
present continuous	The trial **is being held** right now.
present perfect	My car **has been** stolen.
simple past	Jim **was arrested** last month.
past continuous	The theater **was being rebuilt** when it was set on fire.
past perfect	We saw that one of the windows **had been broken**.
future	The prisoner **will be released** next month.
	The verdict **is going to be given** tomorrow.
infinitive	They hoped **to be acquitted** of murder.
base form	You can **be fined** for parking at a bus stop.
gerund	He paid a fine to avoid **being sent** to jail.

- Use the passive when you want to talk about an action, but you are not so interested in saying who or what does / did the action.
- If you also want to mention the person or thing that did the action (the agent), use *by*, e.g., *Prison sentences are decided by judges.* However, in most passive sentences the agent is not mentioned.

***it is said that ..., he is thought to ...*, etc.**

active	passive
1 They say that the company may close.	**It is said that** the company may close.
People think that prices will go up.	**It is thought that** prices will go up.
2 People say the man is in his forties.	**The man is said to be** in his forties.
The police believe he has left the country.	**He is believed to have left** the country.
They think he robbed a bank.	**He is thought to have robbed** a bank.

- This formal structure is used especially in news reports and on TV with the verbs *know, tell, understand, report, expect, say,* and *think*. It makes the information sound more impersonal.

1 You can use *It is said, believed,* etc. + *that* + clause.
2 You can use *He, The man,* etc. (i.e., the subject of the clause) + *is said, believed,* etc. + infinitive (e.g., *to be*) or perfect infinitive (e.g., *to have been*).

3B future perfect and future continuous

future perfect: *will have* + past participle

I'll have finished the article by Friday, so I'll e-mail it to you then.
They'll have built the new terminal in six months.

- Use the future perfect to say something will be finished or completed before a certain time in the future.
- This tense is frequently used with the time expressions ***by*** *Saturday / March / 2030*, etc. or ***in*** *two weeks / months*, etc.
- *By* + a time expression = at the latest.

future continuous: *will be* + verb + *-ing*

Don't call between 7:00 and 8:00. **We'll be having** dinner then.
At this time next week, **I'll be lying** on the beach.

- Use the future continuous to say that an action will be in progress at a certain time in the future.

⚠ We sometimes use the future continuous, like the present continuous, to talk about things that are already planned or decided, e.g., *I'll be going to the supermarket later.*

3C conditionals and future time clauses (with all present and future forms)

zero conditional

If **you want** to stay in shape, **you have to** exercise every day.
If your muscles **ache** every day, **you are** probably **getting** too much exercise.
If you **haven't been** to Rio, you **haven't lived**.

- To talk about something that is always true or always happens as a result of something else, use *if* + simple present, and the simple present in the other clause.
- You can also use the present continuous or present perfect in either clause.

first conditional

If the photos **are** good, **I'll send** them to you.
If **you're not going, I'm not going to go** either.
If **I haven't called** by 8:00, **start** dinner without me.
I'll have finished in an hour **if you don't** disturb me.

- You can use any present tense in the *if* clause (simple present, present continuous, or present perfect) and any future form (*will, going to*, future perfect, or future continuous) or an imperative in the other clause.

future time clauses

We'll probably be watching the game **when you arrive**.
We're not leaving **until** the rain **stops**.
I'm not going to work overtime **unless I get paid**.
Take your umbrella **in case it rains**.
I'll be ready **as soon as I've taken** a shower.

- When you are talking about the future, use a present tense after time or condition expressions, e.g., *as soon as, when, until, unless, before, after,* and *in case*. Use any present tense, e.g., simple present, present continuous, or present perfect.
- We use *in case* when we do something in order to be ready for future situations / problems. Compare the use of *if* and *in case*:
I'll take a jacket if it's cold. = I won't take one if it's not cold.
I'll take a jacket in case it's cold. = I'll take a jacket because it might be cold later on.

3A

a Rewrite the sentences in the passive (without *by* ...).

The police caught the burglar immediately.
The burglar *was caught immediately*.

1 Police closed off the street after the accident. The street ...
2 Somebody has stolen my handbag. My handbag ...
3 The painters are painting my house. My house ...
4 They'll hold a meeting tomorrow. A meeting ...
5 The conductor fined them for traveling without a ticket. They ...
6 The police can arrest you for drunk driving. You ...
7 Miranda thinks someone was following her last night. Miranda thinks she ...
8 They had sold the house five years earlier. The house ...

b Rephrase the sentences to make them more formal.

People think the murderer is a woman.
It *is thought that the murderer is a woman*.
The murderer *is thought to be a woman*.

1 Police believe the burglar is a local man.
It ... The burglar ...
2 People say the muggers are very dangerous.
It ... The muggers ...
3 Police think the robber entered through an open window.
It ... The robber ...
4 Police say the murderer has disappeared.
It ... The murderer ...
5 Lawyers expect that the trial will last three weeks.
It ... The trial ...

3B

a Complete the sentences using the future perfect or future continuous.

The movie starts at 7:00. I will arrive at the theater at 7:15.
When I arrive at the theater, the movie *will have started*. (start)

1 The plane to Taipei takes off at 9:00 and lands at 10:30.
At 10:00 they __________ to Taipei. (fly)
2 I save $200 a month.
By the end of this year, I __________ $2,400. (save)
3 I leave home at 7:30. It takes an hour to drive to work.
At 8:00 tomorrow I __________ to work. (drive)
4 Our meeting starts at 2:00 and finishes at 3:30.
You can't call me at 2:30 because we __________ a meeting. (have)
5 Sam is still paying for his car. The last payment is in November.
By December he __________ for his car. (pay)
6 Their last exam is on May 31st.
By the end of May they __________ their exams. (finish)

b Complete the dialogue with verbs in the future continuous or future perfect.

A It looks like the weather is going to be different in the 22nd century.
B What do you mean?
A Well, they say we*'ll be having* much higher temperatures here in Canada, as high as 90°F. And remember, we [1]__________ on the beach; we [2]__________ in that heat, which is very different. And islands like the Maldives [3]__________ by 2150 because of the rise in the sea level. They say the number of storms and tsunamis [4]__________ by the middle of the century too, so even more people [5]__________ to the cities looking for work. Big cities [6]__________ even bigger by then. Can you imagine the traffic?
B I don't think there will be a problem with the traffic. Gas [7]__________ by then anyway, so nobody will have a car. Someone [8]__________ a new method of transportation, so we [9]__________ around in solar-powered cars or something.

have
not lie
work
disappear
double
move
grow
run out
invent
drive

3C

a Circle the correct form.

Don't worry. Rob (*will pass*) / *has passed* the exam if he studies enough.

1 If *I'm not feeling* / *I won't be feeling* better tomorrow, I'm going to call the doctor.
2 Adam *won't be going* / *doesn't go* to work next week if his children are still sick.
3 Don't call Carla now. If it's eight o'clock, *she'll give* / *she will be giving* the baby a bath.
4 You can be fined if you *aren't wearing* / *won't be wearing* a seat belt in your car.
5 If we're lucky, *we'll have sold* / *we've sold* our house by the first of the year.
6 If plants aren't watered, they *die* / *will have died*.

b Complete the sentence with an expression from the list.

after ~~as soon as~~ before if in case (x2) unless until when

I'll call you *as soon as* I get back from my trip.

1 He's going to pack his suitcase __________ he goes to bed.
2 They're leaving early __________ there's a lot of traffic.
3 Sophie will be leaving work early tomorrow __________ her boss needs her.
4 I'm meeting an old friend __________ I go to Caracas.
5 I'll call you __________ I find out my results.
6 __________ I'm late tomorrow, start the meeting without me.
7 Pat will have packed some sandwiches __________ we get hungry.
8 They'll be playing in the park __________ it gets dark.

4

4A unreal conditionals

second conditional sentences: *if* + simple past, *would* / *wouldn't* + base form

> 1 **If** there **were** a fire in this hotel, it **would be** very difficult to escape.
> I **wouldn't live** in the country **if** I **didn't have** a car.
> 2 **If** you **weren't making** so much noise, I **could concentrate** better.
> 3 **If** I **were** you, **I'd make** Jimmy wear a helmet when he's cycling.

1 Use second conditional sentences to talk about hypothetical or improbable situations in the present or future.
2 In the *if* clause you can also use the past continuous. In the other clause you can use *could* or *might* instead of *would*, e.g., *If you **weren't making** so much noise, I **could concentrate** better.*
3 With the verb *be*, use *were* for all persons in the *if* clause, e.g., *If he were here, he would know what to do.* Conditionals beginning *If I were you...* are often used to give advice.

third conditional sentences: *if* + past perfect, *would* / *wouldn't have* + past participle

> 1 **If** you **had studied** more, you **would have done** better on the test.
> I **wouldn't have been** late **if** I **hadn't** overslept.
> 2 He **would have** died **if** he **hadn't been wearing** a helmet.
> **If** they **had known** you were coming, they **might have** stayed longer.

1 We use third conditional sentences to talk about a hypothetical past situation and its consequence.
2 You can also use the past perfect continuous in the *if* clause, e.g., *if he **hadn't been wearing** a helmet.* You can use *could have* or *might have* instead of *would have* in the other clause.

second or third conditional?

> 1 If you **studied** more, you **would** probably **pass** the exam.
> 2 If you **had studied** more, you **would** probably **have passed** the exam.

- Compare the two conditionals:
  1 = You don't study enough. You need to study more.
  2 = You didn't study enough, so you failed.

> ⚠ We sometimes mix second and third conditionals if a hypothetical situation in the past has a present / future consequence, e.g., *He wouldn't be so relaxed if he hadn't finished his exams.*

4B past modals

***must* / *might* / *couldn't*, etc. + *have* + past participle**

> 1 I **must have passed** the exam. I'm sure I got all the answers right.
> You **must have seen** something. You were there when the robbery happened.
> 2 Somebody **might have stolen** your wallet when you were getting off the train.
> He still hasn't arrived. I **might not have given** him the right directions.
> 3 They **couldn't have gone** to bed yet. It's only ten o'clock.
> They **couldn't have seen** us. It was too dark.

- Use *must* / *may* / *might* / *couldn't* / *can't* + *have* + past participle to make deductions or speculate about past actions.

1 Use *must have* when you are almost sure that something happened or was true.
2 Use *might* / *may have* when you think it's possible that something happened or was true. You can also use *could have* with this meaning, e.g., *They could have stolen your wallet when you were getting off the train.*
3 Use *couldn't have* when you are almost sure something didn't happen or that it is impossible. You can also use *can't have.*

***should* + *have* + past participle**

> It's my fault. I **should have told** you earlier that she was coming.
> We're going the wrong way. We **shouldn't have turned** left at the traffic light.

- Use *should* + *have* + past participle to say that somebody didn't do the right thing.
- You can use *ought to have* as an alternative to *should have*, e.g., *I ought to have told you earlier.* However, *should have* is more common, especially in speaking.

4C verbs of the senses

look* / *feel* / *smell* / *sound* / *taste

> 1 She **looks tired**. That **smells good**! These jeans don't **feel comfortable**.
> 2 He **looks like his father**. This material **feels like silk**. This **tastes like tea**, not coffee.
> 3 She **looks as if she's been crying**. It **smells as if something's burning**. It **sounds as if it's raining**.

1 Use *look, feel,* etc. + adjective.
2 Use *look, feel,* etc. + *like* + noun.

> ⚠ *feel like* can also mean "want / would like," e.g., *I don't feel like going out* = I don't want to go out.

3 Use *look, feel,* etc. + *as if* + clause.
- You can use *like* or *as though* instead of *as if*, e.g., *It sounds **like** / **as though** it's raining.*

4A

a Complete with an appropriate form of the verb in parentheses.

If he _hadn't broken_ his leg, he would have played. (not break)

1 I __________ you a present if I'd known it was your birthday. (buy)
2 If you __________ to bed earlier, you wouldn't have been so tired. (go)
3 I __________ you some money if I had any. (lend)
4 If I __________ money on the street, I'd keep it. (find)
5 Joe wouldn't have crashed if he __________ so fast. (not drive)
6 We would have a dog if we __________ in the country. (live)
7 If you'd watered the plants, they __________. (not die)
8 You __________ the news if you'd been watching TV. (hear)
9 They wouldn't have bought the house if they __________ what the neighbors were like. (know)
10 If she __________ more sociable, she'd have more friends. (be)

b Complete with a second or third conditional.

I didn't wait another minute. I didn't see you.
If I'd waited another minute, *I would have seen you.*

1 Luke missed the train. He was late for the interview.
If Luke hadn't missed the train, …
2 Eva drinks too much coffee. She doesn't sleep well at night.
If Eva didn't drink so much coffee, …
3 It started snowing. We didn't reach the top of the mountain.
If it hadn't started snowing, …
4 Maya didn't buy the jacket. She didn't have enough money.
Maya would have bought the jacket if …
5 I don't drive to work. There's so much traffic.
I'd drive to work if …
6 Matt doesn't speak Chinese fluently. He won't get the job.
If Matt spoke Chinese fluently, …

4B

a Rewrite the **bold sentence** sentence with *must / might (not) / couldn't* + *have* + verb.

I'm sure I left my umbrella at home. I don't have it now.
I must have left my umbrella at home.

1 **I'm sure Ben got my e-mail.** I sent it yesterday.
2 Holly's crying. **Maybe she had an argument with her boyfriend.**
3 **I'm sure Sam and Ginny didn't get lost.** They had a map.
4 **You saw Ellie yesterday?** That's impossible. She was in bed with the flu.
5 **Maybe John didn't hear you.** He's a little bit deaf.
6 **I'm sure Lucy bought a new car.** I saw her driving a Mercedes!
7 **I'm sure Alex wasn't very sick.** He was only off for one day.
8 They didn't come to our party. **Maybe they didn't receive the invitation.**

b Respond to the first sentence using *should / shouldn't have* + a verb in the list.

buy ~~eat~~ go (x2) invite learn write

A Sue is in bed with a stomachache.
B She _shouldn't have eaten_ so much chocolate cake.

1 **A** We couldn't understand anybody in Seoul.
B You __________ some Korean before you went.
2 **A** Tom told me his phone number, but I forgot it.
B You __________ it down.
3 **A** Rob was late because there was so much traffic.
B He __________ by car. The train is much faster.
4 **A** Amanda was rude to everyone at my party.
B You __________ her. She's always like that.
5 **A** I don't have any money left after going shopping yesterday.
B You __________ so many shoes. Did you need three pairs?
6 **A** You look really tired.
B I know. I __________ to bed earlier.

4C

a Circle the correct form.

Your boyfriend *looks* / (*looks like*) a football player.

1 You're so pale! You *look / look as if* you've seen a ghost!
2 What's for dinner? It *smells / smells like* delicious!
3 I think John and Megan have arrived. That *sounds / sounds like* their car.
4 Have you ever tried frogs' legs? I've heard that they *taste like / taste as if* chicken.
5 Are you OK? You *sound / sound as if* you've got a cold.
6 Can you put the heat on? It *feels / feels like* really cold in here.
7 You *look / look like* really happy. Does that mean you got the job?
8 Your new bag *feels / feels like* real leather.
9 Let's throw this milk away. It *tastes / tastes like* a little strange.
10 Can you close the window, please? It *smells / smells as if* someone is having a barbecue.

b Match the two halves of the sentence.

1 That group sounds like	*F*	A	her mother.
2 Those boys look		B	completely out of tune.
3 She looks like		C	very soft.
4 That guitar sounds		D	someone has been smoking in here.
5 He looks as if		E	really sweet.
6 Your car sounds as if		F	~~the Beatles~~.
7 Your new jacket feels		G	too young to be driving
8 This apple tastes		H	it's been overcooked.
9 Ugh! It smells as if		I	roses.
10 Your perfume smells like		J	it's going to break down.
11 This rice tastes as if		K	he just ran a marathon.

5

5A gerunds and infinitives

verbs followed by the gerund, the infinitive, or the base form

1 I **enjoy listening** to music. I **couldn't help laughing**.
2 I **want to speak** to you. They **can't afford to buy** a new car.
3 It **might rain** tonight. I **would rather stay home** than go out tonight.

- When one verb follows another, the first verb determines the form of the second. This can be the gerund (verb + *-ing*), the infinitive, or the base form.

1 Use the **gerund** after certain verbs and expressions, e.g., *admit, avoid, can't help, deny, enjoy, feel like, finish, give up, imagine, involve, keep on, mind, miss, postpone, practice, quit, risk, stop, suggest.*
2 Use the **infinitive** after certain verbs and expressions, e.g., *agree, appear, be able, can't afford, can't wait, decide, expect, happen, learn, manage, offer, plan, pretend, promise, refuse, seem, teach, tend, threaten, want, would like.*
3 Use the **base form** after modal verbs and similar expressions, e.g., *can, could, may, might, must, should, have to, ought to, had better, would rather*, and after the verbs *make* and *let*.

⚠ In the passive, *make* is followed by the infinitive. Compare:
My boss ***makes us work*** *hard. In school we were* ***made to wear*** *a uniform.*

⚠ Some verbs can be followed by either the gerund or the infinitive with very little difference in meaning, for example:
Start / begin + gerund is slightly more common when we talk about a habitual activity, e.g., *She started / began singing when she was five.*
Like / love / hate / continue / prefer + gerund gives a little more emphasis to the action of the verb, e.g., *I like / love / hate / can't stand playing the guitar.*

verbs that can be followed by either gerund or infinitive with a change of meaning

1 **Remember to lock** the door.
I **remember going** to Peru as a child.
2 Sorry, I **forgot to do** it.
I'll never **forget seeing** the Taj Mahal.
3 I **tried to open** the window.
Try calling Su-jin on her cell phone.
4 You **need to clean** the car.
The car **needs cleaning**.

- Some verbs can be followed by the gerund or infinitive with a change of meaning.

1 *Remember* + infinitive = you remember first; then you do something. *Remember* + gerund = you do something; then you remember it.
2 *Forget* + infinitive = you didn't remember to do something. *(Not) forget* + gerund = you did something and you (won't) forget it. It is more common in the negative.
3 *Try* + infinitive = make an effort to do something. *Try* + gerund = experiment to see if something works.
4 *Need* + gerund is a passive construction, e.g., *The car needs cleaning* = The car needs to be cleaned. NOT ~~*needs to clean*~~.

5B *used to, be used to, get used to*

***used to / didn't use to* + base form**

I **used to drink** five cups of coffee a day, but now I only drink tea.
When I lived in Mexico as a child, I **used to have** pan dulce for breakfast.
I didn't recognize him. He **didn't use to have** a beard.

- Use *used to / didn't use to* + base form to talk about past habits or repeated actions or situations / states that have changed.

⚠ *used to* doesn't exist in the present tense. For present habits, use *usually* + the simple present, e.g., *I usually walk to work.* NOT ~~*I use to walk to work.*~~

- You can also use *would* to refer to repeated actions in the past:
When I lived in Mexico as a child, I would always eat pan dulce for breakfast.
But you can't use *would* with non-action verbs:
NOT ~~*I didn't recognize him. He wouldn't have a beard.*~~

***be used to / get used to* + gerund**

1 Carlos has lived in Hong Kong for years.
He's **used to driving** on the left.
I'**m not used to sleeping** with a comforter.
I've always slept with blankets.
2 **A** I can't **get used to working** at night. I feel tired all the time.
B Don't worry. You'll **get used to it** fast.

1 Use *be used to* + gerund to talk about a new situation that is now familiar or less strange.
2 Use *get used to* + gerund to talk about a new situation that is **becoming** familiar or less strange.

- You can't use the base form after *be used to / get used to*. NOT ~~*He's used to drive on the left.*~~

5C reporting verbs

structures after reporting verbs

1 Hiro **offered to drive** me to the airport.
I **promised not to tell** anybody.
2 The doctor **advised me to get** some rest.
I **persuaded my sister not to go out** with Mike.
3 I **apologized for being** so late.
The police **accused Karl of stealing** the car.

- To report what other people have said, you can use *say* or a specific verb, e.g.,
"I'll drive you to the airport."
Hiro ***said*** *he would drive me to the airport.*
Hiro ***offered*** *to drive me to the airport.*

- After specific reporting verbs, there are three different grammatical patterns.

1 + infinitive		2 + person + infinitive		3 + *-ing* form	
agree		advise		apologize for	
offer		ask		accuse sb of	
refuse	**(not) to do**	convince	**somebody**	admit	**(not) doing**
promise	**something**	encourage	**(not) to do**	blame sb for	**something**
threaten		invite	**something**	deny	
		persuade		insist on	
		remind		recommend	
		tell		regret	
		warn		suggest	

- In negative sentences, use the negative infinitive (*not to be*) or the negative gerund (*not being*), e.g.,
He reminded me ***not to*** *be late. She regretted* ***not going*** *to the party.*

5A

a Complete with the gerund, infinitive, or base form of a verb below.

~~call~~ not come do get go go out know see talk wear work

I suggested *calling* a taxi so we wouldn't be late.

1 I'm exhausted! I don't feel like ________ tonight.
2 If you keep on ________, you'll have to leave the room.
3 We'd better ________ some shopping if we want to cook tonight.
4 When I was abroad, I missed ________ my family every day.
5 She tends ________ angry when people disagree with her.
6 Our school used to make us ________ a tie to school.
7 I'd rather ________ tonight. I need to study.
8 I can't wait ________ on vacation!
9 I don't mind ________ late tonight if I can leave early tomorrow.
10 Do you happen ________ her phone number?

b Circle the correct form.

Your hair needs (*cutting*) / *to cut*. It's really long!

1 I'll never forget *to see* / *seeing* the Grand Canyon for the first time.
2 He needs *to call* / *calling* the helpline. His computer crashed.
3 Have you tried *to read* / *reading* a book to help you sleep?
4 I must have my keys somewhere. I can remember *to lock* / *locking* the door this morning.
5 We ran home because we had forgotten *to turn* / *turning* the oven off.
6 Their house needed *to paint* / *painting*, so they called the painters.
7 Did you remember *to send* / *sending* your sister a card? It's her birthday today.
8 She tried *to fix* / *fixing* the TV, but she wasn't able to.

5B

a Right (✔) or wrong (✘)? Correct the wrong phrases.

She isn't used to have a big dinner. ✘
isn't used to having

1 Nowadays I use to go to bed early.
2 The first time we visited China, we couldn't get used to eat with chopsticks.
3 I'm not used to staying up so late. I'm usually in bed by midnight.
4 There used to be a theater in our town, but it closed down three years ago.
5 Paul used to having a beard when he was younger.
6 **A** I don't think I could work at night.
B It's not so bad. I use to it now.
7 Did you used to wear a uniform to school?

b Complete with *used to*, *be used to*, or *get used to* and the verb in parentheses.

He's from Japan, so he *'s used to driving* on the left. (drive)

1 When Jin started his first job, he couldn't ________ at 6:00 a.m. (get up)
2 If you want to lose weight, you'll have to ________ less. (eat)
3 I don't like having dinner at 10:00 – I ________ a meal so late. (not / have)
4 When we were children, we ________ all day playing baseball in the park. (spend)
5 Jasmine has been a nurse all her life, so she ________ nights. (work)
6 I've never worn glasses before, but I'll have to ________ them. (wear)
7 I didn't recognize you! You ________ long hair, didn't you? (have)
8 Amelia is an only child. She ________ her things. (not / share)

5C

a Complete with the gerund or infinitive form of the verb in parentheses.

They advised me *to buy* a new car. (buy)

1 Ted insisted on ________ for the meal. (pay)
2 Lauren agreed ________ with him on the weekend. (go out)
3 I warned Jane ________ through the park at night. (not walk)
4 Jake admitted ________ the woman's handbag. (steal)
5 The doctor advised Pedro ________ coffee. (give up)
6 Our boss persuaded Reiko ________ the company. (not leave)
7 Meg accused me of ________ her pen. (take)
8 I apologized to Eva for ________ her birthday. (not remember)

b Complete with a reporting verb from the list and the verb in parentheses.

deny invite ~~offer~~ refuse remind suggest threaten

She said to me, "I'll take you to the station."
She *offered to take* me to the station. (take)

1 Bruno said, "Let's go for a walk. It's a beautiful day."
Bruno ________ for a walk. (go)
2 "I won't eat the vegetables," said my daughter.
My daughter ________ the vegetables. (eat)
3 Sam's neighbor told him, "I'll call the police if you have any more parties."
Sam's neighbor ________ the police if he had any more parties. (call)
4 The children said, "We did not write on the wall."
The children ________ on the wall. (write)
5 Mi-soon said to me, "Would you like to have dinner with me on Friday night?"
Mi-soon ________ dinner with her on Friday night. (have)
6 Molly said to Jack, "Don't forget to go to the dentist."
Molly ________ to the dentist. (go)

6

6A articles

basic rules: *a / an / the*, no article

1 My neighbor just bought **a** dog.
The dog is **an** Alsatian.
He got into **the** car and drove to **the** courthouse.
2 **Men** are taller than **women** on average.
I don't like **sports** or **classical music**.
I stayed at **home last** weekend.

1 Use *a / an* when you mention somebody / something for the first time or say who / what somebody / something is.
Use *the* when it's clear who / what somebody / something is (e.g., it has been mentioned before or it's unique).
2 Don't use an article to speak in general with plural and uncountable nouns, or in phrases like *at home /work, go home / to bed, next / last (week)*, etc.

institutions (*school, college, prison / jail, church*, etc.)

My son is in **high school**. They are building **a new high school** in our town.

- With *school, college, prison / jail, church*, etc. don't use an article when you are talking about the institution and its usual purpose. To talk about the building, use *a / an* or *the*. (exception: *She's in the hospital.*)

geographical names

1 Korea is in East Asia.
2 Macy's is one of the most famous stores in the US.
3 Lake Maracaibo and Lake Titicaca are both in South America.
4 **The** Danube River flows into **the** Black Sea.
5 **The** Metropolitan Museum is located on Fifth Avenue in New York.

- We **don't usually use** *the* with:
1 most countries, continents, regions ending with the name of a state / country / continent (e.g., *North America, South Asia*), individual islands, states, provinces, towns, cities (exceptions: *the US / United States, the UK, the Philippines, the Czech Republic*).
2 streets, roads, parks, stores, restaurants (exceptions: highways and numbered roads, e.g., *the Trans-Canada Highway, the 80*).
3 individual mountains and lakes.
- We **usually use** *the* with:
4 mountain ranges, oceans, seas, rivers, canals, deserts, island groups.
5 the names of theaters, hotels, museums, galleries, buildings, monuments.

6B uncountable, plural, and collective nouns

uncountable nouns

1 The **weather** was terrible, but at least there wasn't much **traffic**.
The **scenery** is beautiful here, but it's spoiled by all the **trash** people leave.
2 We bought **some new furniture** for the patio. That's **a beautiful piece of furniture**.
3 **Iron** is used for building bridges.
I need to buy **a new iron**. My old one is broken.

1 The following nouns are always uncountable: *behavior, traffic, weather, health, progress, scenery, trash, politics* (and other words ending in *-ics*, e.g., *athletics, economics*).
- They always need a singular verb, they don't have plurals, and they can't be used with *a / an*.
2 These nouns are also uncountable: *furniture, information, advice, homework, research, news, luck, bread, toast, luggage, equipment*. Use *a piece of* to talk about an individual item.
3 Some nouns can be either countable or uncountable, but the meaning changes, e.g., *iron* = the metal, *an iron* = the thing used to press clothes. Other examples: *glass, business, paper, light, time, space, work*.

plural and collective nouns

1 Your **clothes are** filthy! Put a pair of / some clean pants on.
2 Our **staff is** very efficient.

1 *Arms* (=guns, etc.), *belongings, clothes, manners, outskirts, scissors, pants / shorts* are plural nouns with no singular. They need a plural verb and can't be used with *a / an*.
- If a plural noun consists of two parts, e.g., *scissors* or *pants*, it can be used with *a pair of* or *some*.
2 *Crew, staff, team, family, audience* are singular collective nouns and refer to a group of people. They need a singular verb. (exception: *police*)

6C quantifiers: *all / every*, etc.

all, every, most

1 **All** animals need food. **All** fruit contains sugar.
All (of) the animals in this zoo look sad.
The animals **all** looked sad. The animals are **all** sad.
2 **Everybody** is here. **Everything** is very expensive.
3 **Most people** live in cities.
Most of the people in this class are women.
4 **All of** us work hard and **most of** us come to class every week.
5 **Every** room has a view. I work **every** Saturday.

1 Use *all* or *all (of) the* + a plural or uncountable noun.
All = in general, *all (of) the* = specific.
All can be used before a main verb (and after *be*).
2 Use *everything / everybody* + singular verb, e.g., *Everything **is** very expensive.*
3 Use *most* to say the majority.
Most = general; *Most of the* = specific.
4 We often use *all / most of* + an object pronoun, e.g., *all of us, most of them, all of you, most of it*.
5 Use *every* + singular countable noun to mean "all of a group."

⚠ *every* and *all* + time expressions: *Every day* = Monday to Sunday. *All day* = from morning to night.

no, none, any

1 Is there any milk? Sorry, there is **no** milk. There **isn't any** (milk).
2 Is there any food? No, **none**. / There is **none**.
But **none of us** is / are hungry.
3 Come **any** weekend! **Anyone** can come.

1 Use *no* + a noun with an [+] verb or *any* + noun with a [−] verb to refer to zero quantity. *Any* can also be used without a noun.
2 Use *none* in short answers or with an [+] verb to refer to zero quantity. You can also use *none* + *of* + pronoun / noun.
3 Use *any* (and *anything, anyone*, etc.) and an [+] verb to mean "it doesn't matter when, who, etc."

both, neither, either

1 **Both** Pierre **and** Marie Curie were scientists. **Neither** Pierre **nor** Marie was aware of the dangers of radiation.
Marie Curie wanted to study **either** physics **or** mathematics.
In the end she studied **both** subjects at the Sorbonne in Paris.
2 She and her husband **both** won Nobel prizes.
3 **Neither of them** realized how dangerous radium was.

- Use *both, either*, and *neither* to talk about two people, things, actions, etc.: *both* = A **and** B; *either* = A **or** B; *neither* = **not** A **and not** B.
1 Use an [+] verb. The verb is plural with *both*, and either singular or plural with *neither*, depending on the second subject.
2 When *both* refers to the subject of a clause, it can also be used after the subject and before a main verb.
3 We often use *both / either / neither* + *of* + object pronoun, e.g., *us, them*, etc. or + *of the* + noun.

6A

a Circle the correct article.

Marcos bought (a) / *the* / (–) *new suit* last weekend.

1 The weather was awful, so we stayed at *a* / *the* / (–) home.
2 *A* / *The* / (–) dishwasher we bought last week has stopped working already.
3 I love reading *a* / *the* / (–) historical novels.
4 Liz had an exhausting day, so she went to *a* / *the* / (–) bed early.
5 My boyfriend drives *a* / *the* / (–) very cool sports car.
6 The teachers are on strike, so the children aren't going to *a* / *the* / (–) school.
7 Turn left immediately after *a* / *the* / (–) school and go up the hill.
8 My neighbor's in *a* / *the* / (–) prison because she wouldn't pay her taxes.
9 People are complaining because the city council refused to build *a* / *the* / (–) new hospital.
10 Claudia and Joe met in *a* / *the* / (–) college in 2003.

b Complete with *the* or (–).

They're going to *the* US to visit family.

1 ______ Amazon River begins at a small stream in ______ Andes.
2 We didn't have time to visit ______ National Gallery when we were in ______ Washington, D.C.
3 I think ______ Sicily is the largest island in ______ Mediterranean Sea.
4 ______ Mount Fuji is in ______ Japan.
5 Have you ever been to ______ Stanley Park in Vancouver.
6 I'd love to stay at ______ Peninsula Hotel in Hong Kong.
7 ______ Galapagos Islands are situated off the cost of Ecuador.
8 *Romeo and Juliet* is playing at ______ Globe Theater.
9 Manila is the capital of ______ Philippines.
10 ______ Southern California is famous for its beaches and great surfing.

6B

a Right (✔) or wrong (✘)? Correct the wrong phrases.

In our language lab the equipment is all new. ✔
The news are good. ✘ *The news is*

1 We had a beautiful weather when we were on vacation.
2 They have some beautiful furnitures in their house.
3 My brother gave me a useful piece of advice.
4 The team has won every game this season.
5 I need to buy a new pants for my interview tomorrow.
6 I checked two luggages on my flight.
7 Your glasses are really dirty. Can you see anything?
8 The homeworks were very difficult last week.

b Circle the correct form. Check (✔) if both are correct.

The traffic (is) / *are* awful during rush hour.

1 Gymnastics *is* / *are* my favorite sport.
2 I bought *a pair of* / *some* jeans.
3 Marta's clothes *look* / *looks* really expensive.
4 The flight crew *work* / *works* hard to make passengers comfortable.
5 I heard *some* / *a piece of* useful information at the meeting.
6 Is that vase made of *a glass* / *glass*?
7 I think I'll have *a* / *some* time after lunch to help you with that report.
8 I have *a* / *some* good news for you about your job application.
9 We've made a lot of *progresses* / *progress* in the last two weeks.
10 My eyesight is getting worse. I need a new *glasses* / *pair of glasses*.

6C

a Circle the correct word(s).

We ate (*all the*) / *all* cake.

1 *Most of* / *Most* my close friends live near me.
2 I'm afraid there's *no* / *none* room for you in the car.
3 *All* / *Everything* in the stores is expensive nowadays.
4 *Most* / *Most of* people enjoy the summer, but for some it's too hot.
5 She goes dancing *all* / *every* Friday night.
6 We don't have *any* / *no* onions for the soup.
7 *Any* / *None* of us can go out tonight. We're all broke.
8 *Nobody* / *Anybody* can go to the festival. It's free.

b Complete the second sentence so that it means the same as the first. Use the **bold** word.

I like meat. I like fish, too. I like *both meat and fish*. **both**

1 We could go to Hawaii. We could go to Thailand. **either**
We could go ______________________.
2 You didn't stay very long. I didn't stay very long. **neither**
______________________ stayed very long.
3 I think her birthday is on May 6th – but maybe it's May 7th. **either**
Her birthday is on ______________________.
4 One of my children could read when he was four. So could the other one. **both**
______________________ when they were four.
5 My brothers don't smoke. My sisters don't smoke. **neither**
______________________ smoke.

7A structures after *wish*

wish* + simple past, *wish* + *would* / *wouldn't* or *could

1 I wish **I were** taller!
My brother wishes **he could** speak English better.
2 I wish the bus **would come.** I'm freezing.
I wish you **wouldn't leave** your shoes there. I almost tripped over them.

1 Use *wish* + simple past or *could* to talk about things you would like to be different in the present / future (but are impossible or unlikely).
- After *wish* use *were* with *I, he, she,* and *it*, e.g., *I wish I were taller.*

2 Use *wish* + person / thing + *would* to talk about things we want to happen, or stop happening, because they annoy us.

⚠ You don't usually use *would* for a wish about yourself, e.g., NOT ~~*I wish I would...*~~

***wish* + past perfect**

I wish **you had told** me the truth.
I wish **I hadn't bought** those shoes.

Use *wish* + past perfect to talk about things that happened or didn't happen in the past and that you now regret.

⚠ You can also use *If only* instead of *I wish*, e.g.,
If only the bus would come.
If only I hadn't bought those shoes.

7B clauses of contrast and purpose

clauses of contrast

1 **Although** the weather was terrible, we had a good time.
I went to work, **even though** I felt sick.
I like Ann, **though** she sometimes annoys me.
2 **In spite of / Despite** his age, he is still very active.
being 85, he is still very active.
the fact that he's 85, he is still very active.

1 Use *although, though, even though* + a clause. They mean the same thing.
- *Although, though,* and *even though* can be used at the beginning or in the middle of a sentence.
- *Though* is more informal than *although.*

2 After *in spite of* or *despite*, use a noun, a gerund, or *the fact that* + subject + verb.

⚠ Don't use *of* with *despite*. NOT ~~*Despite of the rain...*~~

clauses of purpose

1 I went to the bank **to** / **in order to** / **so as to** talk to the bank manager.
2 I went to the bank **for** a meeting with the bank manager.
3 I went to the bank **so that** I could take out some money.
4 I wrote it down **so as not to** forget it.

- Use *to, in order to, so as to, for,* and *so that* to express purpose.

1 After *to, in order to,* and *so as to,* use the base form.
2 Use *for* + a noun, e.g., *for a meeting.*

⚠ You can also use *for* + gerund to describe the exact purpose of a thing, e.g., *This liquid is for cleaning metal.*

3 *So that* is often followed by a subject + modal verb (*can, could, would,* etc.).
4 To express a negative purpose use *so as not to* or *in order not to* + base form NOT ~~*not to*~~. You can also use *so that* + subject + *won't / wouldn't / don't*, e.g.,
I'm writing it down so that I don't / won't forget.

7C relative clauses

defining relative clauses

1 She's the woman **who / that lives next door**.
That's the book **that / which won a prize**.
2 That's the neighbor **whose dog never stops barking**.
3 James is the man **(who) I met at the party**.
That's the store **(that) I told you about**.
4 My sister is the only person **to whom I can talk**.
My sister is the only person **(who)** I can talk **to**.
That's the drawer **in which** I keep my keys.

- Use *who, that / which, whose,* and *whom* to introduce a defining relative clause, i.e., a clause that gives essential information about somebody or something.

1 You can use *that* instead of *who. That* is more common than *which* in defining clauses.
2 Use *whose* to mean "of who" or "of which."
3 When *who* or *that* is the object of the verb in the relative clause, you can leave it out.
4 After a preposition, use *whom* for a person and *which* for a thing. In informal English, it is more common to leave out the relative pronoun and put the preposition after the verb.

non-defining relative clauses

1 My aunt, **who doesn't like cats**, was given a kitten for her birthday.
The palace, **which was built in the 12th century**, is visited by thousands of tourists.
2 Adriana hasn't come to class for two weeks, **which is worrisome**.

1 A non-defining relative clause gives extra, non-essential information about a person or thing.
- In written English, this kind of clause is separated by commas, or comes between a comma and a period.
- You can't use *that* instead of *who / which* in these clauses.
- In these clauses, the relative pronoun (e.g., *who, which*) can't be omitted.

2 *Which* can also be used to refer to the whole of the preceding clause.

7A

a Circle the correct form.

I wish I (*were*) / *would be* thinner! My clothes don't fit me!

1 I wish I *had* / *would have* curly hair!
2 She wishes her parents *lived* / *would live* closer.
3 You're driving too fast. I wish you *would drive* / *drove* more slowly.
4 I wish it *stopped* / *would stop* raining. I want to go out for a walk!
5 Ben's been wearing the same clothes for years. I wish he *bought* / *would buy* some new clothes.
6 Chloe wishes she *could* / *can* play the guitar.
7 I'm hot. I wish my apartment *had* / *would have* air-conditioning.
8 Their TV is really loud. I wish they *turned* / *would turn* it down.

b Write a sentence with *I wish* + past perfect.

I spent all my money last night and now I'm broke.
I wish I hadn't spent all my money last night.

1 I left my camera in the car, and someone stole it.
2 I didn't set my alarm clock, so I was late for work.
3 I bought a house in the country, but I really miss the city.
4 I dropped my cell phone in the bathtub, and now it doesn't work.
5 I didnt' study for the test, so I didn't pass.
6 I didn't take a vacation last year, and now I'm really stressed.

7B

a Complete the sentences with *one* word.

We're happy in our new house, ___*though*___ there's a lot to do.

1 We enjoyed our vacation, ________ the weather.
2 Carl doesn't like spending money, ________ though he's very rich.
3 They went to the airport ________ catch a plane.
4 Sandy wrote down his number so ________ not to forget it.
5 My mother called the doctor's office in ________ to make an appointment.
6 Bob passed the exam in ________ of the fact that he hadn't studied much.
7 Angela took a jacket so ________ she wouldn't get cold.
8 ________ the service was poor, the meal was delicious.
9 I went home ________ a shower before I went out.
10 ________ being late, he stopped for a coffee.

b Rewrite the sentences.

Despite playing badly, they won the game.
Even though *they played badly, they won the game.*

1 We took a taxi so as not to arrive late.
We took a taxi so that …
2 Despite earning a fortune, she drives a very old car.
Although …
3 Everyone saw the movie, even though the reviews were terrible.
Everyone saw the movie in spite of …
4 The plane managed to land despite the very thick fog.
The plane managed to land, even though …
5 I told her I liked her jacket so that I wouldn't offend her.
I told her I liked her jacket so as …
6 The manager called a meeting so as to explain the new policy.
The manager called a meeting in order …

7C

a Right (✔) or wrong (✘)? Correct the wrong sentences.

That's the man I met on the bus. ✔
She's the woman ~~who her~~ daughter works with me. ✘
whose daughter works

1 This is the quiz show I was telling you about.
2 Is this the train that it goes to the mountains?
3 She told her boss she'd overslept, that was absolutely true.
4 My son, that is very tall, enjoys playing basketball.
5 The employee to who I spoke gave me some incorrect information.
6 My brother, which is a chef, always cooks the Thanksgiving dinner.
7 Easter Island, which is situated off the coast of Chile, is a popular tourist destination.
8 The woman who suitcase disappeared is a friend of mine.
9 Do you know the woman whom is talking to him?
10 This is the book whose review I read in the paper today.

b Join the sentences with a relative pronoun. Be careful with the punctuation.

I just failed my driving test. It's too bad.
I *just failed my driving test, which is too bad.*

1 His girlfriend is very intelligent. She's an architect.
His girlfriend …
2 They gave us a present. This was a complete surprise.
They …
3 He was saying something. I didn't understand it.
He was saying …
4 A car crashed into mine. It was a convertible.
The car …
5 I spoke to a police officer. She was working at the reception desk.
The police officer …
6 We bought our computer two months ago. It keeps on crashing.
Our computer …
7 I left some things on the table. They aren't there anymore.
The things …
8 It's too hot in my room. This makes it impossible to sleep.
It's …

Personality

1 Adjectives and phrases to describe personality

Match the adjectives with phrases 1–20.

~~ambitious~~ ~~arrogant~~ ~~assertive~~ calm /kɑm/ cheerful conscientious /ˌkɑnʃiˈɛnʃəs/ easygoing eccentric /ɪkˈsɛntrɪk/ funny immature impulsive ~~insecure~~ insincere irritable loyal open-minded ~~optimistic~~ possessive reserved ~~self-confident~~ stubborn /ˈstʌbərn/ vain ~~well-balanced~~ wise

She's the kind (sort) of person who ...	She's / He's ...
1 always looks at herself in every mirror she passes.	
2 takes care to do things carefully and correctly.	
3 is ready to accept new and different ideas.	
4 doesn't say what she really thinks.	
5 other people often find different or unusual.	
6 is fairly relaxed about most things.	
7 is emotionally in control, not moody.	*well-balanced*
8 never changes her opinion, even when she's clearly wrong.	
9 expresses her ideas or opinions with confidence.	*assertive*
10 is always in a good mood.	
11 feels sure of her ability to do things	*self-confident*
12 isn't very sure of herself.	*insecure*
13 is determined to be successful	*ambitious*
He's good at ...	
14 supporting his friends.	
15 giving people advice because of his knowledge and experience.	
16 not panicking in a crisis.	
She's not very good at ...	
17 letting other people share her friends.	
18 showing her feelings or expressing her opinions.	
He tends to ...	
19 behave like a child.	
20 act without thinking.	
21 get angry very easily.	
22 think he is better and more important than other people.	*arrogant*
23 expect good things to happen	*optimistic*
She has ...	
24 a great sense of humor.	

Can you remember the words on this page? Test yourself or a partner.

p.9

2 Adjective suffixes

a Many adjectives are formed by adding a suffix to a noun or verb. Look at the typical suffixes in the chart.

-ible	-able	-ful	-y
responsible	*sociable*	*helpful*	*bossy*

-ive	-ous	-al	-ic
assertive	*ambitious*	*practical*	*ironic*

b Add one adjective to each column in **a** by adding a suffix to the nouns / verbs in the list below. You may need to make other small changes. (Be careful with *sense,* which can have two different endings and meanings.)

adventure critic forget mood pessimist rely sense

c Think of definitions for the adjectives you made in **b**.

3 Idioms

a Look at the highlighted idioms and try to guess their meanings.

1 My boss is kind of a cold fish. I don't even know if he likes me or not. ☐
2 She has a heart of gold. She'll always help anyone with anything. ☐
3 She's as hard as nails. She doesn't care who she hurts. ☐
4 I hope Jack doesn't come tonight. He's such a pain in the neck. ☐

b Match the idioms with their meanings.

A annoying, difficult
B very kind, generous
C distant, unfriendly
D shows no sympathy or fear

Illness and treatment

1 Symptoms

a Match the words and pictures.

He has ...

- a temperature /ˈtɛmprətʃər/.
- a cough /kɔf/.
- a headache (earache, stomachache, etc.).
- a rash.
- 1 a blister.
- a pain (in his chest).

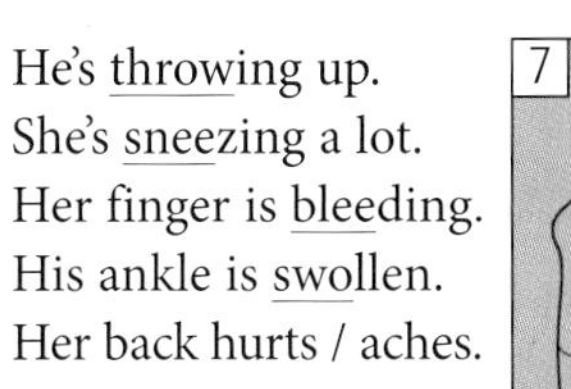

- He's throwing up.
- She's sneezing a lot.
- Her finger is bleeding.
- His ankle is swollen.
- Her back hurts / aches.

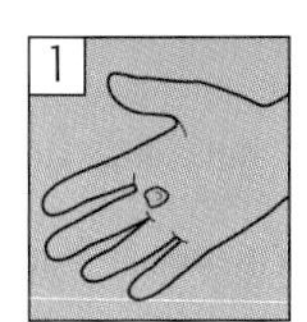

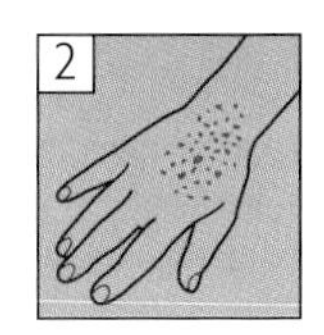

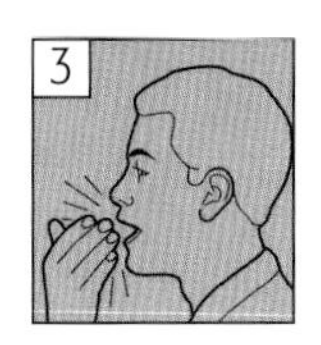

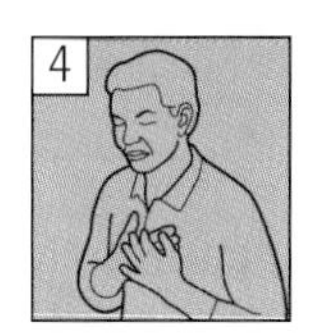

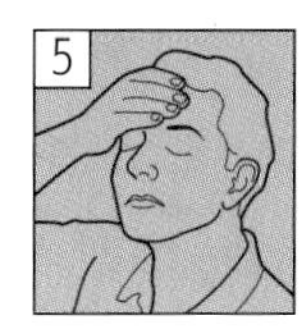

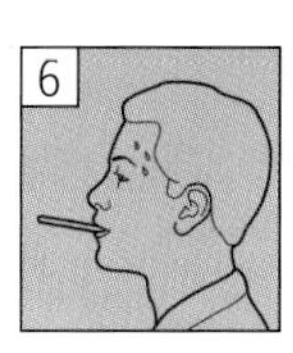

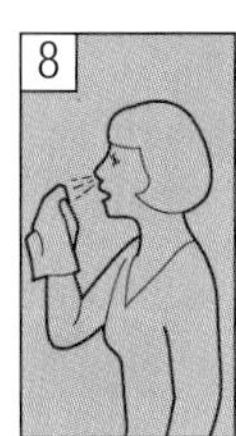

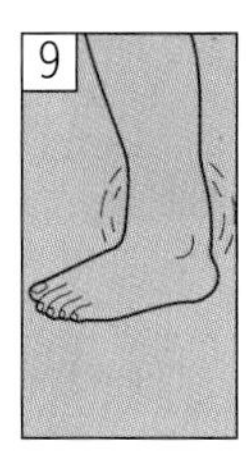

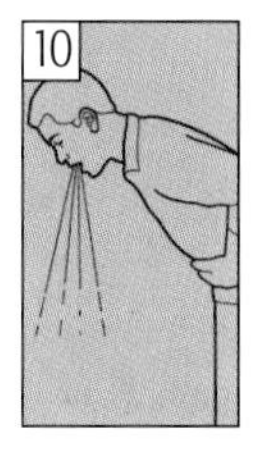

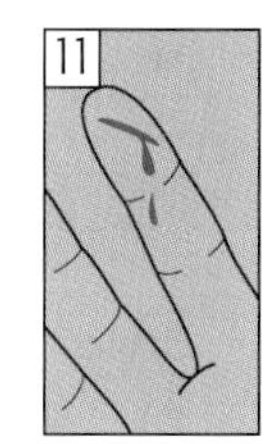

b Match the sentences.

1. She's unconscious /ʌnˈkɑnʃəs/.
2. She has a sore throat.
3. She has diarrhea /ˌdaɪəˈriə/.
4. She feels sick.
5. She fainted.
6. She feels dizzy.

A She's gone to the bathroom five times this morning.
B She's breathing, but her eyes are closed and she can't hear or feel anything.
C She wants to throw up / vomit.
D It was so hot on the train that she lost consciousness.
E She feels that everything is spinning around.
F It hurts when she talks or swallows food.

2 Illnesses and injuries

Match the illnesses / conditions with their causes or symptoms.

1. He has **the flu**.
2. He **caught a cold**.
3. He is **allergic** to cats.
4. He has **asthma** /ˈæzmə/.
5. He has **high** (low) **blood pressure** /blʌd ˈprɛʃər/.
6. He had **a heart attack**.
7. He had **a stroke**.
8. He has **food poisoning**.
9. He **twisted** / **sprained** his ankle.
10. He **burned** himself.
11. He has **a bruise** on his toe.

A It's 150 over 100.
B He was overweight, a smoker, and very highly stressed.
C His right side is paralyzed, and he can't speak.
D He ate some shrimp that weren't fresh.
E He's sneezing a lot and he has a cough.
F He dropped a chair on it, and now it's black and blue.
G He has difficulty breathing.
H He starts sneezing as soon as he's near one.
I He has a temperature, and his body aches.
J He touched a hot iron.
K He fell down, and now it's swollen.

3 Treatment

Write the missing word in the treatment column.

bandage /ˈbændɪdʒ/ injection medicine operation rest specialist stitches X-ray

Go to the doctor's (GP = general practitioner). He / she may tell you to ...	**treatment**
1 take some ______ e.g., **antibiotics** /æntɪbaɪˈɑtɪks/ or **painkillers**.	______
2 stay at home and ______.	______
3 go to the hospital to see a ______.	______
Go to the hospital / to the ER (the Emergency Room). You may have to ...	
4 have an ______ or **scan** to see if anything is broken.	______
5 have ______ if you have a very **deep cut**.	______
6 have an ______, when a **drug** is put into your body through a **needle**.	______
7 have a ______ put on to keep the **wound** /wund/ clean.	______
8 have an ______, when part of your body is cut open to remove or repair a damaged part.	______

Can you remember the words on this page? Test yourself or a partner.  p.12

Clothes and fashion

1 Describing clothes

a Match the adjectives and pictures.

Fit

tight
loose /lus/

Style

sleeveless
long- (short-) sleeved
hooded /hʊdɪd/
V-neck

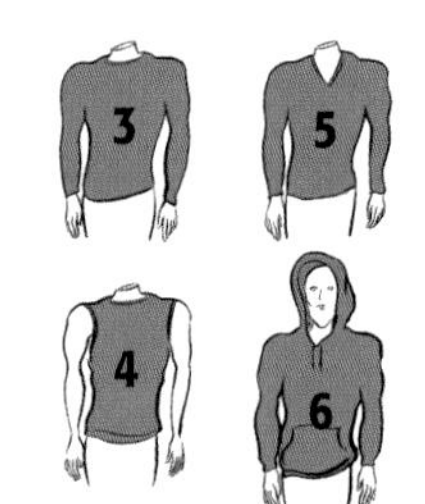

Pattern

polka-dot
solid
striped
checked
patterned

b Match the phrases and pictures

Materials

a cotton undershirt
a silk scarf
leather sandals
nylon /ˈnaɪlɑn/ stockings
a linen /ˈlɪnɪn/ suit
a spandex swimsuit / bathing suit
suede /sweɪd/ slippers
a denim backpack
a velvet bow /boʊ/
a fur /fər/ collar
a wool cardigan / sweater

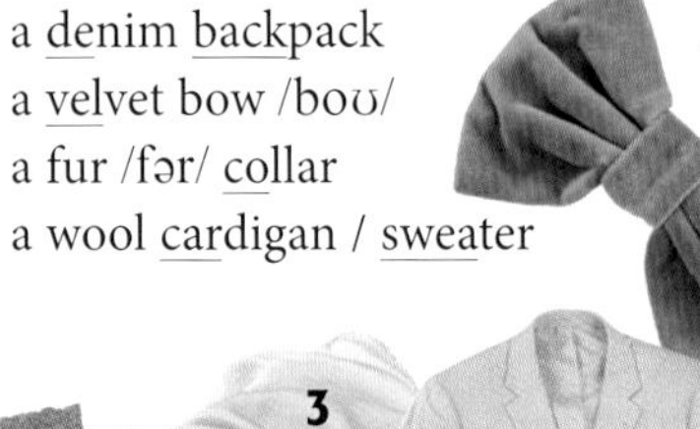

c Write the missing word in the **Opinion** column.

flattering old-fashioned scruffy stylish trendy

Opinion

1 She's very ______. She always wears the latest fashions. ______
2 The Argentinians have a reputation for being very ______ – both men and women dress very well. ______
3 He looks really ______. His clothes are old and kind of dirty, and he hasn't shaved. ______
4 That outfit is very ______ on you – it makes you look slim. ______
5 That tie is very ______. People don't wear such wide ones anymore. ______

2 Verb phrases

a Match the sentences.

1 I'm going to **get dressed up** tonight.
2 Please **hang up** your coat.
3 These jeans don't **fit** me.
4 That suit **looks** great **on you**!
5 Your bag **matches** your shoes.
6 I need to **change clothes**.
7 Hurry up and **get undressed**.
8 Get up and **get dressed**.

A Don't leave it on the chair.
B I just spilled coffee on my dress.
C I'm going to a party.
D Breakfast is on the table.
E It's time for your bath.
F They're too small.
G They're exactly the same color.
H It's very attractive.

b Cover sentences 1–8. Look at A–H. Try to remember 1–8.

3 Idioms

a Look at the highlighted idioms and try to guess their meanings.

1 What a gorgeous outfit! You're really dressed to kill tonight.
2 That suit fits her like a glove. Did she have it especially made for her?
3 Now that you know my secret, please keep it under your hat.
4 That sounds like a difficult situation. I wouldn't like to be in your shoes.

b Match the idioms to their meanings.

A don't tell anyone
B in your place
C wearing clothes that people will notice / admire
D is exactly the right size

Can you remember the words on this page? Test yourself or a partner.

p.22

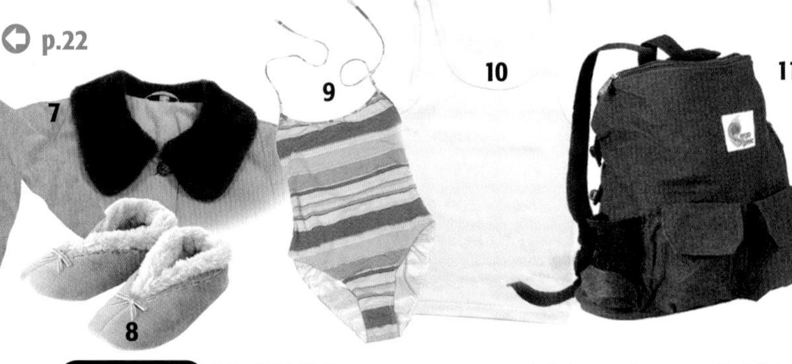

Crime and punishment

1 Crimes and criminals

Match the examples to the crimes in the chart.

A A gang took a rich man's son and asked the family for money.
B She went to her ex-husband's house and shot him dead.
C A passenger on a flight made the pilot land in the desert.
D Someone copied my handwriting and signed my name to a check.
E We came home from vacation and found that our TV was gone.
F Someone tried to sell me some illegal pills at a concert.
G When the border police searched his car, it was full of cigarettes.
H Someone threw paint on the statue in the park.
I She said she'd send the photos to a newspaper if the actor didn't pay her a lot of money.
J An armed man walked into a bank and shouted, "Hands up!"
K A woman transferred company money into her own bank account.
L A builder offered the mayor a free apartment in return for a favor.
M Two men left a bomb in the supermarket parking lot.
N Somebody stole my car last night from outside my house.
O A man held up a knife and made me give him my wallet.

		Crime	Criminal	Verb
1	*I*	blackmail	blackmailer	to blackmail
2		bribery	–	to bribe
3		burglary /'bərgləri/	burglar	to break in / burglarize
4		drug dealing	drug dealer	to sell drugs
5		forgery	forger	to forge
6		fraud /frɔd/	–	to commit fraud
7		hijacking /'haɪdʒækɪŋ/	hijacker	to hijack
8		kidnapping	kidnapper	to kidnap
9		mugging	mugger	to mug
10		murder* /'mərdər/	murderer	to murder
11		robbery	robber	to rob
12		smuggling	smuggler	to smuggle
13		terrorism	terrorist	to set off bombs, etc.
14		theft	thief /θif/	to steal
15		vandalism	vandal	to vandalize

* *manslaughter* /'mænslɔtər/ = killing somebody illegally, but unintentionally
assassination = murder of an important person, usually for political reasons (verb *assassinate*).

2 What happens to a criminal

Complete the sentences.
Write the words in the column.

arrested caught charged ~~committed~~ investigated questioned

The crime

1 Carl and Adam ___ a crime. They murdered a man. *committed*
2 The police ___ the crime. ______
3 Carl and Adam were ___ on the way to the airport. ______
4 They were ___ and taken to a police station. ______
5 The police ___ them for ten hours. ______
6 Finally they were ___ with murder. ______

acquitted court evidence guilty judge jury not guilty proof punishment sentenced verdict witnesses

The trial

7 Two months later, Carl and Adam appeared in ___. ______
8 ___ told the court what they had seen or knew. ______
9 The ___ (of 12 people) looked at and heard all the ___. ______/______
10 After two days the jury reached their ___. ______
11 Carl was found ___. His fingerprints were on the gun. ______
12 The ___ decided what Carl's ___ should be. ______/______
13 He ___ him to life in prison / jail. ______
14 Adam was found ___ (they thought he was innocent). ______
15 There was no ___ that he had committed the crime. ______
16 He was ___ and allowed to go free. ______

Punishments

- community service (doing some work to help society, e.g., painting, cleaning, etc.)
- a ($600) fine
- six months in prison
- a life sentence
- capital punishment (the death penalty)

Can you remember the words on this page? Test yourself or a partner.  p.37

Weather

1 What's the weather like?

a Put the words or phrases in the correct place in the chart.

below zero breeze chilly cool damp drizzling freezing gale-force mild pouring (rain) scorching showers warm

b Complete the text with *fog*, *mist*, and *smog*.

When the weather is foggy or misty, or there is smog, it is difficult to see.
__________ is not usually very thick and often occurs in the mountains or near the ocean.
__________ is thicker and can be found in towns and in the country.
__________ is caused by pollution and usually occurs in big cities.

1 **It's** __________. (a little cold, not extremely cold or hot) 2 **It's** __________. (unpleasantly cold)	5 **It's** __________. (pleasant, not hot or cold) 6 **It's** __________. (a pleasantly high temperature)	8 **It's** __________. (a little wet, but not raining) 9 **It's** __________. (raining lightly) 10 **There are** __________. (short periods of rain)	12 **There's a** __________. (a light wind)
It's cold.	**It's hot.**	**It's raining / wet.**	**It's windy.**
3 **It's** __________. 4 The temperature is __________. (–10º)	7 **It's** __________ / boiling. (unpleasantly hot)	11 **It's** __________. (raining a lot)	13 **There are** __________ (extremely strong) **winds.**

2 Extreme weather

Match the words and definitions.

blizzard drought /draʊt/ flood /flʌd/ hailstorm heat wave hurricane lightning monsoon thunder typhoon

1 __________ (n) a period of unusually hot weather
2 __________ (n) a long, usually hot, dry period when there is little or no rain
3 __________ (n) a storm with small balls of ice that fall like rain
4 __________ (n) a flash of very bright light in the sky caused by electricity
5 __________ (n and v) the loud noise that you hear during a storm
6 __________ (n) a snowstorm with very strong winds
7 __________ (v and n) when everything becomes filled and covered with water
8 __________ (n) a violent storm with very strong winds, especially in the western Atlantic Ocean
9 __________ (n) a violent tropical storm in the Pacific or Indian Ocean with very strong winds
10 __________ (n) the season when it rains a lot in southern Asia

3 Adjectives to describe weather

Complete the weather forecast with these adjectives.

bright changeable clear heavy icy stable strong sunny thick

In the north today it will be very cold, with [1]______ winds and [2]______ rain. There will also be [3]______ fog in the hills and near the coast, though it should clear by noon. Driving will be dangerous as the roads will be [4]______. However, the southern regions will have [5]______ skies and [6]______ sunshine, though the temperature will still be fairly low. Over the next few days, the weather will be [7]______, with some showers but occasional [8]______ periods. However, it should become more [9]______ over the weekend.

4 Adjectives and verbs connected with weather

Match the sentences. Can you guess the meaning of the words in **bold**?

1 You're **shivering**.
2 I'm **sweating** /ˈswetɪŋ/.
3 I **got soaked** this morning.
4 It's very **humid** /ˈhyuməd/ today.
5 The snow is starting to **melt**.
6 Don't **get sunburned**!
7 Be careful! The sidewalk is very **slippery**.

A Come and sit in the shade.
B It will all be gone by tonight.
C You might fall down.
D It's hot and damp, and there's no air.
E Can we turn the heat off?
F Do you want to borrow my jacket?
G It was pouring, and I didn't have an umbrella.

Can you remember the words on this page? Test yourself or a partner. p.41

MultiROM www.oup.com/elt/americanenglishfile/4

Feelings

1 Adjectives

a Match the adjectives with the situations.

~~confused~~ disappointed glad grateful homesick lonely nervous offended relieved ~~shocked~~

How would you feel if ...?

1 two people gave you completely opposite advice *confused*
2 the police told you that your home had been burglarized *shocked*
3 a friend helped you a lot with a problem ______
4 you thought you had lost your passport but then you found it ______
5 you didn't get a present you were hoping to get ______
6 you were studying abroad and missed your family ______
7 you moved to a new town and didn't have any friends ______
8 you were about to speak in public for the first time ______
9 your friend tells you she has just passed her driving test ______ (or *happy*)
10 a very good friend didn't invite you to his / her party ______

Some adjectives describe a mixture of feelings, e.g.:

fed up = bored or frustrated and unhappy (especially with a situation that has gone on too long)
I'm really fed up with my job. I think I'm going to look for something else.

upset = unhappy and worried / anxious
She was very upset when she heard that her cousin had had an accident.

b Match the **strong** adjectives with their definitions.

astonished delighted desperate devastated exhausted /ɪɡˈzɔstɪd/ furious /ˈfyʊriəs/ miserable ~~stunned~~ terrified thrilled

1 very surprised and unable to move or react *stunned*
2 extremely upset and shocked ______
3 very pleased ______ (or *thrilled*)
4 really tired ______
5 very excited ______
6 extremely scared ______
7 really angry ______
8 very surprised ______ (or *amazed*)
9 with little hope, and ready to do anything to improve the situation ______
10 very unhappy ______

⚠ Remember you can't use *very*, *extremely*, etc. with strong adjectives. If you want to use an intensifier, use *absolutely*, e.g., *absolutely astonished* NOT ~~*very astonished*~~.

2 Idioms

a Look at the highlighted idioms and try to guess their meaning.

1 I'm sick and tired of telling you to do your homework. Just do it!
2 When I saw the burglar I was scared to death.
3 He finally passed his driving test! He's jumping for joy!
4 I'm feeling down with all this rain. I can't seem to cheer up.
5 I'm completely worn out. I just want to sit down and put my feet up.
6 When I saw her, I couldn't believe my eyes. She looked ten years younger.

b Match the idioms in **a** above and the feelings below.

A exhausted
B (be) very surprised
C fed up
D terrified
E sad, depressed
F extremely happy

Can you remember the words on this page? Test yourself or a partner.

p.53

1 Parts of the body and organs

Match the words and pictures.

- ☐ ankle
- ☐ calf /kæf/ (pl calves)
- ☐ heel
- ☐ chest
- ☐ waist
- ☐ hip
- ☐ thigh /θaɪ/

- ☐ elbow /ˈɛlboʊ/
- ☐ wrist
- ☐ nails
- ☐ palm /pɑm/
- ☐ brain
- ☐ heart /hɑrt/
- ☐ kidneys
- ☐ liver
- ☐ lungs

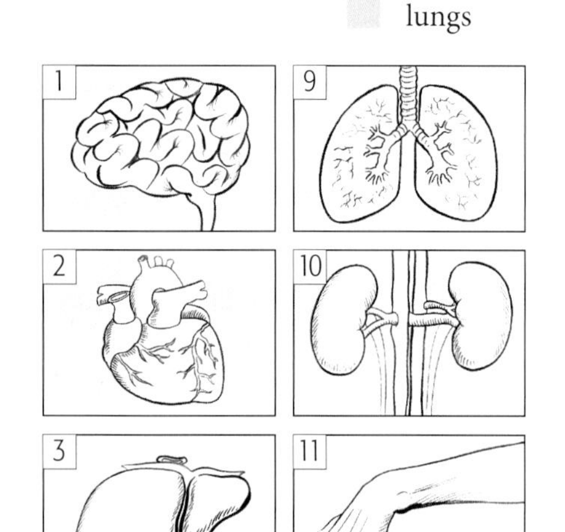

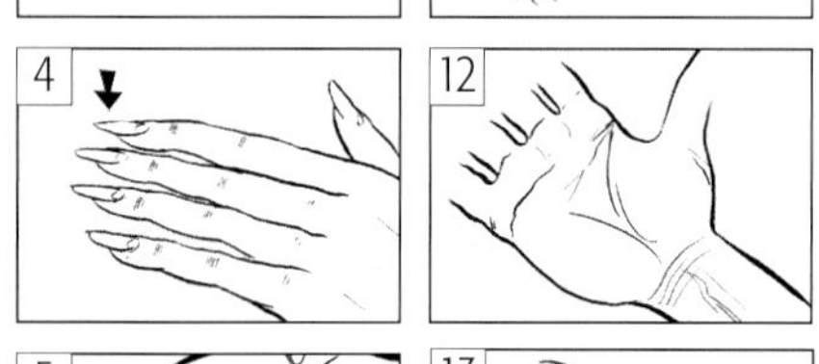

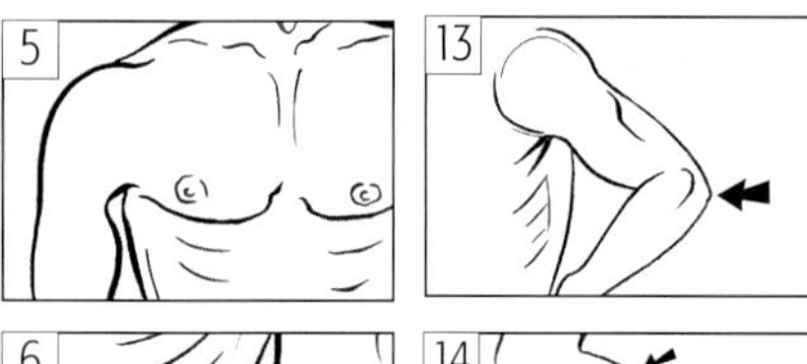

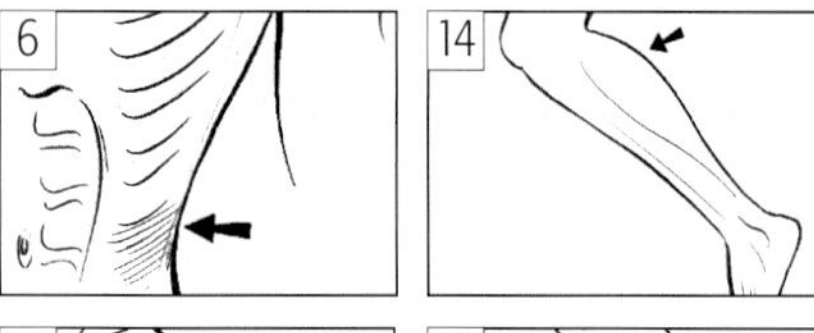

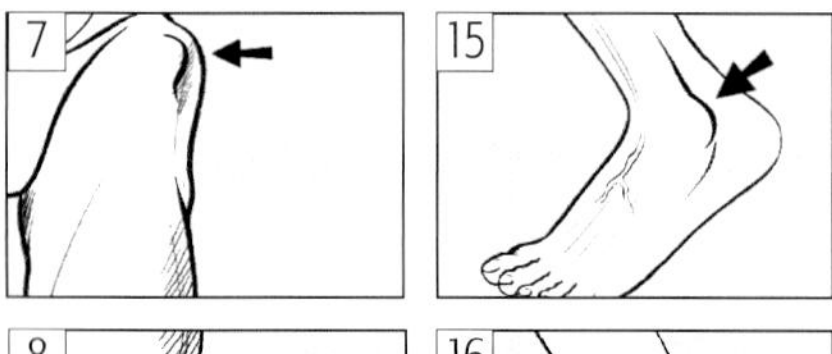

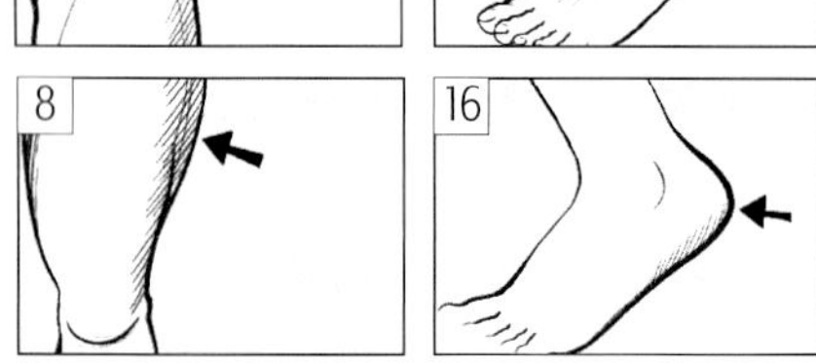

2 Verbs and verb phrases

a Match the verbs with the parts of the body.

arms   eyebrows /ˈaɪbraʊz/   hair (x2)   hand   hands (x2)
head (x2)   ~~nails~~   nose   shoulders   teeth

1 bite your *nails*
2 blow your ______
3 brush your ______ / ______
4 clap your ______
5 comb your ______
6 fold your ______
7 hold somebody's ______
8 nod your ______
9 shake your ______ (to say no)
10 raise your ______ (to show surprise)
11 shake ______ (with someone)
12 shrug your ______

b Read the sentences. Write the part of the body related to the **bold** verb.

1 He **winked** at me to show that he was only joking. *eye*
2 The steak was tough and difficult to **chew**. ______
3 When we met, we were so happy we **hugged** each other. ______
4 Don't **scratch** the mosquito bite. You'll only make it worse. ______
5 She sadly **waved** good-bye to her boyfriend as the train left the station. ______
6 Some women think a man should **kneel down** when he proposes marriage. ______
7 The teacher **frowned** /fraʊnd/ when she saw all the mistakes I had made. ______
8 The painting was so strange I **stared** /stɛrd/ at it for a long time. ______
9 She got out of bed, **yawned** /yɔnd/, and **stretched**. ______ / ______
10 If you don't know the word for something, just **point** at what you want. ______

3 Idioms

Complete the sentences with a part of the body.

chest   foot   feet   hand   head   heart (x2)   leg   stomach   tongue /tʌŋ/

1 Could you **give me a** ☐ with my homework? It's really difficult. ______
2 You really **put your** ☐ **in your mouth** when you told Mark that Jane had been married before. ______
3 You can't be serious. You must be **pulling my** ☐! ______
4 I can't remember her name, but it's **on the tip of my** ☐. ______
5 I'm not sure I want to go climbing anymore. I'm starting to **get cold** ☐. ______
6 The test is on Friday. I have **butterflies in my** ☐! ______
7 When Miriam left David, she **broke his** ☐. ______
8 **I can't get** that song **out of my** ☐. I keep whistling it. ______
9 You need to **learn** the irregular past tenses **by** ☐. ______
10 I need to tell somebody about it and **get it off my** ☐. ______

Can you remember the words on this page? Test yourself or a partner. p.62

1 Instruments and musicians

a Match the words and pictures.

	bass /beɪs/ guitar			piano	
8	cello /ˈtʃɛloʊ/	*cellist*		saxophone	
	drums			trumpet	
	keyboard			violin /ˌvaɪəˈlɪn/	
	flute				

b What do you call the musicians who play each of the instruments above? Write the word next to the name of the instrument. Underline the stressed syllable.

c Match the words and definitions.

bass choir /ˈkwaɪər/ composer conductor DJ (disc jockey) lead singer orchestra /ˈɔrkəstrə/ rapper singer-songwriter soloist soprano tenor

1 a man who sings with a somewhat high-pitched voice ______
2 a man who sings with a low-pitched voice ______
3 a woman who sings with a high-pitched voice ______
4 a large group of musicians who play different musical instruments together ______
5 a group of people who sing together, for example, in a church service ______
6 somebody who writes and sings his / her own songs ______
7 someone who speaks the words of a song that has a strong beat ______
8 somebody who sings or plays an instrument alone ______
9 the main singer in a band ______
10 the person who directs an orchestra ______
11 somebody who writes music ______
12 the person who chooses, introduces, and plays music on the radio or in a club ______

2 Adjectives and phrases to describe music

Match the sentences.

1 This song has **incomprehensible** lyrics.
2 It's a very **catchy** song.
3 This music is so **moving**.
4 It's a song with a very strong **beat**.
5 I think his voice is very **monotonous**.
6 I don't know what it's called, but I recognize the **tune** /tun/.

A The rhythm makes you want to tap your feet.
B It almost puts me to sleep.
C The music sounds familiar.
D I can't understand what it's about.
E I've been humming it all day.
F It almost makes me want to cry.

3 Idioms

Complete the sentences with the correct music idiom.

A tooting his own horn B face the music C good ear for music D music to my ears E out of tune

1 She has a ______. She can sing a tune as soon as she hears it.
2 He's not singing at the same pitch as we are. He's completely ______!
3 He's always ______. He tells everyone how wonderful he is.
4 The others ran away, leaving her to ______. She got punished for what they had all done.
5 When I heard the news, it was ______. It was exactly what I wanted to hear.

Can you remember the words on this page? Test yourself or a partner.  p.70

The media

1 Journalists and people in the media

Match the words and definitions.

critic   editor   freelance journalist   news anchor   paparazzi /ˌpɑpəˈrɑtsi/
press photographer   reporter   sports commentator

1 ________ photographers who follow famous people around to get photos of them to sell to a newspaper
2 ________ a person who writes about the good / bad qualities of books, concerts, theater, movies, etc.
3 ________ a person who describes a sports event while it's happening on TV or radio
4 ________ a person who collects and reports news for newspapers, radio, or TV
5 ________ a person in charge of a newspaper or magazine, or part of one, who decides what should be in it
6 ________ a person who announces the news
7 ________ a person who writes articles for different newspapers and is not employed by a single newspaper
8 ________ a person who takes photos for a newspaper

2 Sections of a newspaper or news website

Match the words and pictures.

- advertisement
- cartoon
- crossword puzzle
- front page
- horoscope
- review /rɪˈvyu/
- classified ads
- weather forecast

3 Adjectives to describe the media

Match the sentences. Then look at the way the **bold** adjectives are used in context, and guess their meaning.

1 The reporting in the paper was very **sensational**.
2 The news on that TV channel is really **biased** /ˈbaɪəst/.
3 This is the most **objective** of the Sunday papers.
4 The movie review was generally **accurate** /ˈækyərət/.
5 I think the report was **censored**.

A It said the plot was poor but the acting good, which I think was true.
B It bases its stories just on facts, not on feelings or beliefs.
C The newspaper wasn't allowed to publish all the details.
D It made the story more shocking than it really was.
E You can't believe anything you hear on it. It's obvious what political party they favor!

Can you remember the words on this page? Test yourself or a partner.

p.78

4 The language of headlines

Match the highlighted "headline phrases" with their meanings.

1 **Famous actress in restaurant bill spat**

2 **Team manager to quit after shock defeat**

3 **Thousands of jobs axed by US companies**

4 **Stock market hit by oil fears**

5 **Prince to wed 18-year-old TV soap star**

6 **Police quiz witness in murder trial**

7 **President backs senator in latest scandal**

8 **Probe finds chemicals in drinking water**

A argument
B have been cut
C question, interrogate
D is going to leave (a job)
E is going to marry
F investigation
G has been badly affected
H supports

Cities and towns

1 Buildings, landmarks, and getting around

Write at least four words in each column.

baseball stadium bicycle lane cable car chapel concert hall courthouse /ˈkɔrthaʊs/ harbor hill mosque pedestrian mall skyscraper square /skwɛr/ statue synagogue /ˈsɪnəgɑg/ taxi stand temple tower

places of worship	other buildings	other landmarks and sights	getting around
cathedral	*town hall*	*bridge*	*subway*

2 Where people live / work

a Match the words and definitions.

1 **downtown**
2 in a (friendly) **neighborhood**
3 in **the suburbs** /ˈsʌbərbz/
4 **on** the **outskirts**
5 in the (financial) **district**
6 in **(the) old town**

A a part of a city / town and the people who live there
B the area outside the central part of a city
C the historic part of a city / town
D an area where, e.g., all the banks (or theaters, etc.) are
E the central part of a city / large town
F part of a city / town farthest from the center; on the edge of the city / town

b Describe where you live.

3 City problems

a Complete the **Problems** column with a word from the list.

beggars homeless people overcrowding pollution poverty slums traffic jams vandalism

	Problems
1 There are a lot of ___ and congestion, especially during rush hour.	
2 There are ___ on the outskirts of the city, where the houses are in very bad condition.	
3 There is a lot of ___, and often pay phones are destroyed and don't work.	
4 In some parts of the city there is a lot of ___ with too many people living in one building.	
5 There is too much ___ caused by car fumes and factory emissions.	
6 There are a lot of ___ who sleep on the streets.	
7 ___ are poor people who stop you on the street and ask you for money.	
8 There is a lot of ___ in this country. Many people are earning less than a dollar a day.	

b Which of these are problems in your country?

4 Adjectives to describe a city / town

Match the sentences.

1 Toronto is a very **cosmopolitan** city.
2 This area of the city is very **run-down**.
3 It's a very **industrial** city.
4 Cuzco is a very **historic** city.
5 I think my town is very **provincial**.
6 Seoul is a **vibrant** /ˈvaɪbrənt/ city.
7 This city is terribly **polluted**.

A It has many interesting old buildings and monuments.
B It's full of life and energy.
C It's full of people from different cultures.
D People here aren't interested in new ideas.
E The air is dirty and dangerous to breathe.
F The buildings are in bad condition.
G There are a lot factories in and around the city.

Can you remember the words on this page? Test yourself or a partner.

p.89

Business and advertising

1 Verbs and expressions

a Complete with verbs from the list.

become expand export import
launch /lɔntʃ/ manufacture
market merge set up take over

1 ________ a company (= start)
2 ________ a product (= make in a factory)
3 ________ a product (= sell using advertising, packaging, etc.)
4 ________ materials (= buy from another country)
5 ________ your product (= sell to other countries)
6 ________ (= get bigger)
7 ________ the market leader (= be the most successful company)
8 ________ another company (= get control of)
9 ________ a new product, an advertising campaign (= show for the first time)
10 ________ with another company (= combine to make one single company)

b *Do* or *make*? Put the words or phrases in the correct column.

business (with) a deal
a decision an investment
a job market research
money a profit

do	make

Can you remember the words on this page? Test yourself or a partner.

p.105

2 Organizations and people

a Organizations. Match the words and definitions.

a branch a business / company / firm /fərm/ a chain
the headquarters a multinational (company)

1 ________ a group of stores, hotels, etc. owned by the same person or company
2 ________ an organization that produces or sells goods or provides a service
3 ________ a company that has offices or factories in many countries
4 ________ the main office of a company
5 ________ an office or store that is part of a larger organization

b People. Match the words and definitions.

thechief executive officer (CEO) a client /ˈklaɪənt/
a coworker a customer an employee an employer
the head of the department a manager the owner the staff

1 ________ the group of people who work for an organization
2 ________ a person who works for somebody
3 ________ a person or company that employs other people
4 ________ someone who buys goods or services, e.g., from a store
5 ________ someone who receives a service from a professional person
6 ________ a person who works with you
7 ________ the leader of a large company or organization
8 ________ the person who owns a business
9 ________ a person who is in charge of a department in an organization
10 ________ a person in charge of part of an organization, e.g., a branch

3 Advertising

Match the words / phrases and pictures.

- [ ] advertisement / ad
- [ ] commercial
- [ ] logo /ˈloʊgoʊ/
- [ ] slogan /ˈsloʊgən/
- [ ] junk mail
- [ ] cold-calling

1

2

3

4

5
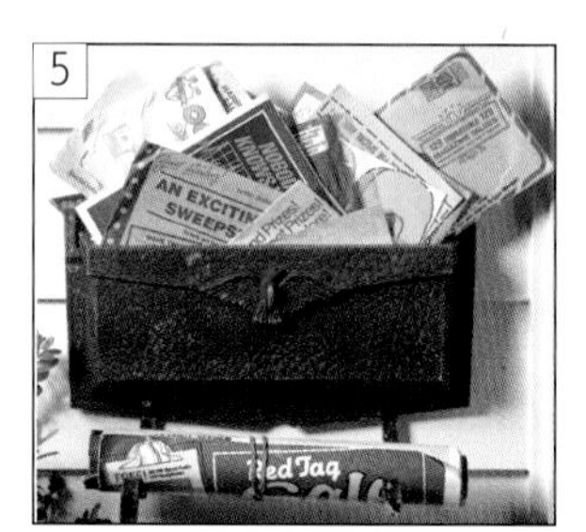

6
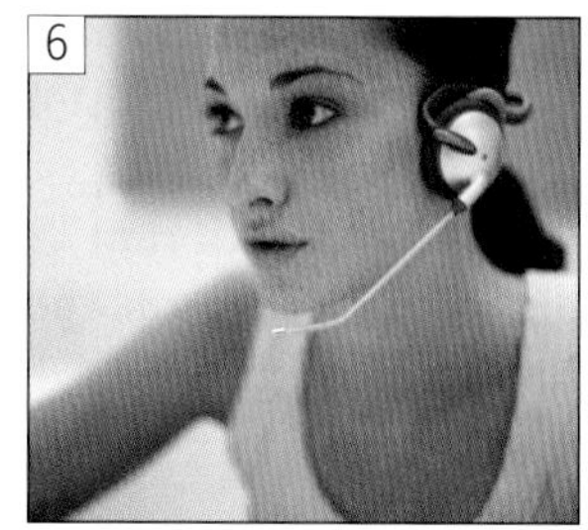

Phrasal verbs in context

FILE 1

Complete the phrasal verbs from File 1 with the correct particle.

back down (x2) up (x3)

1 My brother and his girlfriend **broke** ______ last month.
2 I can't talk now; I'm driving. I'll **call** you ______ in 15 minutes.
3 Scientists have **come** ______ with new ways to save energy.
4 The doctor said that I had to **cut** ______ on coffee.
5 Don't **give** ______. If you keep trying, you'll find a good job soon.
6 **Slow** ______! You're going to get a speeding ticket.

FILE 2

Complete the phrasal verbs from File 2 with a verb in the correct form.

break burst leave put turn

1 Everyone ______ **out** laughing when Jimmy arrived wearing a large, white hat.
2 Can you ______ the TV **up**? I can't hear it with the children shouting in the kitchen.
3 Don't ______ anything **behind** when you get off the plane.
4 Riots ______ **out** in the capital city, and the police were called in.
5 If you take any of my things, please ______ them **back** when you've finished with them.

FILE 3

Match the phrasal verbs from File 3 with a definition A–E.

1 **Watch out**. There are usually pickpockets at this station.
2 The company has been **going through** a bad period recently.
3 The police told us to **get out** because the building wasn't safe.
4 If we **keep on** polluting the planet, we're going to destroy it.
5 The restaurant wasn't popular and it **closed down** last year

A continue
B leave
C stop operating
D be careful
E experience or suffer

FILE 4

Complete the phrasal verbs from File 4 with the correct particle.

down off on out (x2)

1 If there is an emergency, all passengers must **get** ____ of the plane as fast as they can.
2 The tour guide **pointed** ____ some fascinating landmarks to us.
3 Jessica was getting really angry with Tom, so I told her to **calm** _____.
4 **Hold** ___ to me. It's very slippery and you might fall.
5 The teacher **told** me ____ because I hadn't done my homework.

FILE 5

Complete the phrasal verbs from File 5 with the correct verb.

catch eat fall fill lie put

1 I'm exhausted. I'm going to ______ **down** for half an hour.
2 I'm not very good at ice skating. I always ______ **down** at least 20 times!
3 We stopped at a gas station to ______ **up** with gas.
4 I'm looking forward to the party. It'll be a good chance to ______ **up with** some old friends.
5 It's very easy to ______ **on** weight if you ______ **out** several times a week.

FILE 6

Match the phrasal verbs from File 6 with a definition A–E.

1 The teacher **hurried through** the last part of the class.
2 I'll only call you if something interesting **comes up** in the meeting.
3 James **thought up** a brilliant new idea for our new product.
4 An old man was **run over** in the crosswalk.
5 A truck **crashed into** my car when it was parked outside my house.

A hit something, usually violently, while moving
B hit and knocked to the ground by a vehicle
C produce or invent
D rush to complete something quickly
E mentioned in a discussion

FILE 7

Complete the phrasal verbs from File 7 with the correct form of the verb.

end go pick take

1 I don't know what's ______ **on**. Can anyone tell me what's happening?
2 We got completely lost and we ______ **up** miles away from where we wanted to go.
3 I'll ______ you **up** at the station if you tell me what time your train arrives.
4 I've decided to ______ **up** a new hobby – I'm going to learn to dance salsa.

English sounds

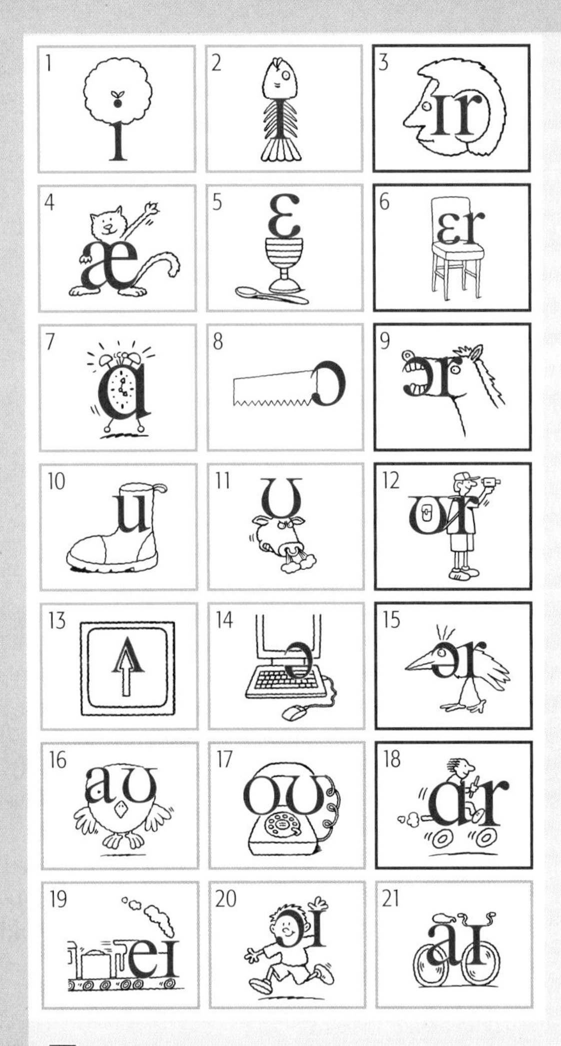

vowels followed by /r/

diphthongs

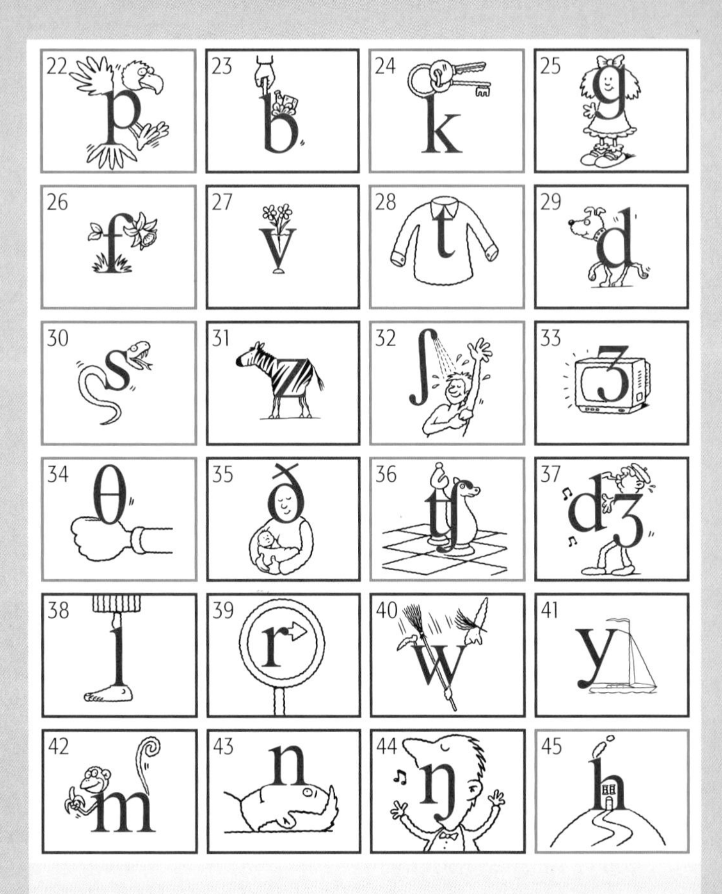

voiced

unvoiced

1 tree /tri/
2 fish /fɪʃ/
3 ear /ɪr/
4 cat /kæt/
5 egg /ɛg/
6 chair /tʃɛr/
7 clock /klɑk/
8 saw /sɔ/
9 horse /hɔrs/
10 boot /but/
11 bull /bʊl/
12 tourist /'tʊrɪst/
13 up /ʌp/
14 computer /kəm'pyutər/
15 bird /bərd/
16 owl /aʊl/
17 phone /foʊn/
18 car /kɑr/
19 train /treɪn/
20 boy /bɔɪ/
21 bike /baɪk/

22 parrot /'pærət/
23 bag /bæg/
24 keys /kiz/
25 girl /gərl/
26 flower /'flaʊər/
27 vase /veɪs/
28 tie /taɪ/
29 dog /dɔg/
30 snake /sneɪk/
31 zebra /'zibrə/
32 shower /'ʃaʊər/
33 television /'tɛləvɪʒn/
34 thumb /θʌm/
35 mother /'mʌðər/
36 chess /tʃɛs/
37 jazz /dʒæz/
38 leg /lɛg/
39 right /raɪt/
40 witch /wɪtʃ/
41 yacht /yɑt/
42 monkey /'mʌŋki/
43 nose /noʊz/
44 singer /'sɪŋər/
45 house /haʊs/

Sounds and spelling – vowels

	usual spelling	but also
tree	**ee** sneeze feel **ea** easy team **e** even recent	believe key people ski heavy police
fish	**i** twisted blister silk fitness sick slipper	reliable women bandage business build symptoms
ear	**eer** cheerful volunteer **ere** atmosphere sincere **ear** appear fear	series experience souvenir
cat	**a** act glad classic pattern scratch vandal	
egg	**e** energy pessimist credit else rest velvet	leather friend many says said guest
chair	**air** airline repair wheelchair **are** square stare	everywhere bear scary area their
clock	**o** opera obvious rob body optimist	swallow knowledge father
saw	**al** walk talk **aw** awful thaw **augh** manslaughter caught	thought bought cough fraud autograph
horse	**or** boring forgery scorching sports **ore** explore snore	warm course floor board court
boot	**oo** loose moody **u*** confused flu **ew** chew news	routine juice move soup shoe beautiful through

* especially before consonant + **e**

	usual spelling	but also
bull	**u** fully push **oo** bookcase hooded stood wool	could would woman
tourist	A very unusual sound. assure surely plural jury	
up	**u** punish jungle impulsive scruffy trumpet stunned **o** become money	flood blood rough enough couple trouble
computer	Many different spellings, always unstressed. opinion obviously immature psychology terrified genetics podium paralyzed	
bird	**er** reserved allergic **ir** firm thirsty **ur** burn hurt **er / or** (unstressed) concert doctor	earth learn world worse journey blizzard treasure
owl	**ou** ground council amount drought **ow** frown tower	
phone	**o*** lonely choke both don't **oa** throat load **ow** elbow blow	soul though shoulders toe
car	**ar** scarf alarm harmful landmark scorecard	heart guard
train	**a*** danger gale **ai** vain faint **ay** may say gray	great break neighbor suede survey they
boy	**oi** disappointed avoid voice choice **oy** annoy toy	
bike	**i*** crime wise **y** style nylon **igh** high tight	eyebrow height buy guy tried good-bye

Sounds and spelling – consonants

	usual spelling		but also
parrot	**p** **pp**	press plain export hip kidnapping disappear	
bag	**b** **bb**	burglar bribe vibrant job stubborn robbery	
keys	**c** **k** **ck** **que**	calm ironic kind link trick neck mosque antique	chemist choir chaos ache
girl	**g** **gg**	global guilty drug forget mugger beggar	ghost
flower	**f** **ph** **ff**	fed up grateful photo elephant traffic offended	tough cough
vase	**v** **ve**	violin velvet provincial review sleeve wave	of
tie	**t** **tt**	trendy terrorist storm strict settled patterned	worked passed debt doubt receipt
dog	**d** **dd**	dream denim hand confident address middle	failed bored
snake	**s** **ss** **ce/se** **c**	strange responsible depressing possessive peace promise celebrity city cyclist (before **e**, **i**, **y**)	scientist psychologist
zebra	**z** **zz** **s**	zero freezing dizzy blizzard drizzle miserable museum loves reserved	dessert
shower	**sh** **ti** **ci**	shocked shy cash selfish operation injection (+ vowel) unconcious sociable (+ vowel)	sugar sure brochure mustache pressure machine ocean
television	An unusual sound. decision confusion pleasure usually garage		

	usual spelling		but also
thumb	**th**	theory thrilled healthy truth thief both	
mother	**th**	although breathe neither rhythm weather	
chess	**ch** **tch** **t (+ure)** **ti**	cheerful chest stitches match immature question suggestion (after **s**)	cello
jazz	**j** **g** **-dge**	jealous injury generous original judge	soldier graduate
leg	**l** **ll**	launch employ deal blackmail college chilly	
right	**r** **rr**	relieved reporter breeze critic terrified hurricane	wrist wrinkled rhythm
witch	**w** **wh**	wave waist windy highway whatever wheel	one once language quiet
yacht	**y** **u**	yoga yawn yogurt yourself university music	view
monkey	**m** **mm**	medicine media damp homeless commercial recommend	thumb comb column
nose	**n** **nn**	needle nervous kidney monotonous tennis connection	kneel knew design foreign
singer	**-ng** before **k**	lightning pouring tongue scorching wink ankle	
house	**h**	hijack horoscope historic incomprehensible unhappy behave	whoever whose whole